W9-DHT-495

LEFT BEHIND IN ROSEDALE

LEFT BEHIND IN ROSEDALE

Race Relations and the Collapse of Community Institutions

SCOTT CUMMINGS

WestviewPress
A Division of HarperCollins*Publishers*

F
394
.F7
C86
1998

Copyright © 1998 by Westview Press, A Division of HarperCollins Publishers, Inc.

Published in 1998 in the United States of America by Westview Press, 5500 Central Avenue, Boulder, Colorado 80301-2877, and in the United Kingdom by Westview Press, 12 Hid's Copse Road, Cumnor Hill, Oxford OX2 9JJ

Library of Congress Cataloging-in-Publication Data
Cummings, Scott, 1944–
    Left behind in Rosedale : race relations and the collapse of
community institutions / Scott Cummings.
        p.   cm.
    Includes index.
    ISBN 0-8133-3420-9.—ISBN 0-8133-3421-7 (pbk.)
    1. Rosedale (Fort Worth, Tex.)—Race relations.   2. Fort Worth
(Tex.)—Race relations.   3. Afro-Americans—Texas—Fort Worth—
Social conditions.   4. Rosedale (Fort Worth, Tex.)—Social
conditions.   5.Fort Worth (Tex.)—Social conditions.   6. Community
development—Texas—Fort Worth.   I. Title.
F394.F7C86   1998
305.8'0097645315—dc21
                                                                              97-32511
                                                                              CIP

The paper used in this publication meets the requirements of the American National Standard for Permanence of Paper for Printed Library Materials Z39.48-1984.

10   9   8   7   6   5   4   3   2   1

To Juanita, Roy, and Jeannette,
with love and appreciation

CONTENTS

List of Illustrations   *ix*
Acknowledgments   *xi*

1 Race Relations and Urban Neighborhoods   1

Background and Overview, 3
A Retrospective Overview, 12

2 The Ghettoization of Rosedale   17

A Brief History of Rosedale, 18
The Racial Transformation of Rosedale, 20
Suburban Development and Racial Change, 23

3 Racial Transition and the Loss of Community   28

The Elderly of Rosedale: A Window to the Past, 31
Grief and the Loss of Community, 36
Commitment and Entrapment, 38
The Transformation of Neighborhood Life and Culture, 40
The Transformation of Community Standards, 41
The Loss of the White Middle Class, 43
The Loss of Community Business, 43
The Intrusion of Government, 44
Summary, 46

**4 Racism and Residential Transition:
Old Myths and New Realities**   48

Rosedale and the American Racial Legacy, 51
Residential Integration and the Violation of Racial Etiquette, 55
The Erosion of Mental and Physical Health, 59
Crime, Isolation, and Withdrawal, 63

5 The Adolescent Menace: Beyond Racial Stereotypes   68

Crime in Rosedale, 70
The Subjective Side of Criminal Victimization, 74
Cars and Outside Equipment, 74
Household Robberies, 75
Street Crimes, 80

6 Sexual Violence in Rosedale   84

The Roots Rapist, 93
The Rosedale Rapist, 97

7 The Wilding Incidents of 1982   102

8 The Underclass of Rosedale:
   Community Institutions in Crisis   126

9 The Struggle to Create New Institutions:
   The Crisis Deepens, *with Elise Bright and Richard Cole*   146

Commercial Redevelopment, 148
The Effort to Save Rosedale's Housing, 159
Gangs and the New Wave of Adolescent Crime, 165

10 Public Policy, Social Change, and the Fall of Rosedale   171

Rosedale as a Victim of Social Change, 172
Rosedale as a Victim of Liberal Public Policy, 178
Federal Housing Policy, School Desegregation,
   and the Fall of Rosedale, 182

11 Race Relations, Social Justice, and the Future of
    Urban Neighborhoods   193

A Conflict of Rights, 197
Social Justice and Residential Integration, 200
African American Youth and the Future of Race Relations, 204

Notes   209
Index   217

ILLUSTRATIONS

Tables

2.1 The Socioeconomic Characteristics of Rosedale's
     Current Residents, 1990 Census   27

3.1 Social Characteristics of Rosedale's Elderly   31
3.2 The Social Roots of Rosedale's Elderly   32
3.3 Homeownership Among Rosedale's Elderly   33
3.4 Living and Employment Situation of Rosedale's Elderly   33
3.5 The Social Class Composition of Rosedale's Elderly   33
3.6 Source of Income for Rosedale's Elderly   34

4.1 Perceived Safety During Daylight and Evening Hours   61

5.1 Rate of Criminal Victimization Among Rosedale's Elderly   74

Photo Section

The Rosedale Senior Center
Abandoned housing and arson
The houses of the elderly are easily identified
The business district in Rosedale before renovation
Street scenes from Rosedale's commercial district

ACKNOWLEDGMENTS

WHILE WRITING LEFT BEHIND IN ROSEDALE, I relied upon the goodwill and help of many individuals. Without the aid and support of these people, the job of telling the story of Rosedale would have been much more difficult. I am especially indebted to the elderly residents of Rosedale, both African American and white, for allowing me to spend so much time with them. I learned an immense amount from them. Their grace and wisdom, displayed under very difficult living conditions, made me grateful for the many blessings of my own life that I had taken for granted.

Many people opened doors for me and provided critical pieces of information that made the story of Rosedale more compelling. I wish to thank my colleague Allen Butcher for helping me find my way through the local criminal justice system. I thank my colleague Wayne Zatopek for keeping me informed about critical changes taking place in Rosedale over the years. Both of these men make significant contributions to my work, and I wish to express my thanks to them and acknowledge their valued assistance.

Many former and current colleagues have listened patiently to me work through the political and ethical dilemmas raised by the story of Rosedale. I thank Paul Giesel, Mark Rosentraub, Del Taebel, Peter Meyer, Tom Keil, and Jerry Vito for listening and responding wisely to my thoughts and ideas about public policy and the case of Rosedale.

Some special individuals shared in the evolution of my thinking about Rosedale and its residents. I thank Michele, Lenora, and Angie for their kind support. I thank Kim, Kristin, Katie, and Sophia for patiently sharing me with Rosedale when I should have been paying more attention to them. I dedicate this book to the memory of my mother, Juanita, who left us much too early, and to my aunt and uncle, Roy and Jeannette Adams, for their warmth and support over the years.

Scott Cummings
Key West, Florida

The Rosedale Senior Center shortly after the wilding incidents of 1982. Courtesy of Albert G. Mogor.

Abandoned housing and arson. Courtesy of Albert G. Mogor.

The houses of
the elderly
are easily
identified.
Courtesy of
Albert G.
Mogor.

The business
district in
Rosedale be-
fore the reno-
vation efforts
of 1986.
Courtesy of
Albert G.
Mogor.

Jesus said,
"I am the way, and the truth, and
the life; no one comes to the Father
but through Me."
John

Street scenes from Rosedale's commercial district. Courtesy of Albert G. Mogor.

1

RACE RELATIONS AND URBAN NEIGHBORHOODS

FEW ISSUES HAVE GENERATED MORE CONTROVERSY in American cities than the racial integration of urban neighborhoods. Public officials, civic leaders, and civil rights activists have all struggled with the serious problems that accompany residential integration. Since the 1970s, "white flight," "block-busting," and "neighborhood racial transition and change" have all become familiar terms in both the academic and popular vocabulary. Racial transformation in urban neighborhoods is not a new topic for social scientists. The social science and planning literature abounds with the case studies and theoretical treatises describing the process of invasion and succession.[1] Drawing from our accumulated knowledge of the topic, we know that residential transition from one group to another is seldom smooth or devoid of serious conflict.[2]

Disputes among groups over control of urban space is not a recent problem or one limited to blacks and whites. American urban history was largely shaped by the dynamics of immigration and industrialization.[3] The urban neighborhoods of Boston, Philadelphia, New York, and Chicago are rich in ethnic diversity and tradition. Because ethnic residential segregation was so prevalent in most major industrialized cities, strong ties developed between immigrant minorities and their neighborhoods. Little Italy, Poletown, and South End are all names reflecting ethnic allegiance to urban space and denoting a strongly developed sense of community and neighborhood. Historians inform us that the psychological sense of community among immigrant minorities was intensely felt and aggressively defended, especially under conditions when one group appeared ready to invade their turf and territory.[4] Nor did the sense of neighborhood fade in the face of urban renewal or gentrification.[5] Even today, most major cities reflect patterns of residential and neighborhood settlement rooted in immigration history, cultural diversity, ethnic competition, and conflict.[6]

Despite the persistence of ethnicity in American life, it is clear that neighborhood institutions and values do not remain stable when control of urban space changes from one group to another. New groups entering a community and eventually gaining control over it do not simply take over or acquire the institutions and lifeways of prior residents. Old institutions change and new ones are created. Over time, neighborhood businesses not only change hands but often alter the commodities and services provided to the new arrivals. Churches become occupied by different denominations, thus changing the religious culture of the neighborhood. Local schools typically experience gradual but steady modifications in the type of academic programs offered and in the socioeconomic composition of their student bodies. Street life and patterns of neighboring change, as do the content and form of family relations. The nature of everyday events changes in the wake of neighborhood transition. In most urban neighborhoods, racial and ethnic succession permanently and radically transforms community life and culture, especially under conditions where the religious, racial, and ethnic characteristics of residents are different.

This book examines the institutional, cultural, and psychological changes that accompanied racial transition in a single community over several years. Few popular or academic accounts of racial and ethnic change in urban neighborhoods describe the psychological and emotional circumstances that confront those individuals and families who are the direct participants in residential succession. Although demographic statistics profile important changes in our cities, they do not capture the human side of neighborhood succession. Seldom is the process of invasion and succession totally complete. Many of the previous residents do not move; they remain in the old neighborhood. This book examines the transformation of a once cohesive and stable community I will call Rosedale. The study spans two decades of institutional and cultural change. Particular attention is given to the ways in which community and cultural institutions change during the course of residential transition.

Special attention is also given to the influence of numerous social policies initiated during the 1960s and 1970s upon the process of institutional change within urban neighborhoods. During the era now referred to as the War on Poverty, a number of significant social programs were passed by the federal government and implemented as public policy.[7] Many of these programs were designed to provide equal opportunity for urban minorities in the areas of housing, education, social welfare, and job training. Additionally, important federal initiatives took place in the areas of urban renewal, community development, and model cities, all with the intention of revitalizing the nation's cities.

These programs constituted an important political watershed in the history of American public policy. Not since the Great Depression and the legislation initiated by the Roosevelt administration have so many programs designed to provide equal opportunity dominated the public policy arena. This book is critical of many programs initiated during the 1960s and 1970s. In the book, I examine the relationship between federal urban policy and the collapse of one neighborhood's social and cultural institutions.

The book is also about crime, violence, and personal crisis among older people; it is about human suffering, fear, and entrapment. The book is about racial oppression and social inequality; it is about insensitivity and neglect. The book describes the failure of public officials, public policy, and community residents to manage the process of racial succession in an effective and humane manner. The book pays special attention to the problems of the elderly, both white and African American, and minority underclass families and their collective inability to forge any sense of solidarity and mutual support during the process of institutional and cultural change. Special attention is also given to African American youth, the social problems that confront them, and the increasingly serious challenges they pose to community residents, public officials, and civil rights leaders.

Background and Overview

I was originally drawn to Rosedale during the mid-1970s. At that time I was involved in community organizing. Attempting to provide technical assistance and university services to tenants' rights activists, minority organizations, and those involved in the fair-housing movement, I established professional and political affiliations with neighborhood and grassroots political organizers in the community. In 1978, the executive director of a community center located in the heart of a predominantly African American neighborhood asked me to assist in designing and seeking funds for a community development corporation. The corporation would eventually address housing needs in the area by rehabilitating existing and vacant structures, arranging home improvement loans with local financial institutions, and renovating multiple- and single-family dwellings. After several months of planning, a proposal was developed and ultimately funded with local and federal dollars.

University professors who have been active in community and neighborhood politics know that attempts to create any type of progressive social program require constant lobbying of city officials, potential funding agencies, and neighborhood leaders. Neighborhood political organizing, to quote George Bernard Shaw's description of socialism, "is an endless meeting." It was during meetings that occurred five times each week, sometimes five times each day—evenings, afternoons, mornings, on weekends—that I became involved in the events described in this book.

Rosedale is situated in the Dallas–Fort Worth metropolitan area, one of the largest urban regions in the nation. The neighborhood is adjacent to that part of Fort Worth in which the community development corporation was eventually established. The Rosedale Community Center was part of a social service program funded by a consortium of urban churches. Like the community in which I had been working for two years, the neighborhood was composed predominately of a few low- to moderate-income whites, African Americans, and Hispanics. The community, according to social science terminology, was "in transition," that is, rapidly changing from white to African American. In fact, the transition was nearly complete. By 1980, Rosedale was considered "black" by city officials and by most residents of that area.

The community center in Rosedale was located next to a church and used primarily to house a youth program. Being unfamiliar with all programs offered through the church consortium, I initially overlooked the fact that all the meetings I attended were held on the second floor of the community center. All of the personnel there were of African American descent, as were all the children participating in the youth program. It was a noisy place to meet; our discussions were constantly interrupted by the boisterous "rapping" and unruly behavior of youngsters. Arriving early for an afternoon meeting one hot summer day, I inadvertently interrupted a conversation between the executive director and several members of his staff. They were trying to devise a way to deal with the numerous complaints from the "old people" downstairs. The old people had apparently complained about the kids being too rowdy and disrespectful. It was also apparent that several of the kids had been accused of breaking into the downstairs facility. Not wanting to intrude, I simply made a mental note to meet the "seniors" downstairs sometime in the future.

It was several weeks later that I finally had an opportunity to visit what I assumed was a program for minority elders, housed on the first floor of the community center. The executive director of the youth program introduced me to Mrs. Rollins, the director of the Rosedale Senior Citizen's Center. She was a pleasant white woman, about sixty-five years old, neat, very tidy, and energetic. I soon realized that nearly all of the other senior citizens in the program were also white. The men were playing dominoes or checkers or shooting pool. Many of the women were just talking and sipping a soft drink or iced tea.

As I stood between the two directors, I noted a submerged but obvious tension between Mrs. Rollins and Mr. Ellins, the director of the youth facility. Their relationship appeared guarded but cordial, respectful but lacking in trust. Ellins appeared polite yet cavalier. Rollins seemed superordinate but also defeated, intimidated but resolved not to show signs of fear. I explained to Mrs. Rollins that I was from the university and had been working with numerous community leaders in the adjacent neighborhood, Southside. We talked briefly about the kinds of programs the senior center offered. When I expressed interest in knowing more about the program, she insisted that I return at a later date so that we could talk more extensively. As she walked me to the door, she stated, being sure that Ellins heard: "We need help. Please come back and talk with us." I was not able to return to the senior center for another several weeks. By this time, the obligations associated with the community development corporation had been largely satisfied. More significant, I kept recalling the desperation in the voice of Mrs. Rollins when she said she wanted help. I called her and arranged to have lunch the next afternoon with the seniors at the Rosedale Center.

Before eating lunch, I talked with Mrs. Rollins about the center's programs. We quickly established a first-name relationship. Ruth was a pleasant woman, dressed stylishly, and seemed intensely committed to the center. She took phone calls about every ten minutes during our conversation, answered a steady stream of questions from the staff, and managed to say hello to numerous seniors getting ready to have lunch. Even though she was fast approaching senior status herself, she displayed a strongly nurturing and maternal orientation toward her clients. She explained proudly that the most popular program at the center was lunch. People in the neighborhood "can get a hot meal and just come and talk to each other," she said. Explaining in more detail, she said, "Our people like to come and play dominoes. . . . We have tournaments every month." Crafts, cards, dancing, and singing were also popular activities. The center often invited outside people to make speeches or "present a talk" to the seniors. "They just love to do crafts too," she said. "We have two brand-new kilns, and we use them all the time."

Despite Mrs. Rollins's commitment to her program and enthusiastic promotion of it, I could not help but notice that the downstairs facility was stark and devoid of color. The gray walls needed paint. The tile floors were stained and reflected years of sustained service. A small kitchen was packed into a tiny room at one end of the large, open hall. The appliances in the kitchen were old but apparently adequate. At the other end of the hall was a small stage. A pulpit, a large crucifix attached to its front, stood boldly in the center of the stage. A microphone and a Bible were placed neatly on top of the portable pulpit. Numerous tables were carefully organized in the middle of the hall. Off to one side were two pool tables and several smaller table-and-chair arrangements for dominoes, cards, and checkers. A small room housed the ceramics equipment and various craft activities about which she had boasted. The windows were covered with strong steel mesh. The front door, the solitary entrance and exit, was ensconced with a large dead-bolt lock. The stairway leading to the youth facility upstairs was nailed shut with plywood and two-by-fours, all painted black. Occasionally, youthful pranksters would sneak down the stairway and pound violently on the plywood, yelling and shrieking as they did so.

When it was time for lunch, I waited in line with "the folks" and made small talk. Most of those lunching that day were women. I learned later that their numbers accurately reflected the female presence in the white elderly population of Rosedale Heights. The tables in the center, arranged cafeteria-style, each accommodated about eight people. My plate was filled with carefully rationed amounts of boiled carrots and chipped beef on egg noodles as well as a carton of milk and a small wedge of apple pie. I took a seat at one of the tables. Ruth took a place behind the pulpit and said grace over the loudspeaker. She announced my presence to the group. She said that Dr. Cummings was "here to try and help us with our problems." Still very much uncertain as to what the problems actually were, I realized that Ruth had publicly committed me to find their solutions. I stood and stated that I was glad to be a guest at the center and was looking forward to talking with many of those present.

At the table I had selected, three women sat on one side, with myself, another male, and two women on the other. The only elderly African American woman present at the center that day was also sitting at the table. The conversation that unfolded that afternoon clarified and partially explained the tension I had perceived between Mrs. Rollins and Mr. Ellins several weeks earlier. The conversation also served as the door through which I eventually passed to observe and document the experiences described in this book. The women at the table talked enthusiastically. To them, most of the questions they asked me had major significance. "Do you have children?" "How old are they?" "Are you from around here?" "Are you really a professor?"

We chatted amiably about their own children and grandchildren. I asked how long they had lived in the community and what they thought about the center. The one male at the table—a blunt, feisty character tired of the small talk—could restrain himself no longer. "Well, what are you going to do about it?" he said, looking me directly in the eyes.

"Well, sir," I responded, "do about what?"

"The kids, the kids," he said, showing some degree of impatience with my stupidity. I asked him and others at the table to tell me about "the kids."

For the next half-hour, I was hit with a barrage of stories and allegations about the kids who attended the youth program "upstairs." When they said "upstairs," their eyes moved toward the black wooden mass blocking the upstairs entrance. Everyone at the table, excluding the one elderly black woman, explained that the center was "broken into" about once a week. The windows were smashed, and the place was always left in a mess. "We can't even keep a Coke or a candy machine here anymore; they just bust it up and take the money and all the candy and drinks; they take our radios and dominoes and checkers; we have to lock everything up but they still find them." The police would come, but "they don't do anything," insisted one woman.

"Are you sure that the children upstairs are the ones who break in?" I asked. Several responded they were not positive, but they were almost sure. One of the women explained that they no longer had any night programs at the center because "we're too afraid to walk from the parking lot to the center."

"But the parking lot is just across the street," I responded with some skepticism. One of the women explained that on several occasions, kids had surrounded her car in the parking lot and she didn't dare to get out to cross the street. Others told stories of friends who could not enter their cars after an evening program because teens were milling around the auto or sitting on the hood or roof or blocking the door. Another claimed that several youths had lined the sidewalk between the center and the parking lot and hit the pavement with sticks as the seniors passed by. One story led to another—from intimidation to theft to assault to rape and murder.

The luncheon situation was beginning to make me uncomfortable. It was obvious that the problem Mrs. Rollins had referred to was black youth victimizing elderly whites. The discomfort that I experienced was only partly related to the racial aspects of the victimization being described. At that time, other cities had reported similar events. In fact, the criminal victimization of the elderly had reached epidemic proportions in some cities by the early 1980s. And in some instances, the interracial dimensions of the victimization had pushed intergroup tension to the brink of rioting. In Boston, an African American youth had murdered an elderly white man while he was fishing; a woman had been burned to death by teens in the same city. Although systematic white retaliation did not always materialize, fear of such was always widespread. All of this occurred over a decade before the Rodney King riots in Los Angeles.

At that time, these events were abstractions, newspaper accounts of racial crises in some other community, hatred in someone else's backyard. I had even heard liberal, white colleagues within the university rationalize these events as somehow being just retribution for America's violent legacy of racial oppression. One colleague remarked to me: "Their ancestors were probably yukking it up when blacks were being lynched by Klansmen."

The events described at the luncheon table, however, could not be dismissed by political or ideological schemes designed to rationalize the brutality of interracial violence, irrespective of the skin color of the victims or the victimizers. The awkwardness and discomfort inherent in the luncheon situation were maximized by the free and open manner with which the man at my table was beginning to express his racial views. The women were either less infected with racial intolerance or surmised that it would be inappropriate (what we now call politically incorrect) to express their feelings to me in such an unabashed manner. The one elderly African American woman at the table, by this time, had psychologically withdrawn from the situation and was looking off into space, singing softly to herself.

The man, Mr. Huggins, said, "Haven't you heard about the Rosedale rapist?"

I told him that I had heard of that person. "Rosedale rapist" was the name the local media had given to the perpetrator of a series of violent rapes that occurred in the neighborhood during summer 1977. Over forty rapes had been committed. The victims were mostly old and white. Eventually two rapists were caught and convicted. Both were young blacks. The elderly had lived in constant fear until the rapists were apprehended. Even though I had read about the Rosedale rapist in the local papers and heard accounts of the sexual violence on local television, Huggins was intent on making some sort of public statement about the incidents. "There's only one way to deal with a person like that," he said confidently. I had a sinking feeling because I had a pretty clear idea of what was about to be said. "You have to make a good nigger out of him, and the only good one is a dead one," he proclaimed. He stood up, pointed his finger at me, and emphasized: "That's what I would have done." And he walked away from the table for emphasis. Those at the table were silent. The conversation was over. So was the meal.

I spent the next hour talking with Mrs. Rollins about "the problem." She corroborated many of the stories told at the luncheon table. The problem was quite simple: About 250–300 elderly whites were still living in selected areas of Rosedale. They were the residue, those left behind, the ones who could not afford to be part of the massive wave of white flight that had taken place earlier in the community. The elderly were frequent victims of crime. They did not feel secure on the streets or within their homes. The center was the target of numerous break-ins and the object of frequent vandalism. People at the center were afraid. They had lost their courage and their reasons for living. She looked at me and said, "Do you think you can help us?"

I tried to be honest, both to her and to myself. "I'm just one person, Mrs. Rollins; I'm not sure what I can really do." I asked if she had talked with the police about the vandalism and the break-ins.

She said that the police were trying, but they really couldn't do anything. "They come out and put markings on the property and tell people to install dead-bolt locks and get alarms in their house. But the people here can't afford new locks and alarms," she said, "and they don't work anyway." She thought the police didn't really believe their stories or just had too much else to do. "They just don't pay any attention to old people," she insisted. "They think we exaggerate." I asked about the racial attitudes of the seniors at the center. I tried to suggest that some of the people might invite harassment simply because of their racial bigotry. Thoughts of Mr. Huggins were obviously fresh in my mind.

She was prepared for my question. "I can't deny that some people here are prejudiced; most people, though, are not." She said that even if some people were prejudiced, they had learned that they had to get along with "blacks." They had to because they were living in a black neighborhood. "Old people," she argued, "don't have time to be prejudiced anymore. They just want to go to the center, go to church, and live the rest of their life in peace in their own home."

I asked about the youth program upstairs. "Have you talked with Mr. Ellins about the break-ins?"

She said that she had. She expressed respect for Mr. Ellins and claimed that he had been quite cooperative. "Frankly," she said, "I don't think it's the kids upstairs." She explained that some of the kids there had been problems but that Ellins had punished them. "He does what he can, but it doesn't help much. He's like the policemen," she explained; "he listens but doesn't really believe us."

I told Mrs. Rollins that I would try to think about what I had been told that day. I tried to make it clear that I had no ready-made solutions to her problems but that I would talk to more people and try to get a clearer idea of possible remedies. Needless to say, the afternoon was not the most pleasant one I had experienced, and I was glad to return to my office at the university. Over the next few weeks, I tried to think through honestly the implications of what I had learned that day. It was tempting to hide behind the mask of academic objectivity, to seize upon what my academic colleagues call "ethical neutrality" as a convenient excuse to walk away from the situation. Every time that option crossed my mind, however, I kept thinking that everyone, including the police, seemed to be turning away from Rosedale, a community fast becoming a racial powder keg. It was too easy to dismiss the immediate anguish of the elderly and return to the university classroom. At the same time, there was really nothing I could do for them. They were unwelcome and disturbing intruders into my political and intellectual activities.

The following week, I had occasion to meet with Lee Ellins, director of the youth program. Our relationship was such that I could pose a straightforward question and expect an honest answer. At the appropriate time, I asked: "What's going on downstairs?" His eyes squinted at me, correctly assuming that I had talked with Mrs. Rollins. "They make it sound like they're getting the shit kicked out of them on a regular basis down there," I said.

He made it clear that there was definitely some degree of exaggeration going on. "They're old, and uptight," he said, "and part of the problem is their own attitudes." He explained that some of his kids had been problems, but they were "taken care of." He and Mrs. Rollins had apparently established a cooperative relationship and tried to avoid complicating each other's lives. Part of the tension between the seniors and the youth, he contended, was simply related to age differences. The kids were noisy, and the old people wanted peace and quiet. The kids threw rocks and occasionally stole a hubcap or two. Some kids knew there was a Coke machine downstairs and wanted a free Coke. Some of that "type of stuff" was going to happen, he contended. "You got to expect it."

Sensing a degree of defensiveness about his own kids and program, I asked about crime in the area generally. "Come on, Scott," he said, "you know what this neighborhood is like. The crime rate is high; we do the best we can with the kids."

"Do you think the elderly whites are getting singled out as easy marks?" I asked.

Thinking for a minute, he responded, "Probably." We talked more about the problem. He thought that both elderly whites and black elders in Rosedale were being victimized by teenagers. Both were easy marks; but old whites were likely considered easier. The people downstairs, he thought, were exaggerating their problems only insofar as many laid the blame at the doorstep of the youth program. "Our kids are pretty good," he said. Otherwise, he observed, "Yeah, they're probably gettin' fucked over."

"What do you think can be done with the situation?" I asked. "With old white people living in a black neighborhood?"

"Do you want a straight answer?" he asked.

"Yes," I replied.

He said that in a couple of years the problem would go away. Pretty soon there would be no elderly whites in Rosedale. Consequently, it wasn't worth investing a lot of time and energy worrying about it. There were too many other issues and problems confronting the neighborhood and black people generally.

Whereas his position on the matter was not ethically satisfying to me, it was not altogether irrational, with one major exception. I said, "Lee, this situation is racial dynamite. If old white people keep getting harassed and beat up, you'll have every redneck and Klansman in Texas riding shotgun on the streets of Rosedale."

He responded, "I'm not saying it's not important; I'm saying there is only so much I can do, and there's just too much to do. You deal with it." I could not argue with his answer.

Over the next three years, I became extensively involved with the people at the Rosedale Senior Citizen's Center. This involvement included numerous visits to the center itself as well as with the various funding agencies that supported programs for the elderly throughout the city. In tandem with community leaders, I designed a proposal to establish a crime-prevention program for Rosedale Heights in which the elderly were to play a major role. I suggested numerous ways that the elderly could serve as an educational resource for minority youth in the area. I also proposed programs in which minority youth could provide escort services for the elderly. This program was designed to promote some degree of security for the elderly when they shopped or moved around the neighborhood. I surveyed most of the seniors attending the center. The survey established accurate rates of victimization. I and a team of graduate students from the university taped extensive interviews with about 100 senior citizens both at the center and in their homes. We also interviewed numerous African American youth in the area. These interviews were taped and transcribed.

Reports were written. Funds for programs were sought. Presentations were made to various organizations. I pressed my beliefs that crisis was imminent, that the community was teetering on the brink of serious racial violence. Presentations and proposals were politely received, considered, and dismissed. Support for programs was solicited from community and church leaders, city officials and administrators, and nonprofit organizations and agencies serving the elderly. All of these efforts accomplished very little by way of additional funds, programs, or services for the community.

Maybe those involved in the effort to assist the elderly could have tried harder. Maybe we could have been more effective in organizing political support for the programs proposed. Maybe our efforts were lacking in quality and substance. Having acknowledged these likely possibilities, I am more convinced that our initial failure to accomplish anything was based primarily on the intractable nature of race relations in American society and our collective inability as a society to transcend the problems deriving from it. The white elderly of Rosedale were and continue to be politically irrelevant to city elections. They are on the fringes of neighborhood life and culture. Their purchasing power makes them only marginally supportive of business vitality in the community. They are surplus commodities, relics from another era. They are dew about to vanish in the hot Texas sun.

The immediate problems of Rosedale's white elders, and the apparent lack of interest in dealing with them, however, have to be understood in a larger context of race relations and community change. During the time of my initial involvement in the community, Rosedale was evolving into a black ghetto. In retrospect, it is clear that systematic disregard of the white elderly was a simple by-product of America's racial legacy. Like their black neighbors, the white elders were powerless to alter the institutional changes taking place around them and unable to capture the attention or compassion of the larger society in which they lived.

A Retrospective Overview

Nearly two decades have passed since my initial involvement with the black and white residents of Rosedale. During these years, many additional changes have occurred in the community. Many of the white elders have passed on. The institutions and lifeways found in the old neighborhood continue to shift and change. The racial powder keg about which I was so concerned in the late 1970s did in fact ignite and explode. In 1997, problems in the community have become even more divisive, serious, and difficult to solve. For a brief period in the mid-1980s, a much publicized effort to revitalize Rosedale surfaced. It eventually failed. Today, the residents of Rosedale remain unable to shape a common destiny. Public concern over the area fluctuates radically. At this moment, Rosedale's future remains uncertain and problematic.

I have returned to Rosedale on numerous occasions over the past several years and continue to monitor its vital signs. In retrospect, it is clear to me that the story of Rosedale's white elders is only part of a much larger set of problems and issues confronting our nation's cities and their neighborhoods. After numerous years of studying Rosedale and its residents, I also feel it is clear that the community represents much more than a case history of one city's inability to manage residential integration. Rosedale represents a national failure to deal with the continuing problems of race relations in American urban life. As a student of American urban policy, I remain amazed that we as a nation remain spectators while communities like Rosedale collapse in the face of racial transition and change. It is ironic that in pursuit of racial harmony and equal opportunity, some of our public policies helped to undermine many of the institutions we were attempting to strengthen. In pursuit of the public good, we seemed to make things worse for those we were attempting to assist. The events described in this book document the development, growth, and decline of the community of Rosedale and explain the unique role played by national urban policy in unwittingly promoting its collapse as a stable urban neighborhood.

Over the years, a unique combination of racial antagonism and federal efforts to reduce or eliminate this antagonism produced in Rosedale a complicated pathology of social forces. Racism produced cycles of neighborhood growth, decline, and decay. Racism eventually transformed Rosedale from a prosperous and stable community into an urban ghetto. All the negative symptoms of ghettoization were present in the area during the course of this study, and they show no signs of abating at the current time. These include spiraling crime rates, rapid deterioration of business and commercial vitality, declining city services, alienation and despair, family breakdown and disorganization, and youth violence and juvenile gangs.

How did our national policies contribute to Rosedale's collapse? How did this once stable and pleasant community reach its current state of deterioration? How does the case of Rosedale relate to other communities in American cities undergoing racial transition and change? What can we learn from the case of Rosedale? How can public officials, civic leaders, and civil rights activists better manage racial integration? All of these important questions will be addressed in the pages that follow. Before I tell the story of Rosedale, let me explain how the book is organized and how I gathered the information appearing in it.

The subject matter addressed in the book is complicated and has many facets. It is part of a much larger academic literature within the social sciences drawn from the field of race relations. Because this book is written for students, public officials, and the general public, I will inform the reader periodically just how the material presented relates to this wider set of intellectual traditions, but I will not do so in a manner that distracts from the real people and events described in the book. Although references are made to the field of race relations throughout the book, I am primarily concerned with how various public policies contributed to Rosedale's decline and what new policies can be created to better enable cities to preserve, protect, and revitalize their neighborhoods. Of special importance are policies dealing with intergroup relations and programs designed to promote community development.

Because Rosedale was studied over a period of several years, it was possible to observe and analyze the process of racial transition. The longitudinal analysis of transition enabled me to understand more clearly the larger problem of ghetto formation in American cities. Two populations helped shape my thinking on this topic: the white and African American elderly and the African American youth of Rosedale. The problems encountered by these two marginal groups magnify the institutional breakdown that accompanies the ghettoization of urban neighborhoods. For the white elderly, the ghettoization of Rosedale produced fear, isolation, and withdrawal. For adolescents, it produced rage, hostility, and violence.

I learned a great deal from the elderly people of Rosedale, both African American and white. I learned a great deal from African American adolescents and their parents. I could see in the elderly of Rosedale my own grandparents and better understand their physical and emotional vulnerabilities. I could also experience the rage shown by the sons and daughters of Rosedale's elderly when their parents were attacked or assaulted by gangs of young people. The elderly of Rosedale revealed to me the vitality of the human spirit in the face of constant fear, oppression, and victimization. Their courage and persistence were inspirational.

I also developed a tremendous awe and respect for the problems faced by many African American parents, especially single women, attempting to raise children in the jaws of ghetto life. Having four children, I have developed some understanding of the difficulties of parenting even in circumstances where adults are present and contribute to a stable, middle-class lifestyle. Because I was raised in a single-parent household, I can also appreciate the financial and psychological burdens confronting a woman responsible for meeting her children's social, emotional, and financial needs. In a neighborhood milieu where no jobs are available, where informal mechanisms of social control do not exist, and where adolescents feel they have little future, the odds are clearly stacked against African American women who must simultaneously perform as mother, father, and breadwinner.

An African American social worker I interviewed during the course of this study told me that depression was the single most frequent problem encountered among the younger and middle-aged mothers of Rosedale. Contending their depression was directly related to the economic and familial burdens they shouldered, he said:

> It's one thing to say single-parent home, but it's another thing to understand that the person is black and is a woman. That that person does not receive alimony checks and does not receive support from her family. That she's working a job and that she has two or three kids to raise at home. And she makes phone calls to see if they went to school. And then you have to understand the fact that the woman really wants to have a husband. She wants to have somebody with her, and she doesn't. She's very lonely, and she gets depressed. She probably drinks some, and she may even smoke some dope. And she still has to take care of kids and do her job at the same time. She has to meet her bills by herself. You have to understand the depression and the despair of that one parent that these kids do have. That is a big problem. The kid sees his mama depressed. He sees Mama lonely. He sees her going through all that stuff and either decides to get out of her way and find something else on the street, or sometimes he puts even more demands on her. The demands only reinforce her sense of inadequacy and failure and deepen the depression.

Every time I visit Rosedale, I come away with a much greater understanding of the everyday struggles experienced by minority parents in raising their children. Their efforts to keep their children in school, out of trouble, off the streets, and off drugs are constant. There is no relief. When children and adolescents drift into the violent street and drug culture of the urban ghetto, their parents are devastated. When African American adolescents become involved in gang activities that involve violent attacks on elderly whites, their parents, like the community generally, are horrified. They feel they have failed as parents. The working- and lower-class African American families of Rosedale confront failure on a daily basis: on the job, on the streets, and in the family. Violence, drugs, and street crime are the demons that ravage the lives of African American parents in Rosedale. Their struggles, like those of the elderly whites, touched me very deeply.

Over and above the field data, numerous sources of information and analytical approaches were used in this study. Extensive surveys were conducted. Demographic and census information was compiled. Evidence was gathered from police records, court transcripts, newspapers, and various other municipal agencies. Numerous people were interviewed besides elders and adolescents. I talked extensively with neighborhood leaders and community organizers, church officials and ministers, local business figures and merchants, policemen and judges, attorneys and public defenders. I spent hours in the county jail interviewing adolescents awaiting trial for capital murder. I also interviewed their attorneys. I talked with social workers and juvenile detention officers, all having extensive caseloads within the Rosedale area. I talked with local teachers and administrators.

The volume and variety of data collected in a study of this type are overwhelming. Further, there is no foolproof methodological scheme that nicely defines what to include in the final text and what to omit. The social and psychological realities of life in Rosedale are not easily sifted through a canned statistical program or a sophisticated methodological plan lifted from a social science textbook. In writing this book, I was guided by the ethnographic principle that a field researcher should try to suspend preconceptions and let the subjects speak for themselves. Although a researcher certainly must interpret and analyze the contents of what is said by subjects, I was compelled to allow those directly involved in the action being investigated to speak what they believed to be the truth. At the same time, I have not always followed orthodox social science wisdom and suspended my own values and political opinions. When expressed, however, they are clearly and candidly identified.

Wherever possible, I have used direct quotations from subjects. Whereas these verbatim responses have been edited and carefully selected to illustrate specific analytical or theoretical observations, they are the exact words of the people of Rosedale as they spoke them to me. In the chapters that follow, I will try to present to the reader the nature of life in Rosedale, its history and future, as it was subjectively perceived and experienced by those directly involved in it.

I have chosen to maintain the anonymity of all subjects discussed in this book. I have also used fictitious names for some of the communities studied. I have done this for both ethical and practical reasons. Many of the adolescents I interviewed are on probation, have been convicted of serious crimes, or are currently serving time in prison. Some of the criminal convictions are being appealed. Many of the elderly feared retribution should their comments be made public. Although their concerns may not have been based on a realistic assessment of potential retaliation, their apprehensions must be honored and respected. Many subjects forthrightly expressed their racial views. Many officials, social workers, lawyers, police officers, and minority leaders revealed positions and attitudes that they might not have otherwise shared without my pledge of keeping their identities hidden.

Most important, I gave my word to all those interviewed that their comments would remain confidential.

The chapter that follows this introduction examines the demographic transformation of Rosedale. Chapter 3 explores the gradual erosion of community and neighborhood institutions in Rosedale. The psychological impact of the loss of community among the elderly is described and discussed, as is the failure of the new residents to develop sound and sustainable neighborhood institutions. In Chapter 4, the social and psychological bases of fear among the elderly are described. The senior citizens of Rosedale live in constant fear. As a result of their apprehensions about neighborhood change and decline, they withdraw from community and neighborhood life and retreat into private thoughts and personal memories. By and large, their fears are rooted in racial biases, largely tied to black males. Chapter 5 details the magnitude and extent of criminal victimization among Rosedale's elderly during the initial phases of the research, especially by minority adolescents. Not only the elderly live in fear. All residents of Rosedale fear street crime, violence, and the increasingly violent behavior of African American adolescents. Chapter 6 describes a series of interracial rapes that polarized Rosedale and pushed the city to the brink of racial crisis. In Chapter 7, the emergence in Rosedale of "wilding" gangs is discussed. The wilding episodes racially polarized the city and dramatically emphasized the magnitude of problems emerging in the community. Chapter 8 discusses the forces that have transformed and undermined the African American family in Rosedale. Particular attention is given to intergenerational changes in the African American community and their implications for the management and control of youth violence in the neighborhood. Chapter 9 describes recent efforts to rebuild Rosedale and explains why they failed. In Chapter 10, a critical analysis of national urban policy is presented along with an extended explanation of how larger patterns of social change undermined efforts to save the community. In Chapter 11, recommendations on how cities and residents can better manage racial transition and change are presented.

2

THE GHETTOIZATION
OF ROSEDALE

This was the prettiest street in Rosedale, trees all up and down it. Everybody kept their yards clean. It's different now. The neighborhood was the most friendly little neighborhood that you've ever moved into.

—Woman, age 78

I've lived here since 1928. It was the best part of town then. I used to work as a clerk in the 40s and 50s. If they lived in the Rosedale area or had a Rosedale telephone, that check was good. It was known to have the best rating over any part of the whole city [with pride]. And if I'm not mistaken, back in the 30s when they were serving free lunches, Rosedale served more than any other part of the city. Rosedale was known as a working class of people. They weren't really rich people, but they weren't that poor either, a middle class of people that were self-sustaining.

—Man, age 82

ROSEDALE HEIGHTS, a community of about 10,000 people, is located in the Dallas–Fort Worth metropolitan area, one of the largest and most rapidly growing urban regions in the nation. In the early 1900s, Rosedale was considered "one of the more fashionable areas" in which to live. Characterized by single-family brick homes and wooden bungalows with large open porches and tall shade trees in the yards, Rosedale was a "nice, quiet place to live."

It was a cohesive and intimate community, a place where residents shared collective feelings of neighborhood and civic pride and expressed mutual bonds of solidarity. Rosedale's face has long since changed, as has its collective sense of community. The central business district, once housing independent merchants and shopkeepers, continues to decay and deteriorate. By the early 1980s, the neighborhood meeting halls and voluntary association centers had been closed. Some of the schools had been boarded up, along with the old firehouse and post office.

In 1980, Rosedale hovered on the edge of urban blight. The community was devastated by the forces of urban decline and disinvestment. Ghettoization had stripped its once proud features, gutted the core of its physical infrastructure and housing stock, and undermined the social fabric that once bound neighbor to neighbor, business to community, and old to young. The ghettoization of Rosedale occurred within a few decades.

A Brief History of Rosedale

Despite its current predicament, Rosedale has a vital and significant history, a fact proudly stated by its elderly residents. Prior to 1890, the geographic area that became the community of Rosedale was primarily farmland. Cotton, corn, and wheat were grown there commercially. In the early 1890s, residential growth in the area was stimulated by the development of a large cotton mill. The production of various types of cloth in tandem with the processing of raw cotton promoted the residential development of Rosedale and its gradual movement away from an exclusively agricultural economy.

The establishment of Rosedale College, founded by the Methodist Church in 1891, was a major impetus in the growth and development of the community. Today, the college is still considered one of the most important assets of the community. The community's first grocery store was established in 1892. When the area was initially developed, its only transportation link to the city of Fort Worth was one streetcar pulled by a donkey. By the late 1890s, Rosedale was considered a small suburban community that developed around the cotton industry and Rosedale College.

Many of the families that eventually settled there were drawn to the area because of Rosedale College. They built homes in the community so that their children could be educated at the college and receive the kind of moral and intellectual training they thought desirable. The college, its faculty, staff, and student body, provided the core around which to build a stable community.

By the turn of the century, a small business district emerged. It is estimated that in 1904, approximately 80 households could be found in Rosedale. By 1908, there were about 315 residences with fewer than 6 vacant structures. Historical records establish that the area had four grocery stores by 1908 and one "up-to-date" drugstore. Between 1904 and 1908, the number of real estate agents increased from one to twelve, and subscriptions to the city newspaper increased from eighteen to twenty-five. In 1904, only 20 to 30 students attended a one-room school. By 1908, over 400 students were housed in a two-story, concrete school heated by a furnace and illuminated by electricity.

In 1910, the citizens of Rosedale debated the merits of incorporating as a separate city. The debate centered around tax policies and the need to provide city services to the expanding population. One faction supported annexation by the city of Fort Worth; the other favored incorporation as a separate governmental entity. Those favoring annexation argued that the community's tax base was too small to adequately fund the volume of new services required. The financial arguments notwithstanding, the city of Rosedale was incorporated as a separate governmental entity in November 1910.

Those supporting annexation on financial grounds eventually proved correct in their prognoses. Historical accounts show that between 1910 and 1920, "a never ending line of citizens request[ed] the city to grade their streets and clean their gutters." According to the city directory, by 1915 Rosedale had 540 occupied residences (only 1 occupied by a black person), 29 vacant houses, 37 businesses, 7 doctors, and 17 preachers. The population was estimated as being between 3,500 and 4,000.

By 1915, the city of Rosedale had drilled two artisan wells, created a community reservoir, built a city hall, purchased fire equipment, graded streets, and poured concrete sidewalks. In its city directory, Rosedale community officials boasted about the numerous modern conveniences available to Rosedale's citizens. It was stated in the directory that these modern conveniences were achieved through the low tax rate made possible by the city's superb public officials, who ran local government efficiently and professionally. Reflecting a high degree of civic pride in the community, the city directory of 1915 boldly proclaimed that Rosedale was "rapidly becoming the most beautiful and healthful residential locality about the city of Fort Worth."

By 1921, however, it was apparent that local boosterism had come face-to-face with the realities of financing local governmental services. In January 1922, a petition was presented to the city of Fort Worth asking that the community of Rosedale be merged with the larger governmental entity. In February 1922, Rosedale dissolved its corporate existence and merged with the city of Fort Worth. Its annexation by the larger city in 1922 was a harbinger of the social turmoil and cultural upheaval that emerged much later in its brief history as an autonomous community. Like a small town absorbed within the institutional network of urban society, Rosedale's incorporation into the larger metropolitan area ensured its inability to escape the racial and political conflicts that surfaced during the 1960s and 1970s.

Immediately following annexation, its city hall was converted into a municipal police and fire station; it also served as a branch of the municipal waterworks facility. Its trash and garbage were also collected by the centralized city system. Its voluntary associations became merged with the larger municipal chapters, as did its libraries, charities, and related community activities.

Despite incorporation as part of the larger metropolitan area, Rosedale continued to grow and prosper during the 1920s. It even remained fairly stable during the Great Depression. According to local historians, "Many beautiful homes were built during the 1920s and even during the 1930s. As Fort Worth continued to expand, Rosedale became an inner-city bedroom community." Throughout the 1940s and 1950s, Rosedale remained one of the more prosperous and desirable urban communities in which to reside.

Rosedale developed as an exclusively white community. In the 1940s and 1950s, it was virtually isolated from residential contact with either the African American or Hispanic populations. Many residents of Rosedale employed African Americans and Mexican Americans as domestics or in related service jobs, but relationships among blacks, Hispanics, and whites were systematically regulated by southern racial etiquette. Blacks and whites resided in totally separate areas of the city.

The Racial Transformation of Rosedale

By the 1950s, racial changes in Rosedale were beginning to surface. These early warning signs telegraphed the more serious racial problems that would fully surface in the 1960s. Located about four miles southeast of Ft. Worth's central business district, a strategic geographic position, Rosedale forecast the radical demographic changes that were beginning to take shape as early as 1960.

Immediately to the southwest of Rosedale is a community I will call Freetown. Settled after the Civil War by freed, rural blacks, its primary economic focus was agriculture. The early population of this community served as a pool of domestic help and service workers for the residents of Rosedale and other more prosperous neighborhoods in the metroplex. Freetown grew steadily during the decades after the Civil War as former slaves left the farms of rural Texas and sought employment in larger urban settlements. By the 1940s, Freetown was a thoroughly segregated community. Numerous public-housing projects were constructed there during the late 1940s. These projects publicly sealed and confirmed the reputation of the area as "colored." Older white residents of Rosedale still refer to it as Niggertown.

Directly west of Rosedale is another African American community. This area is immediately south of Ft. Worth's central business district. One of the original residential neighborhoods of the city, Southside was settled more than a century ago. Around the turn of the century, however, sections of Southside became the heart of the city's African American community. The city's first black businesses and banks emerged there, as well as minority artisans and community theater. Prominent minority political leaders were drawn from this neighborhood. The more fashionable streets of Southside housed the community's prosperous minority families and members of the black bourgeoisie. Many of the city's established minority politicians and power brokers still reside there. Also, some of the more affluent African American merchants continue to conduct business in this area.

Over the years, Southside expanded eastward to the fringes of Rosedale. In the 1960s, Rosedale and Southside were divided by a major interstate highway, eventually renamed in the memory of Martin Luther King, Jr. It was only a matter of time before this artificial boundary lost its effectiveness as a barrier between the two racially separate neighborhoods.

On the southeast side of Rosedale is Rolling Plains, known for its magnificent view of the city's skyline. After World War II, enterprising developers engineered one of the region's first suburban communities in this area. With the assistance of the private automobile and the rudimentary beginnings of public transportation in the city, Rolling Plains became a popular residential neighborhood for whites. In the 1960s, limited racial integration emerged there. Professional minority families bought homes in Rolling Plains, as did the more prosperous African American residents of Southside.

Presently, Rolling Plains is one of the few residential areas in the metropolitan region that passed through the racial integration era of the 1960s and 1970s in a reasonably stable manner. As Southside continued to lose its more prosperous residents to the lure of black suburbanization, however, it began to deteriorate. The age composition of residents shifted upward, as did the proportion of tenant-occupied houses. As Rolling Plains "opened up" to the black middle class, the prosperity of Southside "went down," according to residents who have lived there over the past thirty years.

To the northeast of Rosedale is the semirural and suburban community of Hammond. Historically the home of rural whites, Hammond is referred to with pride as "redneck" by local residents. It is known as a place where "niggers" are not welcome. In the late 1970s, an attempt to locate a scattered-site public-housing project in the community initiated widespread public opposition and Ku Klux Klan activities. By the early 1980s, the farmland in Hammond had increasingly fallen to suburban development. By and large, development accommodated white families. Because the new construction was designed to attract middle- and upper-income residents and because of its history, the area remained residentially segregated throughout the 1980s.

Because of its unique geographic location, Rosedale was destined to be pulled into the turbulent waters of racial transition and change. Population growth in Southside and in Freetown and the migration of rural blacks to the metropolitan area increased pressure on the existing housing stock available to African Americans in the city. As more prosperous African American families set their sights on the attractive dwellings and suburban lifestyle offered by Rolling Plains, many looked first toward Rosedale. Rosedale, however, proved to be a temporary stepping-stone for prosperous minority families. Racial steering among real estate brokers, informal agreements among homeowners, and overt discrimination initially kept many African American families out of Rosedale. Busing, court-ordered school integration, federal housing policies, and public transportation helped to erode some of the early resistance. Eventually, a residential trickle broke through the walls of racial exclusion. By the late 1960s, major weaknesses in the walls of racial exclusion were evident. By the late 1970s, white resistance had collapsed, white flight had accelerated, and Rosedale was well on its way to becoming a predominantly black neighborhood.

The first wave of African American migration to Rosedale was primarily middle and upper income. The later residents consisted mainly of working- and lower-class black families. The current residents are the urban poor. White flight and the movement of the black bourgeoisie to the more prosperous suburbs sealed the fate of Rosedale as an unstable, decaying neighborhood. In 1950, the three census tracts that composed the geographic center of Rosedale were close to 100 percent white in racial composition. Even in 1960, racial patterns of residential settlement showed remarkable stability in the three tracts. The 1960 census showed that about 98 percent of the households in the community were occupied by white families.

In 1970, however, the magnitude of the racial transition was beginning to surface in official statistics, which revealed that in the two tracts composing the residential and commercial core of Rosedale, 30 and 40 percent of the residents, respectively, were African American. By 1980, these two areas had shifted to 63 and 82 percent African American. The one remaining tract, an area that stretches north into Hammond, shifted from less than 1 percent African American in 1970 to over 31 percent in 1980. By the mid-1990s, the community had become resegregated with whites composing approximately 12 percent of Rosedale's population.

Census tracts often do not correspond to the actual boundaries of urban neighborhoods. Within the natural geographic boundaries that have historically defined the community of Rosedale, there is an even greater concentration of black families. And when driving or walking through the streets and blocks of Rosedale, one now encounters clusters of Chicano families; their houses tend to group along specific streets in selected blocks. One also encounters young, white, working- and lower-class families and a small but growing Asian community. They moved to Rosedale in response to the drop in housing prices or rental fees that accompanied white flight. The bulk of those currently living in Rosedale are poor African American and Hispanic families, poor whites, and recent Asian immigrants: The urban underclass now dominates the community.

Sprinkled throughout the area, one finds a few white elderly. Their homes are easy to identify. They are marked by steel or iron bars covering windows and by doors displaying one or more dead-bolt locks. The homes of the elderly are surrounded by other security measures such as chain-link fences and floodlights. Many have small gardens in the backyard or flowers planted along the sides of the house or by the front porch. The dwellings of the white elderly look neater, more secure, and tend to be in better repair than those of their poor minority neighbors.

Suburban Development and Racial Change

Why did Rosedale become an urban ghetto in such a short time? What exactly happened to its neighborhood institutions, community life, and culture during the period of change? Why did its housing stock quickly fall into disrepair? Why did the established residents of Rosedale abandon the community so rapidly? Why didn't they stay in Rosedale and try to protect their financial and social investments? In order to answer these questions, it is necessary to understand why the price of real estate fluctuates in cities and what causes people and financial institutions to stop investing in certain neighborhoods. The value of real estate in cities is strongly influenced by the process of competitive bidding for urban space. As a result of competitive bidding, land acquisition, rental fees, and the price of real estate, generally, are higher nearer the centers of economic activity. In cities, rich and poor families have very different residential choices available to them. According to urban geographer David Harvey,

> For the poor group, the bid rent curve is characteristically steep since the poor have very little money to spend on transportation; and therefore their ability to bid for the use of the land declines rapidly with distance from the place of employment. The rich group, on the other hand, characteristically has a shallow bid rent curve since its ability to bid is not greatly affected by the amount of money spent on transportation. When put in competition with each other, we find the poor group forced to live in the center of the city, and the rich group living outside.[1]

Rosedale's rapid ghettoization can be partially understood by viewing it in relationship to the real estate development taking place in the larger metropolitan area of which it is a part. Over the past three decades, the entire Dallas–Fort Worth metropolitan area has experienced rapid development. Urban development in this part of Texas is not only regional in nature but reflects the emergence of the Sun Belt as a major growth area in the American economy. Dallas–Fort Worth has become a centerpiece of banking and finance in the Southwest. Urban growth and development in this region has been shaped by multimillion-dollar investments on the part of national and international financial conglomerates and corporations. The growth of suburbs in this region rapidly accelerated during the 1970s and 1980s.

By most objective standards, Dallas–Fort Worth is a prosperous metropolitan region. Despite fluctuations in the housing market in the 1980s, its unemployment rate has remained fairly low by national standards, and the potential quality of life there is considered to be among the best in the nation. Reflecting Dallas's emergence as a center of developmental prosperity, its population grew from 434,462 in 1950 to 679,684 in 1960. By 1970, the U.S. census established the population of Dallas at 844,401. It grew to over 900,000 in 1980, and presently there are over 1 million residents living in the city. Fort Worth grew less rapidly over the past four decades. Between 1950 and 1960, the population increased from 278,778 to 356,268. By 1970, there were 393,467 residents living in the city. In 1980, the population of Fort Worth declined slightly to 385,164. But by 1990, it registered an increase to more than 448,000 residents. Most significant, the Dallas–Fort Worth metropolitan region as a whole grew from 3 million to more than 4 million residents between 1980 and 1990.

Despite all the outward indications of growth and development, the emergence of Dallas–Fort Worth as a regional center of southwestern business prosperity was largely a suburban and not an urban event. The rural area between Dallas and Fort Worth rapidly developed between 1970 and 1990. Associated with suburban growth and development was a concomitant shift in the racial and class composition within the city limits of Dallas and its sister city thirty miles away, Fort Worth.

In 1950, African Americans composed about 13 percent of Dallas's population. By 1960, the proportion had grown to 19 percent, and by 1970 the figure exceeded 25 percent. In 1980, the proportion of African Americans residing in Dallas approached 30 percent. By 1990, 29.5 percent of Dallas's residents were of African American descent and nearly 21 percent were of Hispanic origin. In 1950, only 13.2 percent of the population of Fort Worth was reported in the census as African American. By 1960, this figure had risen to 15.8 percent, and in 1970 the African American population of the city was reported at 19.9 percent. In 1980, almost 23 percent of the city was populated by African Americans. By 1990, 22 percent of the city was of African American descent, and about 20 percent was of Hispanic origin.

The degree of racial polarization and residential segregation in both cities is extremely high. In 1980, African American and Hispanic segregation in Dallas and Fort Worth was higher than national averages for all southern cities.[2] By 1990, rates of segregation had registered no significant declines. Further, the ghettos and barrios of Fort Worth and Dallas reveal all the symptoms of neglect and decay that are found in central cities all over the nation. In this sense, the ghettoization of Rosedale is a direct reflection of the growing impoverishment of the inner-city population of Forth Worth itself and the suburban development that contributed to this outcome.

While these population transformations were taking place within the two cities, the suburbs between Dallas and Fort Worth were experiencing equally rapid growth and change. Suburban growth, however, was qualitatively different. The major suburbs between and surrounding the two cities—Arlington, Irving, Richardson, Mesquite, Plano, Grapevine, Hurst, Euless, Bedford, Garland, and Lancaster—are predominately white in racial composition, professional and managerial in occupational characteristics, and high in income. The homogenous class and racial composition of the suburbs has been reinforced by public policies promoting racial equality and civil rights. Court-ordered busing in Dallas and Fort Worth could be avoided by simply moving to the suburbs, an option reinforced by the refusal on the part of most suburban jurisdictions to participate in HUD-sponsored housing or community development programs. Suburban political autonomy, white flight, and the suburbanization of industry, although contributing to the prosperity of the metropolitan region as a whole, eroded the business and commercial vitality of the central cities. The price of real estate is much higher in the suburbs, as are the profits to be realized from real estate speculation in housing development and shopping malls.

The ghettoization of Rosedale and the declining value of its housing stock simply mirrored the changing land use and development patterns in the metropolitan region of which it is a part. Rosedale was initially conceived as a white suburban community; its racial composition was eventually changed by the tremendous expansion in the size of the city's minority community, a trend reinforced by larger patterns of real estate development and growth. As the farmland between Dallas and Fort Worth became developed and suburbanized, it eventually housed residents being displaced from older communities like Rosedale. Land use and development patterns in the metropolitan region were shaped by the investment activities of suburban builders, bankers, real estate speculators, and industrialists.

Arlington, the major suburb between Dallas and Fort Worth and immediately east of Rosedale, established itself as one of the fastest-growing communities in the nation during the 1980s. Arlington grew from 90,000 in 1970 to 262,000 in 1990. Between 1980 and 1990, it reported a 63.5 percent increase in population. In 1990, it reported that 8.2 percent of its population was of African American origin and 8.9 percent was of Hispanic descent. The population of Plano experienced a 78 percent increase between 1980 and 1990. Only about 4 percent of its population was of African American decent in 1990, and around 6 percent was of Hispanic background. Very similar population trends are found in the other suburbs between and around the Dallas–Fort Worth metropolitan area.

During the period 1970 to 1990, the population of the metropolitan region became more racially separated and socioeconomically differentiated. These demographic trends were reinforced by the development of major transportation systems and arteries, making it possible for the region's more affluent citizens to commute to places of employment downtown. Additionally, a major new airport facility was strategically located directly between the two metropolitan areas in the small rural community of Grapevine. The Dallas–Fort Worth airport project stimulated rapid growth in the suburban communities of Hurst, Euless, and Bedford and promoted construction of additional roadways linking these suburbs with the two downtowns.

The rapid development of Arlington was facilitated by massive investments in a major amusement park and by the related construction and expansion of the stadium housing the Texas Rangers baseball franchise. Even the Dallas Cowboys left the city of Dallas for Texas Stadium, located in the suburban facilities of Irvine. The Cotton Bowl, former home of the Cowboys, is located in South Dallas, one of the worst black ghettos of the city.

The racial composition of Rosedale began to shift in response to the larger demographic and developmental transformations taking place in the metropolitan region as a whole. By 1970, white flight in Rosedale closely followed patterns of demographic change in the region generally. Between 1980 and 1990, the accelerated transformation of Rosedale dramatically revealed itself in official census statistics. The proportion of whites living there dropped steadily after the 1970s. Between 1980 and 1990, the proportion of African Americans living in Rosedale remained fairly stable, and the proportion of Hispanics living in the community increased sharply.

By 1990, Rosedale was approaching a triethnic urban neighborhood, populated exclusively by poor African Americans and Hispanics and low-income whites. By 1990, the white middle class had long since left the community. The white population still residing there consisted of the elderly original residents of Rosedale, and younger poor whites who had moved there from rural communities or relocated from other impoverished neighborhoods in the city.

Contrary to its once proud history, recent information shows that Rosedale's current occupants are much poorer than residents of the metropolitan area. Whereas Rosedale's earlier residents could boast that their community and its residents were well above the average, those now living there are among the poorest in the metropolitan region. The median household, median family, and per capita income figures are well below countywide averages. Whites, African Americans, and Hispanics living in Rosedale's three census tracts report consistently lower income figures than their counterparts living in other areas of the city.

Table 2.1 shows that in the county as a whole, 11 percent live below the official poverty level. The Rosedale figures are well above that amount. On virtually every measure of poverty, Rosedale reports figures well above countywide averages. In certain sections of Rosedale, over 50 percent of families with children live in poverty, and over one-half of female-headed households reside in poverty.

Census data can accurately describe demographic transitions and identify the number of people living in poverty in a particular community. Census

TABLE 2.1   The Socioeconomic Characteristics of Rosedale's Current Residents, 1990 Census

	Countrywide Averages	Rosedale's Census Tracts		
		A	B	C
Income				
Median household	$32,335	$13,946	$14,063	$15,938
Median family	38,279	17,515	15,645	16,511
Per capita				
White	16,935	7,446	5,833	5,402
Black	8,775	5,455	4,718	5,763
Hispanic	8,147	4,271	4,626	5,286
Poverty				
% persons below	11.0	41.3	38.8	27.4
% persons 65 or older	11.7	29.1	47.3	34.9
% all families	8.2	36.8	32.5	22.5
% families with children under 18	11.6	45.9	36.3	26.7
% female head	24.8	45.9	55.2	25.7
% female head with children under 18	31.2	52.0	54.3	24.8

information, however, does not illuminate the psychological and cultural dimensions of neighborhood decline and change. How did racial change affect the nature of neighborhood life and culture in Rosedale? What happened to established neighborhood institutions in the face of racial change? How did residents deal with the process of change?

3

RACIAL TRANSITION AND THE LOSS OF COMMUNITY

SOCIOLOGISTS AND URBAN PLANNERS have studied the serious social and psychological traumas that accompany radical changes in community institutions. According to many social scientists, the relationships between individuals and their social institutions are profoundly affected by rapid social change. Many of the positive feelings bonding individuals to each other, to neighborhood institutions, and to their larger communities have weakened in cities and in rapidly changing urban neighborhoods in particular. More important, the bond between individuals and their institutions is what provides moral order to community life and culture.

Robert Nisbet maintains that the loss of community is one of the central ideas dominating social science thinking about city life over the past century. The sense of community, according to Nisbet,

> encompasses all forms of relationships which are characterized by a high degree of personal intimacy, emotional depth, moral commitment, social cohesion, and continuity in time. Community is founded on man conceived in his wholeness rather than in one or another of the roles, taken separately, that he may hold in the social order. It draws its psychological strength from levels of motivation deeper than those of mere volition or interest. . . . Community is a fusion of feeling and thought, of tradition and commitment, of membership and volition.[1]

Nisbet claims that positive feelings of community have collapsed in the wake of industrialization and the increasing rationalization of social life and culture. According to this interpretation of urban life, major technological and economic changes have eroded the institutions and sentiments that make up the psychological sense of community. Other students of city life and culture have analyzed the trend toward increasing rationality that accompanies the shift from agricultural to industrial society.[2] According to many contemporary social critics, social relationships in the modern metropolis have become increasingly secondary, impersonal, and fragmented.[3] Few social scientists, however, have identified race relations as a major source of institutional decline in cities.

Contrary to critics of contemporary urban life, we know that many ethnic communities in cities exhibit qualities and sentiments similar to those found in rural villages. Many urban communities are characterized by sentiments that produce a strong commitment to collective institutions and a shared sense of values and moral standards. Herbert Gans refers to city neighborhoods that display these qualities as "urban villages."[4] Industrial growth and development do not inevitably destroy the fabric of neighborhood life and culture. Nor do simple demographic shifts transform a stable community into an urban ghetto. The case of Rosedale shows that racial antagonism was a much more potent and salient factor undermining a sense of community than were the sinister forces of technological and industrial change.

The Rosedale that exists in the memories of the white elderly was a community in the traditional sense, an area compatible with Gans's urban village and consistent with Nisbet's idea of a "moral commitment" to place. To the elderly, Rosedale was and continues to be much more than a geographic area. The neighborhood institutions and social relationships remembered by the elderly were primary and characterized by face-to-face intimacy. They knew the merchants of Rosedale on a first-name basis. They considered the schools collective property and expressed similar feelings about neighborhood churches and voluntary organizations. They were psychologically, socially, and economically bonded with local institutions and practices.

Well-manicured yards were considered by the elderly a moral obligation, part of a collective responsibility to maintain community standards. Disciplining disrespectful and rowdy children on the streets of Rosedale was a community as well as a family and an individual responsibility. Family life was the centerpiece of life and culture in Rosedale, and a family's worth was typically measured by the manners and public demeanor exhibited by its children on neighborhood streets and in meeting places. For the elderly, neighboring in Rosedale represented the kind of social bonding and mutual support found in small-town rural America.

Sociologist Gerald Suttles maintains that modern urban neighborhoods are highly organized territorial units; the social and cultural order found within spatially segregated urban neighborhoods provides "a common arena within which people arrive at a fairly standard code for deciphering and evaluating one another's behavior."[5] If geographic segregation among groups remains stable, he claims, some form of "ordered segmentation" preserves the relationship between locality and culture. If, however, groups are pitted against one another in competition for common urban space, the relationship between locality and culture becomes severely fragmented and unstable. Further, if one group chooses to leave a contested area or is forced out, it is logical to expect that the entire social fabric of neighborhood life and culture will be destroyed or significantly transformed or eventually replaced by new social forms, patterns, and behaviors.

Suttles maintains that some cities are characterized by stable, territorial enclaves. In other situations, however, chaos and conflict seem to be more prevalent: "Ethnic invasion, the encroachment of industry, and economic conditions constantly reshuffle slum residents and relocate them around new neighborhoods."[6] If relocation produces intergroup conflict and succession, established residents usually follow one of two possible behavioral options. First, they can restrict social relations to members of their own group or retreat and withdraw from community and neighborhood life altogether, possibly by physically relocating.

Second, long-term residents can establish social relationships with the new group. These new relationships can provide a cultural and institutional foundation upon which to formulate and build strategies of intergroup cooperation and, ultimately, peaceful coexistence. New relationships, however, do not emerge easily. They are often created through tough negotiation, compromise, and reluctantly accepted trade-offs. More often than not, new community relationships are created through conflict and confrontation. Some communities never achieve the compromises required in a stable multiethnic neighborhood.

At an earlier point in history, the black and white communities of Rosedale, Southside, Freetown, and Hammond existed in a state very similar to what Suttles calls "ordered segmentation." Each territorial unit was not only spatially separate and distinct, but morally and culturally isolated as well. Relationships among groups were highly structured and formalized through well-established codes of racial etiquette. Blacks did not travel into Rosedale, and whites seldom set foot in Southside or Freetown. Each community had its own culture and lifestyle and its own set of neighborhood institutions and practices. The ghettoization of Rosedale, however, transformed neighborhood life and culture in that community. I have described briefly the demographic changes that transformed Rosedale. It is equally important to understand the social and cultural aspects of community and neighborhood change. By viewing the process of racial change through the eyes of Rosedale's original residents, those now left behind, we can understand more clearly the emotional, psychological, and cultural barriers preventing peaceful coexistence there. It is also possible to understand why the racial integration of Rosedale was managed so poorly and why racial harmony was nearly impossible to achieve.

TABLE 3.1   Social Characteristics of Rosedale's Elderly (percent)

Sex	
Male	26.6
Female	72.4
	N = 124.0
Race	
White	95.2
Black	4.0
No response	0.8
	N = 125.0
Age	
Between 56 and 62	9.6
Between 63 and 67	12.8
Between 68 and 72	19.2
Between 73 and 77	19.2
Between 78 and 82	22.4
No response	5.6
	N = 125.0

The Elderly of Rosedale: A Window to the Past

In 1980, there were approximately 280 elderly white households in Rosedale. This estimate was obtained from Mrs. Rollins at the Rosedale Senior Citizen's Center and also corroborated by estimates from the Fort Worth Police Department. Administrative personnel at the center believed they had compiled a fairly comprehensive list of all senior citizens in the neighborhood. Even though the center's services were available to all the elderly of Rosedale, in the early 1980s the clientele was almost exclusively white. For whatever reason, the African American elderly rarely used the facility. In order to understand exactly who was left behind in Rosedale, I forwarded a comprehensive survey to all seniors on the center's mailing list. Of the 280 families receiving questionnaires, 125 returned them with complete information, a response rate of approximately 45 percent. The survey data uncovered the social and cultural roots of Rosedale's white elderly and enabled us to establish a racial and economic context in which to interpret the changes taking place there.

Table 3.1 shows selected social characteristics of Rosedale's white elderly. Most were female (72 percent), white (95 percent), and over 70 years old. The median age of respondents was 73.2 years. By and large, those left behind in Rosedale were elderly, white women. Most of the elderly had personal roots deeply embedded in Rosedale's community history.

Table 3.2 shows that the respondents had been living in Rosedale for an average of twenty-one years. Almost 33 percent had lived there for more

TABLE 3.2   The Social Roots of Rosedale's Elderly (percent)

Length of residence	
1–5 years	23.2
6–10 years	8.8
11–20 years	17.6
21–30 years	17.6
31–40 years	12.8
41–50 years	8.8
51–65 years	6.4
No response	4.8
	N = 125.0
Place of residence prior to Rosedale	
Somewhere else in the city	81.6
Other city in the metropolitan area	4.8
Other part of Texas	7.2
East coast of U.S.	–
West coast of U.S.	–
Midwest of U.S.	1.6
Rocky Mountain area	–
Outside U.S.	–
No response	4.8
	N = 124.0

than thirty years. Over 80 percent were residents of the larger metropolitan area before moving to Rosedale. Quite clearly, the elderly of Rosedale were "hometown" people with strong bonds to the city, the community, and the neighborhood. They considered themselves to be natives of the area.

The strong, local ties of the elderly are further revealed in Table 3.3. Most of the elderly not only owned their own home but had completely retired their mortgage debt, a fact that financially tied them to the area. Homeownership, however, had become a dream gone sour. Many of the elderly told us, with pride, that they had neighborhood parties during the 1950s and 1960s to burn their mortgage notes. The presumed security of paying off the mortgage was symbolically displayed to neighbors through the public act of setting the note ablaze.

Table 3.4 shows the economic circumstances of those surveyed. The majority of the elderly were living alone, their spouses having died several years earlier. Over 70 percent were retired or identified themselves as housewives. This information in and of itself did not fully reveal the financial circumstances of Rosedale's elderly females. Table 3.5, however, shows their occupational, educational, and financial characteristics.

The elderly males of Rosedale represented all levels of the occupational hierarchy. Most had had white-collar occupations or been employed in the crafts sector. These data are consistent with historical descriptions of Rosedale as a stable, middle-class community. Most of the respondents had

TABLE 3.3   Homeownership Among Rosedale's Elderly (percent)

Homeownership	
Own and making mortgage payments	8.8
Own and completely paid off mortgage	66.4
Renting	21.6
No response	3.2
	N = 125.0

TABLE 3.4   Living and Employment Situation of Rosedale's Elderly (percent)

Living situation	
Living with husband or wife	25.6
Living alone; husband/wife deceased	52.0
Living with relatives	9.6
Other	10.4
No response	2.4
	N = 125.0
Employment situation	
Retired	70.4
Working	10.4
Housewife	17.6
No response	1.6
	N = 125.0

TABLE 3.5   The Social Class Composition of Rosedale's Elderly (percent)

Occupation of male head of household before retirement or death	
Professional	10.4
Managerial	9.6
Clerical and sales	16.8
Craftsmen	16.0
Semi-skilled	12.8
Unskilled	1.6
No response	32.8
	N = 125.0
Annual family income	
Less than $4,000	57.6
Between $4,001 and $8,000	20.8
Over $8,000	12.0
No response	9.6
	N = 125.0
Educational level	
Less than high school	52.0
High school	24.0
Trade school or some college	12.8
College	4.0
No response	7.2
	N = 125.0

TABLE 3.6   Source of Income for Rosedale's Elderly

Source of Income	Yes		No	
Social security	82.4%	(103)	17.6%	(22)
Welfare	4.8	(6)	95.2	(119)
Disability	5.6	(7)	94.4	(118)
Employment pension	22.4	(28)	77.6	(97)
Insurance	5.6	(7)	94.4	(118)
Other	20.8	(26)	79.2	(99)

achieved a high school diploma or less. These findings are consistent with the educational attainment levels expected for women raised in an earlier era. Most important in Table 3.5 are the income data. Over 57 percent of the families in our survey were carrying out their lives on less than $4,000 per year, and cumulatively, over 75 percent received less than $8,000 each year.

Table 3.6 reveals the sources from which Rosedale's elderly drew their income. Over 80 percent received benefits from the social security system. This was the single most important source of income for the elderly women of Rosedale. The other major source of financial support was employment pensions (about 22 percent). The category "other" in Table 3.6 largely represents family support networks, including income from children, brothers, and sisters. Only a very small proportion of the elderly derived income from stocks, bonds, insurance, and related kinds of investments.

The social and financial profiles of Rosedale's elderly, as shown in the survey data, presented a clear picture of their circumstances. They were elderly women living on fixed incomes. Many lived alone in a house paid for by a lifetime of collective family labor. Their pension or social security income was adequate, just about enough to meet the expenses of running a household and keeping food on the table. Little was available for anything else but the basics of life. But their house was fully paid. The mortgage, like the occupant of the house, had been retired for several years.

The elderly were "natives," having moved to Rosedale several decades earlier. They had raised their children there and were now retired. They had taken meticulous care of their homes, their piece of the American dream. During interviews with them, it was clear that they knew how many times they had painted the kitchen or papered the living room. They knew when the new bathroom was installed and what color tile they had argued over. They knew when the trees on the front lawn were planted and how much they had grown over the years. Their homes were filled with memories— pictures of a departed husband, of a son who was killed in Korea, of a daughter's family that now lived in California. The major part of their adult lives had been carried out in Rosedale, and it was there that they were going to stay. As one man told me, "I'm not going to leave this house until they carry me out in a pine box."

Because many of the elderly remained in Rosedale, they witnessed its turbulent transformation from white to African American and Hispanic. When the racial transition began to take shape in the community, according to them, those who left first were those who could afford to do so or who were able to market their homes quickly. Local market opportunities and personal financial circumstances made it possible for many families to leave the neighborhood "early on." Panic selling and blockbusting, whether rational or irrational, stimulate sales in the local real estate market. Panic selling creates an oversupply of units in a concentrated geographic area; an abrupt decline in the price of units in that area is an inevitable by-product of blockbusting. Strong incentives exist, therefore, to sell quickly before prices drop.

Real estate brokers interested in maximizing commissions have a direct stake in volume selling. A drop in market prices can be compensated for by increasing the volume of sales. If white owners are convinced that the value of their investment in real estate is about to plummet because of black invasion, it makes sense to sell quickly in order to minimize losses. Brokers, no doubt, do little to discourage this interpretation of market realities. If a broker has access to willing buyers, even though these buyers are black, the incentive for white owners to bail out before things get worse must indeed be very high.

Lost in the panic psychology of white flight, however, are the economic parameters that establish the limits of real-life options. In the case of Rosedale, middle-aged and younger whites, because they were employed and thus able to obtain mortgage financing, sold their property and moved to other neighborhoods first. Many of the elderly, because they were without sufficient resources to sustain a move or to finance the purchase of another home, did not flee in the face of black invasion. Most of the elderly were surely not able to obtain mortgage financing; they were considered bad credit risks. And even though a sale might return to them all of the equity accumulated in their homes, the capital would be insufficient to cover the cost of similar housing in other, more prosperous areas of the city. Furthermore, they had no way to service the mortgage debt.

Those left behind in Rosedale, therefore, composed a significant population of eyewitness informants capable of providing a unique perspective on the racial transformation of the neighborhood. Even if they desired, many of the elderly could not afford to leave Rosedale. Equally significant, they had lived in Rosedale so long that the thought of leaving was painful. As explained by one elderly woman, "Why should we leave Rosedale? We have just as much right here as anybody. Even though I can't afford to leave, I feel I should stay. This is my home. My house is paid for, and I'm not going to leave."

This statement captures important psychological, emotional, and cultural issues that must be addressed in order to manage more effectively the integration of established urban neighborhoods, especially those in the midst of rapid social change. As the demographic information indicated, the age distribution of Rosedale's white population shifted dramatically in response to the racial transition. Those left behind might hold different racial attitudes and values than those who fled, but it is more likely that the elders' opinions and perspectives revealed why so many others had felt compelled to leave. This is why their opinions are so important. It is probably fair to conclude that some groups remaining in an urban neighborhood are not psychologically or culturally capable of accepting the changes required to coexist peacefully when another, culturally different group enters the same geographic space. Nonetheless, it is clear that flight from a community leaves its institutions imperiled and its history and culture devastated. What follows is a social accounting of what was lost, abandoned, or thrown away in the community of Rosedale as reported by those left behind.

Grief and the Loss of Community

Social scientists studying families who have been forced to relocate because of urban renewal projects describe a painful psychological state that they label "grieving for a lost home."[7] Neighborhoods slated for slum-clearance programs were physically destroyed, crushed by what critics of urban renewal called the "federal bulldozer."[8] Not only were the physical manifestations of neighborhood life and culture demolished by slum clearance but also the human and emotional dimensions of community life were undermined and destroyed.

Families displaced by urban renewal lose access to neighborhood life and culture. Familiar places and institutions are no longer available to them. Friendship ties and bonds of neighborhood social life are permanently severed. Since displaced residents are eventually scattered throughout a metropolitan region, they typically lose access to each other and to the psychological gratification that access provided. Individuals and families affected by profound changes taking place within their immediate environment recognize but often do not often accept the legitimacy of the external forces confronting them and sometimes mobilize against these forces.

For the elderly, the racial transformation of Rosedale was very similar to a slum-clearance project in that the federal government was seen as the agency primarily responsible for destroying their lives and their community, both physically and psychologically. They viewed the change as being initiated by forces external to them, completely independent of their volition and will. They were angry about the distant and powerful forces changing their lives and frustrated by their inability to reverse them.

After interviewing numerous elderly residents, I sensed that they viewed the changes taking place in Rosedale as comparable to a natural disaster. Kai Erikson, in his analysis of the Buffalo Creek flood, reports that natural disasters produce collective trauma. At the basis of collective trauma is the psychological loss of community.[9]

Erikson explains that when a community is destroyed by a natural disaster, profound emotional consequences follow: "The difficulty is that when you invest so much of yourself in that kind of social arrangement you become absorbed by it, almost captive to it, and the larger collective around you becomes an extension of your own personality, an extension of your own flesh. This means that not only are you diminished as a person when that surrounding tissue is stripped away, but that you are no longer able to reclaim as your own the emotional resources you invested in it."[10]

A deep form of grief has been reported by those studying individuals who have been displaced by slum-clearance projects or who are the victims of natural disasters. Perhaps this is not the kind of grief that is produced by the loss of a spouse, a child, or a parent or the kind of grief that follows the loss of a close friend. Nonetheless, the sense of loss is profound. The residents grieve for a lost home and all that is represented by that home. They miss the old neighborhood and the emotional security it provided. They miss the things they used to do there.

Many cope with the loss by mentally retreating from their present surroundings and immersing themselves in memories. The physical aspects of community life are crushed under the powerful treads of the urban bulldozer or submerged by rising floodwaters. Also destroyed by these powerful external forces are the psychological and emotional elements of neighborhood existence.

The dimensions of grief expressed by the elderly of Rosedale closely parallel those reported by families displaced by urban renewal projects or uprooted by natural disasters. Extreme grief was evident in the way they recalled how the neighborhood used to be before the racial transition took place. Most were bitter, alleging that irresponsible outside forces had allowed the community to be taken away from them. Like the victims of natural disasters, the elderly of Rosedale felt they had been "cheated out" of what was rightfully theirs. Unlike victims of a natural disaster, however, few conceded that "God's will" was at work. Instead, they held the "government" and "politicians" responsible for destroying their beloved neighborhood.

Like most people who grieve over a serious loss, many of the elderly initially denied that the changes in Rosedale would be permanent. Others simply denied the fact that the neighborhood had changed. Denial eventually produced anger. Over time, most accepted the change. But acceptance was often expressed as sorrow, as grief over what had happened to their community. The neighborhood as they knew it had died; it was gone, and part of them had died with it. Acceptance of their situation, however, produced other emotions, few of which were positive or contributed to the creation of new community and neighborhood institutions.

Commitment and Entrapment

Those left behind in Rosedale had to deal with the fact that although the neighborhood had changed, they still resided there. As a result, they were compelled to search for ways to cope with the new lifeways and values emerging around them. Many coped with immediate realities by psychologically withdrawing. They loved the community, but their love was sustained only by memories. They lived in the past. They grieved over what had taken place in the community and were powerless to alter or change the course of external events. They expressed a desire to leave but could not voluntarily uproot themselves from the neighborhood. They were trapped—both by their memories and by the financial circumstances that controlled their life options.

One man with whom I talked had lived in Rosedale for forty-nine years. He was living in the home of his parents; he was a second-generation resident of the area. Recalling how Rosedale used to be before the transition, he said with pride and conviction:

> Actually, it was just a great little area. I remember that my parents really struggled hard to get a down payment on the house. It was an achievement to them. You know what I mean? They were stepping up; they had a sense of pride of "look we are in a little better neighborhood and we have a little better this and that." The school was good and, oh, Rosedale High, was just, oh, you can't imagine it. The Marching 100 went all over Texas and I think New York or somewhere like that. It was really a nice community, the kind that you would be proud to send your kids to its schools. Now, it wasn't a rich community, but everybody took care of the yards and took pride in painting and that sort of thing. And now you go down and you see old filthy mattresses out on the curbs and it is taking on a ghetto look.

The ghettoization of Rosedale compelled the elderly to come to grips with being trapped in a neighborhood they couldn't leave. They rationalized their sense of powerlessness by clinging to the old ways and by hoping that the Rosedale they once knew would eventually return. Revealing a sense of entrapment and strongly expressing feelings of ambivalence, one elderly man explained:

> You're damned right I would move if I could. I'd get out of here if I could. But you have to give your home away, and the market in another section of town is

prohibitive. You couldn't buy anything. You wouldn't qualify for a loan. At my age, you haven't got time for those long loans. Our houses are paid for, and that was the whole idea of buying this house back in the 30s and 40s. When you were older you wouldn't have to make payments. You would live on less money. We could live on less money. I'm not complaining about that. There's ways to cut back, to get by on less money. But elderly persons here wouldn't move if they could. It's just that simple.

The themes of powerlessness, entrapment, and the loss of community appeared frequently in personal interviews with the elderly. Explaining that most of her friends had already left Rosedale, one elderly woman said with bitterness: "They are still moving out, the whites. In other words, it's not abandoned yet. But we are in a minority now. We are a minority, and nobody considers that we are a minority. Like the police chief told my friend, 'Why do you want to live in a town that's predominately black; why don't you move?' What she said back is something unusual, you know. She said she's lived here all her life and she intends to stay."

Many people interviewed took great pains to explain to me the importance of Rosedale to their lives. One elderly woman said that her daughter had been putting a great deal of pressure on her to leave Rosedale and relocate in a nearby city:

Yeah, I went down there and found a nice apartment, but I have a dog. And we had this dog ten years, and she's my protection; she protects me like anything. She is really a wonderful dog, and I just couldn't turn that dog over to somebody else now. Any apartment that you get wouldn't have a fenced yard. We just looked and looked and looked and couldn't find anything that was acceptable that had a fenced yard. So then, finally, he [her son-in-law] had two rented houses. A good businessman. One of them was vacant and so she wanted me to move down there and take that one, and it was fenced in the back with a chain-link fence, and that's when I got ready to move and began packing. But I just couldn't do it. It was just too much for me. You see I am eighty-five years old and I've lived here since 1928, and I've just got so much stuff and I don't have time to get rid of it.

She confessed that her ties to Rosedale were too strong. Her memories were too important to extinguish by leaving the area. A move somehow represented symbolic death, a termination of life as she had lived it for more than five decades. For her, life in Rosedale was life itself. As Erikson contends, the merger of individual identity with community institutions makes it unlikely that social change can be accomplished without profound personal consequences. These deeply ingrained attitudes constitute major emotional and psychological barriers affecting the course of residential integration within urban neighborhoods. Without adequate attention to them, public policies promoting racial integration are destined to fail.

The Transformation of Neighborhood Life and Culture

Neighboring and street socializing are no longer evident in the lives of the elderly. Neighborhood life and culture as the elderly knew it no longer exists. Deep down, they know this to be true but lack the resources or the will to reorient their lives along different lines. They try to continue the old ways, but their efforts are futile. They act out a cultural script written and created for another era and for another time. The elderly no longer have supper with friends on the next block. They don't play cards on Saturday evening or get together for a few drinks and conversation. They don't chat over the back fence or organize a group to watch Rosedale High School play football on Friday evening.

One woman told me about her efforts to be neighborly:

Oh, I know the next neighbor over. But I don't know the one next to her, or the one next to that one. The one I know is white. The other places have all been transients, so to speak. Some of them you might refer to as black and some of them you might call wetbacks. Well, you know people today, they come and go and we come and go. One thing about our property here, we're located fifty feet off the street and then we [her husband was deceased] have a lot about 40 feet deep and the lot is say 114 feet wide. Well, I may get in my car [she seldom drove] and get completely out and see a neighbor and throw up my hand like that [gesturing]. It's such a distance, but we can get out in the yard and hang over the fence and communicate, so to speak. Like the old saying is, "Get out in the backyard and hang over the fence and visit with your neighbor." But we just don't have time for that anymore. We just don't do that anymore.

Another woman's comment revealed the impact white flight had on her web of friendship affiliations and habits of neighboring:

Well, I don't visit my neighbors as much because I have, well, right across the street I had some good friends. Not directly across, but the two houses next to the one right opposite me. I had good friends there that I visited with quite often, and next door was one of the nicest neighbors anybody ever had. But they moved out and went to Granger and went into one of these trailer camps in a trailer home and are just living there in their trailer. As far as [a blank pause and retreat into memories] I visit this neighbor right next to me here, and across the street. They're about the only ones I can visit now. Well, I don't ever see these people next door, and the Negroes just beyond this first house. There is one Negro home down the street, farther across the street. I just don't go and see them anymore. I don't do much visiting now because most of my close friends moved out. And I don't dare go out at night here.

In a melancholy tone, another lady explained to me that she just had one friend left in Rosedale. "Nobody visits. My friend just comes to see me once in a while. But as far as visiting, nobody does anymore. You know that. Not anymore. They don't have time, or they are afraid to cross the street, you know, in the evening or late at night."

A woman who lived close by, equally pensive about the changes that had taken place, put it this way:

> I like neighbors. I'm old fashioned, enough in that I like neighbors, but of course that's, ah [withdraws and lapses into memories and private thoughts]. You don't have that much anymore. In other words, I like people. I used to take walks. I used to visit friends. Used to have lunch with neighbors, and sometimes come back at 9:00 or 10:00 at night [with pride]. And then when I worked, I went anywhere I wanted at night. And I don't do any of those things anymore. You're taking too big a chance.

Atomized and detached from collective social relationships, the lives of the elderly were fragmented and incomplete. They searched for elusive social relations that were no longer available to them. The emotional trauma experienced by Rosedale's elderly was enhanced as they watched the collapse of the institutions upon which they once relied. Residents harbored strong feelings of resentment and anger toward public officials who "sold them a bill of goods." They complained about merchants who fled from the area and left them without a stable economic base. They were outraged by unscrupulous realtors who used racial fear to enhance personal gain. They were angry at their former neighbors who "fled" from Rosedale. The flight from Rosedale violated their own life accomplishments and somehow made them feel their personal worth was diminished. Considerable rage was reserved for the federal government and the social programs that they believed forced blacks and whites to live together. As a result of these changes, the community was opened to the kinds of people they thought were highly undesirable.

The Transformation of Community Standards

Many elderly residents lashed out at the real estate brokers who participated in the panic selling that spurred white flight. But they were most concerned about the drop in community standards that accompanied the racial transition. One angry man contended: "The real estate blockbusters let the community go down. They tried to sell houses to every trash that came in here. I'm not saying anything bad about the 'coloreds,' because those that bought their homes, they appreciate them, and they keep them up. It's not the colored people that's the problem, it's the real estate blockbusters that let people in with no option but to rent."

Some of the elderly insisted that they did not object to living in the same neighborhood with black people, but most were very concerned about the "type of colored" that were moving in. The elderly of Rosedale were highly critical of certain classes of people regardless of racial or ethnic origin. The following kinds of observations were frequently offered by numerous seniors interviewed:

> Oh, yes, the neighborhood is really different now. It's just a different class of people that's around you all the time. Now, you see, like over there in those two apartments [pointing across the street]. There's been every type of person in the world that's lived there. And they get black and white married. And there's been such trash, white trash [wrinkles nose in disgust] and Mexican and just a little bit of everything. And over there [pointing up the street], it's all white people, but they are so dirty. They throw old tires out in that vacant lot over there, just use it for a dump. Over there [points in the other direction], that's colored people. They're O.K. They don't keep their place up like they should, but they're O.K.

A man who had lived in Rosedale for nearly fifty years echoed similar sentiments: "Well, the people that live here no longer keep it up like they did, and so many of my neighbors have moved away because of the colored situation. It is still my home and I'm trying to keep my part up but the people that have moved in next door, that's the trashiest place you have ever seen in your life. They are white people. The two dark families in my block have two of the nicest places on the block."

An elderly woman said: "Right next door, three black families live there. One took care of their house, the other two didn't. A Mexican family lived there for a while as well. They were filthy. They left trash in the garage and put it right there in the yard. The dogs would always get in it and put it all over everything. There were rats all over, and bugs, and it smelled. It was terrible."

This woman knew who lived in every house on her block and most of those who lived in the adjacent block. Although she did not know the residents personally, she had ample commentary on their living habits, personal standards of cleanliness, and how well they kept their houses and yards. Like many elderly in Rosedale, she viewed the lifestyle and personal habits of recent residents as directly contributing to the deterioration of community standards. The elderly felt that the living habits of recent arrivals were offensive to established traditions of community life in Rosedale and further undermined standards of common decency.

Irrespective of feelings toward individual African Americans, it was clear that nearly all those interviewed associated the deterioration of community standards in Rosedale with the racial transition and the drop in the class of people that accompanied it. Explaining why Rosedale had "gone down," one woman captured the overwhelming sentiment of the elderly: "In this neighborhood, it is linked to the racial change, because blacks are coming into this area and the younger blacks are coming in here with teenagers and children. And in this situation those are the ones who are giving the problems."

Another lady maintained: "People aren't permanent anymore. These people will buy a house and live in it until they tear it up, just to put it bluntly, and then they'll move on to another one. They just won't take interest in their homes."

The Loss of the White Middle Class

Many of the elderly revealed strong feelings of resentment toward whites who had abandoned Rosedale, especially those with children. Those who left Rosedale "made it possible for the undesirable element" to invade the community. The whites should "not have quit; they should have stayed and fought." White homeowners were replaced by lower-class transients: "I don't like the fact that so many of our good neighbors moved out since the colored people began to come in. We have just gotten well acquainted with the people that moved out and so that part has been bad. The moving out and the colored coming in."

Another senior citizen explained:

> Well, you know when the younger people with younger children moved, they are really the "stabling" part of the community because they are in the activity of schools and churches and things. And when they move out and leave the elderly, and then these vacant houses that the government moves and welfare moves people that have never achieved on their own at all, they don't really have that sense of pride in the community, and it starts running down. If there was a death in the neighborhood or something, it was when they left.

The Loss of Community Business

Negative feelings about abandonment were not limited to former friends and neighbors; nor was hostility reserved only for those new residents who had just entered the community. The elderly were also angry about the businesses and merchants who had moved from Rosedale to set up shop in other parts of the city. Many of the elderly expressed a sense of personal loss when discussing the deterioration of Rosedale's business center: "It's a lot different now. The buildings are different. A lot of the buildings they removed or wrecked them, and they put up different ones. You can't recognize them anymore. You can tell the difference, you can tell the same buildings aren't here. Now it changes pretty quick overnight. Sometimes over an hour it changes."

Much like in Erickson's description of flood victims, the physical changes in Rosedale's commercial structure were seen primarily in personal and emotional terms. One lady, a person who had run a small gift shop in Rosedale for thirty years, said: "What makes me sick is to see the business go down. When the community began to change, many of the businesses began to run, which they should not have done. It just ruined the community. They should not have run. You can sell to blacks just as easy as whites. They just left us here."

Another woman explained her dismay over the commercial abandonment of Rosedale in a way that suggested both a loss of symbolic status and a drop in self-esteem: "Rosedale is run down. And what is really hurtin' it in my estimation is partly our businesses. We don't have any. There's not a Dairy Queen or anything like that where you can get you a hamburger. And you know we lost our drugstore and our florist has moved. I was very disappointed when the druggist left. You depend on a good druggist for your life."

Her neighbor expressed similar sentiments: "No, we don't shop here anymore. I'm sorry they run out all the businesses in what used to be Rosedale. We used to have a lot of businesses here, and they've all left. It's beer joints now, predominately. We used to have a lady that had the best restaurant here, named Mrs. Duke; she had the best home-cooked restaurant that they had in this neighborhood. Well, she was run out."

Another said: "Well, we have a few stores left. I don't know about the grocery stores. I don't go in them. They used to be just marvelous stores, but Lordy mercy, it's just been ruined."

The Intrusion of Government

City government was also identified as having abandoned Rosedale. The elderly claimed that the quality of city services had deteriorated since the neighborhood had changed from white to black. One elderly man complained: "Sometimes they don't haul the trash out for about a week, and you put it out front and they let it sit there a long time. It stays long and then the cats and dogs, they scatter it."

Another woman explained: "Well, the streets are really run down. When the city don't keep up the streets, the people don't keep up the houses." During the course of the early fieldwork, it appeared that the perceptions of the elderly were correct. Rosedale seemed to have more than its share of uncollected trash and litter.

In addition to expressing anger about the curtailment of city services, many of those left behind in Rosedale voiced special contempt toward the federal government. Some elderly residents of the neighborhood saw court-ordered busing and school integration as the beginning of the end in Rosedale. In 1973, the federal court ordered major changes in the city's school desegregation plan. Busing provisions were included in the new plan as well as new attendance boundaries. Later modifications in the plan produced additional changes in attendance boundaries, some school closings, and further revisions in the mission and programmatic emphasis of neighborhood schools. Rosedale's neighborhood schools were directly affected.

Initially, minority children were bused to Rosedale's community schools. By the late 1970s, the number of white children in Rosedale was rapidly declining. By 1983, the pool of white children living in Rosedale was insufficient to accomplish busing objectives.

Busing and court-ordered integration severed the bond between Rosedale's residents and its neighborhood schools. Alienation from the school system was summarized by an elderly resident: "We don't get involved because it's, as we say, the schools are predominately black. When my children attended schools here we did. We took care of the things that were going on. But because it's gone predominately black we don't have anything to do with the schools anymore. It's just out of this world; it's another world."

I spent several hours in the home of a retired English teacher, a sixty-eight-year-old man who still lives two blocks from Rosedale High School. His entire career was spent at Rosedale High School; his professional identity was heavily invested in the community and its secondary school. He explained that the racial transition made it next to impossible to carry on many important traditions that gave Rosedale High a special identity.

Thumbing through a large collection of yearbooks on his bookshelf, he explained: "You know, there were just a lot of activities we could not continue after busing. All of our alumni clubs and reunions broke down after the change. People just didn't want to come back because it was so different. And you know, the donations for our library and other programs just dropped way off. People [white residents and alumni] just lost interest in the school and it really hurt us."

The assistant principal at Rosedale High School, an energetic and enthusiastic African American woman, echoed his sentiments. She told me: "It's nearly impossible to continue some of the traditions at Rosedale High. It's not that we don't necessarily want to continue them. But we've got to recognize that some of the traditions our kids just can't do. For example, the Marching 100. Our students can't afford the instruments much less the cost of the lessons to learn how to play them." The Marching 100 was a Rosedale High School institution, a precision drill band that won statewide and national recognition for performance excellence during the 1950s and 1960s.

Unwitting participants in the abandonment process themselves, the white elderly revealed why they no longer supported the schools of Rosedale. "Well, you know when it started? When the government [bitterly emphasized] invaded the schools. When they started busing blacks to Rosedale. Those that had children in Rosedale High moved out; I know some that moved to Burlton and Evans."

An elderly man explained that he just didn't understand what the federal government was trying to do by integrating the schools. He argued that busing had only increased white flight. Busing, he contended, had changed Rosedale High school from all white to 95 percent black. He saw the deterioration of the schools as the symbolic death of Rosedale itself. All social institutions tied to public education, he contended, were negatively affected by the racial integration of neighborhood schools.

According to this respondent, the sense of neighborhood cohesion was smashed by busing and federal intrusion into community affairs:

> I can remember when new people moved here we took over dishes and helped serve the families that came in. And well, I can remember sickness in the neighborhood, that you helped out, take a dish over for supper. Two or three would go over when the mother of the family couldn't cook that night. That's all gone. Well, I've seen people help out in sickness on their block and just a lot of things, and a good community spirit among the kids. They were proud to go to that school, and now they are bused. They are standing on the corner waiting for a bus to take them to another place where they have no ties in the community. I think when you destroy a community, you have destroyed something important. And I really think our politicians are destroying that. Merely for a vote, you know. To my idea, I think politics entered in it. You can see that it entered in the schools and made a big hassle over segregation. Now I'm not against desegregation, but I am against tearing down a community because I do think young people learn a lot in a community. I think there is a sense of morals that is learned, a sense of standards, in a good high school. There are always those that are a little outstanding that are good examples, and the others try to live up to it. You know what I mean? As far as I know, that is all gone. But I do think it really helps children to have other children that are outstanding church-going, morally conscious and all that sort of thing. It gives them a pattern among their own, not necessarily their peers. It might be a girl or boy in a grade or two higher than them, but it gives you a sense, you want to be like them. I've seen it work in my kids ... and it worked in me. But I think the schools are being destroyed and it's laughable to me when I hear this "all we want is higher-quality education." And we don't have higher-quality education. We have education that is lowering in value all the time, I think.

Federal housing policy was also viewed with contempt by the elderly. Many claimed that programs like Section 8 rental assistance had contributed to the lowering of community standards. "It creates problems because they don't buy these houses; they lease them. They get involved in this program where the federal government pays part of the rent and that's what the problem is. They are not homeowners."

Summary

As perceived through the eyes of the elderly, the transition of Rosedale from white to black revealed all the negative symptoms associated with the loss of community. Responding to racial fears and biases, those whites who were able to flee the black invasion did so. Real estate brokers, responding to opportunities in the marketplace, attempted to maximize housing turnover. Their efforts hastened the pace of racial transition, lowered the cost of housing in the area, and accelerated the transition from owner-occupied to rental housing.

Businesses, fearing spiraling crime rates and unpredictable changes in consumer tastes, moved elsewhere. Chain stores and franchises shut their doors and sought better markets in other parts of the city. The city no longer provided services to the neighborhood with the same degree of efficiency or frequency that was evident in the past. White families with children moved into suburban school districts that were exempted from court-ordered integration. The black middle class also left Rosedale, seeking housing opportunities more consistent with its income levels and occupational status.

Informal patterns of neighboring weakened and eventually stopped altogether. Voluntary organizations and community support networks ceased to function. That elusive psychic energy, that collective sense of commitment to a neighborhood that urban sociologists call "community," eroded and gradually vanished. Like victims of a natural disaster, the elderly were left in the midst of institutional devastation. Unlike with victims of disaster, however, there was no possibility of rebuilding or recapturing the life that had been swept away. Like individuals in perpetual mourning, they simply pined for the way life used to be.

The sentiments of the elderly partially explain why it has been so difficult to manage the successful integration of changing neighborhoods in American cities. Long-term residents of many neighborhoods hold strong feelings about their community and express a profound commitment to its established institutions. These feelings are often intergenerational and inextricably tied to the perpetuation of existing behaviors, beliefs, and cultural practices. To the extent that newly arriving groups subscribe to different values, cultural standards, and beliefs, it is unlikely that they will be able to peacefully share common geographic space with established groups. New arrivals to urban neighborhoods are usually not interested in or inclined to continue established institutional and cultural practices. Nor are established groups enthusiastic about adopting the lifeways and values of the new arrivals. In this situation, conflict is an inevitable consequence.

Social institutions and cultural practices do not simply pass from one group to another when ethnic and racial transition takes place. Peaceful coexistence within racially changing urban neighborhoods is extremely difficult to achieve and maintain. Likewise, new social forms and emergent cultural institutions are not easily created when control of urban space passes from one group to another. Social change is accomplished at very high personal and institutional costs. These costs are complicated by the intensity of intergroup hostility, especially when community and neighborhood change involves blacks and whites. America's racial legacy is deeply rooted within its urban neighborhoods.

4

RACISM AND RESIDENTIAL TRANSITION: OLD MYTHS AND NEW REALITIES

I used to walk. I used to walk every day, but I don't do it anymore. Now Mrs. Prewitt, she's afraid to ever go outside because she's afraid that something's going to happen to her. She even calls me when she goes to the mailbox so I can watch her.

They're hanging around the center when we come in, and we just pretend we don't see them. We don't know what they're up to or why. I keep the windows fastened and bolted. I have a small gun. I feel the safest when I'm locked up in my house.

Sometimes I wonder what we would do at the center if they came in. If they came in we would just have to sit there and do what they said. Anybody can walk in. The church too; they can just walk in. I read in the paper where they robbed people in church. I think about that a lot. We have just one door in front and one on the side. They can just walk in and we can't get out.

FEAR IS A BASIC HUMAN EMOTION. Psychologists maintain that anxiety and fear are among the most important emotions shaping human behavior. Fear is a potent psychological and physiological reaction to an unknown or unidentified stimulus. It may be activated by a premonition or suspicion that something terrible is about to happen. If one is convinced that one's physical well-being is constantly endangered, fear may turn to terror. Terror is an intense form of fear, capable of overwhelming the human personality with dread, hysteria, or panic. Social scientists contend that most of us will do almost anything to avoid or escape from a situation that produces fear.

Fear is also a socially constructed response to the human environment, an emotional reaction that is learned and transmitted through social experiences and cultural predispositions. William James maintained that emotions could be viewed as direct and immediate responses to powerful external stimuli.[1] In order to illustrate his observations, he asked us to imagine a situation in which we were confronted by a ferocious beast in the wilderness. If we encounter such a creature and flee in terror, do we scramble for safety because we are afraid, or are we afraid because we are running from the perceived danger?

He suggests that fleeing in terror is but one of several possible options that might be chosen. Options are typically selected according to our analysis of various subtleties and contingencies that characterize the situation itself.

But once a decision is made to flee, a powerful surge of psychological and physiological consequences occurs within the human organism. The immediate set of responses may be raw and uninhibited. The situation and the subsequent wave of emotional responses, however, require interpretation and classification. The interpretation is provided by locating the event within a larger cultural scheme capable of processing and accurately coding both the external stimuli and the internal emotional responses. In James's hypothetical situation, it is clear that the beast has caused us to run away. It is also clear that cultural traditions and practices provide us with numerous cognitive schemes that help us classify and define various situations encountered in everyday life. These cultural road maps structure our perceptions of the social world.

Fear among Rosedale's elderly is a way of life. The elderly of Rosedale perceive danger in all facets of their lives. They feel there are no safe havens in the neighborhood. Many feel anxious about safety in their own homes, on the streets, in the stores, and in the churches. They are afraid to go out at night. They are afraid to park their cars in their garages and walk the distance between the garage and the front door. When they pause to insert the key in the front door and unlock it, they fear they will be attacked from behind or that someone awaits them inside.

Fear overwhelms the consciousness of the elderly. There is no place to seek refuge from fear. It hunts them down and eventually finds them even when they are behind the locked doors and bolted windows of their homes. Fear reveals itself in many ways in the neighborhood: iron bars on windows, complex locking devices on doors, chain-link fences surrounding the yard. Many of the elderly even lock their bedroom doors at night. During the course of the initial interviews, some of the elderly withdrew to the presumed security of their home, never to go outside.

But for many of the elderly, even the house itself had become intimidating. One woman confined her daily activities to one or two rooms inside her home. The closed rooms were perceived as danger zones, areas in which someone might be lurking, waiting to harm her. Like a child imagining demons looming in a dark closet or in isolated corners of the room, the woman spent her evening hours consumed by terror.

Fear among the elderly of Rosedale is activated by two interrelated concerns: (1) African American people in general, but especially males, and (2) the assumption that they will be potential victims of crime at any moment. Because many of the elderly are physically weak, they are powerless to defend themselves against victimization. Their fear of criminal victimization is not limited to simple acts of verbal abuse and intimidation or more serious crimes like purse snatchings and vandalism. They also fear they will eventually be violently assaulted, raped, or murdered. Since those who victimize the elderly in Rosedale are usually black youths, the elderly's fear of crime and of black people generally are strongly related.

Fear of blacks is partly rooted in racial myths and stereotypes. Assumptions about the nature and behavior of black Americans are intricately woven into a complex mosaic of personal beliefs and values. The elderly accept as fact the many notions and legends that constitute American racial beliefs. At the same time, the aggressive and violent behavior of some young African American males does little to alter the elderly's beliefs about the criminal inclinations of all black males irrespective of age.

Nationally, fear of crime has been identified as one of the most important problems facing the urban elderly. In some cities, crime rates against the elderly are very high, and adolescents seem to be disproportionately involved in victimizing them. The director of Criminal Justice Services for the American Association of Retired Persons recently reported that juveniles commit 90 percent of the crimes against the elderly.

Terms such as "house arrest" and "prisoners of fear" have frequently been used to illustrate the magnitude of the crime problems confronting the urban elderly. Among those elderly citizens who have been left behind in racially changing neighborhoods, the psychological problems accompanying fear of crime have been magnified and reinforced by traditional racial attitudes and beliefs. Yona Ginsberg reported, for example, that many elderly Jews in Mattapan, New Jersey, were terrified not only of crime but of black adolescents in particular.[2] Whereas the fears of Matapan's elderly might have been intensified by racial stereotypes, the assessment of potential danger was not without factual basis.

Racist ideology, actual rates of crime, and fear of victimization are three potent forces having a strongly negative effect on the successful integration of urban neighborhoods. Racism was a strong contributor to the ghettoization of Rosedale. As illustrated through the commentary of those left behind in the community, rather than coexist with African Americans in the same geographic area, most whites chose to leave Rosedale. Our research made it clear that racism and related attitudes supporting white supremacy strongly contributed to the collapse of social institutions in the community.

It was also clear from our research that the criminal victimization of the elderly, part of a crime wave initiated and sustained by African American adolescents, reinforced many of the most negative components of the racist ideologies of Rosedale's elderly citizens. I examine adolescent crime in greater detail in Chapter 5. It is important at this point, however, to describe in more detail the historical and cultural roots of white attitudes toward African Americans and explain how these beliefs contributed to the transformation of Rosedale and its institutions.

Rosedale and the American Racial Legacy

Classic studies of minority relations in the South amply describe the racial beliefs and ideologies that have historically legitimated the oppression of African Americans. Those case studies of race relations in the South help us better understand the racial beliefs to which most elderly residents of Rosedale subscribe and, by inference, the attitudes of those who left the area earlier in the wake of racial transition and change.

Many early studies of American race relations described segregation as a unique type of caste system. Similar to more traditional forms in India and other parts of the world, caste relations in southern cities defined and maintained an exploitative and oppressive system of social relationships among the races.

The ideology of white supremacy has historically regulated relations between blacks and whites in the same manner that Hindu religious principles structured social relations among members of the upper and lower castes in India. Like the beliefs and myths surrounding the "untouchable" caste in traditional India, southern racial ideologies required that whites and blacks avoid physical contact, especially intermarriage and sexual liaisons. Additionally, southern traditions required that blacks and whites conduct their lives in a separate and unequal manner and live in geographically separate areas.

Similar dictates composed the traditional Indian caste system. As explained by Gerald Berreman, "In the United States, color is a conspicuous mark of caste, while in India there are complex religious features which do not appear in America: but in both cases dwelling area, occupation, place of worship, and cultural behavior, and so on, are important symbols associated with caste status."[3]

Membership in a caste or in a racial group is hereditary and permanent; it is determined at birth. Irrespective of one's occupational or financial accomplishments, caste or racial status is assigned and not earned. Sociologists studying southern racial traditions also make note of the fact that segregation has produced a system of social classes on each side of the color line. A caste arrangement and a system of racial separation not only produce spatial isolation but also generate internal differentiation and stratification on both sides of color and caste lines.

As a result of racist traditions in American society, many whites consider blacks beneath them irrespective of the latter's educational or professional accomplishments. At the same time, many whites perceive an array of important differences separating categories of individuals within black society. Some studies of southern race relations reveal that whereas most whites rejected the idea of showing any deference toward professional and middle-class blacks, they perceived gradations in status between this group and those blacks of very low social status.

Despite their unwillingness to acknowledge publicly higher levels of status achieved by individual African Americans, most whites strongly supported the need to maintain the color line: "The very nature of the caste system is such that white people must, perforce, view Negroes in terms of their relation to that system rather than in relation to the system of social classes. It is far more important to the preservation of white rank for whites to evaluate Negroes as 'uppity' as contrasted with 'good,' rather than as 'better class' or 'common class' except when these class differences are felt to constitute a threat to 'correct' Negro-white relations."[4]

Established social science literature describing southern racial traditions helps us better understand the fears and suspicions dominating the lives of Rosedale's elderly during the process of residential transition. These traditions also clarify how many of the elderly perceived and classified the external events occurring during the racial transition. Some of the most important contributions to the study of American race relations were written during the 1930s and 1940s, important eras in the lives of Rosedale's elderly.[5]

Some of the institutions and practices supporting overt segregation and racial oppression have surely faded with time. Social change, racial enlightenment, and the civil rights movement have erased many of the more blatant behavioral and institutional mechanisms supporting segregation, prejudice, and discrimination. Irrespective of the recent progress made in the civil rights arena, these early accounts provide an important gateway through which to enter the past. And the present in Rosedale is surely a reflection of its past. Based on two decades of research in the community, I am comfortable concluding that the racial attitudes of Rosedale's elderly are consistent with traditional beliefs about African Americans described in earlier social science literature.

The elderly of Rosedale grew up and reached adulthood in a racial era characterized by high degrees of segregation, prejudice, and discrimination. The features of segregation and oppression described in the early studies of

American race relations are undoubtedly strong components of the childhood and early adult memories of Rosedale's elderly. It is probably safe to assume that many of the personal and ideological beliefs of Rosedale's elderly are living artifacts of southern racial history.

The racial attitudes and beliefs of Rosedale's elderly were shaped in an intensely racist historical period. Because this is the case, it is important to interpret their racial beliefs and attitudes in a historical as well as contemporary framework. Of special interest are those racial beliefs and ideas that explain why the elderly are so fearful of blacks, especially males.

Many students of race relations contend that patterns of inequality between the races were established so that whites could maintain a competitive advantage over blacks. These advantages extended to all areas of social life, including jobs, housing, education, sex, power, and prestige. Of particular concern to a better understanding of whites' beliefs in Rosedale are the elaborate ideologies created to justify racial separation and segregation. Many of these beliefs generate fear as a psychological by-product.

Explaining the complex of whites' beliefs and sentiments created to justify violence against blacks, John Dollard observed in 1937: "Another line of belief about Negroes is that they are immoral, liars, and thieves, which is the equivalent of saying that they do not follow our mores on one point and therefore cannot claim their benefits at any other, i.e., such as voting. We must remember the crime of rape in this connection and the defensive belief that lynchings are mainly done as a result of sexual attacks on white women."[6]

According to Dollard, the assumption of immoral and evil intentions on the part of all blacks was widespread in the southern community he studied. The need to keep blacks "in their place" was based largely on the attempt to maintain economic, sexual, and political advantages over them. The system of racial inequality, however, was legitimated by beliefs about the perverse and wicked tendencies dominating the character of all black people. Self-interest, therefore, dovetailed nicely with a belief system requiring that blacks be perceived as a menace, especially to white women.

Other early accounts of southern racial traditions reported similar observations. In *Deep South*, published in 1941, the authors described the predominant view of black males held by whites: "Since he is regarded as a primitive being, emotionally unrestrained and sexually uncontrolled, the Negro man is thought by whites to be always a potential rapist. Thus, white women are expected to fear strange Negro men, and they usually feel it unsafe to go out alone in Negro districts or to stay alone at night in isolated houses."[7]

In Gunnar Myrdal's seminal study of race relations, *An American Dilemma*, published in 1944, similar conclusions were reported: "Whites believe the Negro to be innately addicted to crime. . . . This belief is connected with two more basic beliefs: that the Negro cannot control his passions and so is addicted to crimes against persons; that the Negro has no sense of morals and thus is addicted to crimes against property."[8]

The strongest fear dominating white perceptions of blacks were those beliefs and taboos related to sexual contact between black males and white women. In addition to a well-developed system of southern racial etiquette that has historically restricted even elementary forms of physical contact between blacks and whites (e.g., handshaking, drinking from common fountains, or eating at the same table), the most rigidly enforced racial norm was found in the mandate to protect white women from being sexually violated by black men. Myrdal referred to this sexual preoccupation in pathological terms through the use of the concept "southern rape complex."[9]

Fear of sexual contact between black males and white women has been critically examined by numerous contemporary writers, primarily in psychoanalytical terms.[10] I am not concerned here with the psychoanalytic explanations of this "complex" or in commenting on the mental health of those who subscribe to its credibility. My primary concern is to stress the existence of the belief itself, to show how it contributed to the terror experienced by the elderly women of Rosedale and to illustrate how it assisted the ghettoization of the community.

William Cash, in his widely acclaimed study of southern culture *The Mind of the South*, interprets the "rape complex" as an exaggerated preoccupation on the part of most Southerners. Suggesting that the chances of a white woman actually being raped by a black man were about the same as being "struck by lightning," Cash sympathetically explained:

> There was real fear, and in some districts even terror, on the part of white women themselves. And there were neurotic old maids and wives, hysterical young girls, to react to all this in a fashion well enough understood now, but understood by almost no one then. . . . Hence if the actual danger was small, it was nevertheless the most natural thing in the world for the South to see it as very great, to believe in it, fully and in all honesty, as a menace requiring the most desperate measures if it was to be held off.[11]

When the walls of residential segregation in Rosedale collapsed, the deepseated racial suspicions and fears of white residents were undoubtedly unleashed. Not only were the historical conventions endorsing segregation violated by integration but the entire ideological belief system supporting separation between the races was challenged. Because traditional racial ideologies are part of the elderly's personal belief system, it is logical to posit that integration itself initiated emotional instability and personal disorientation, forms of psychological stress avoided by those who left the community.

Because many elderly are genuinely convinced they are in serious danger when in the presence of black people, it is not surprising to find that fear dominates their lives. As long as the objects of their fears are confined to specific geographic areas of the city, a sense of well-being can be preserved. Residential integration, however, makes it impossible for them to flee from the source of their fear. Under conditions of neighborhood integration, they feel vulnerable, unprotected, and defenseless. And as a traditional female without a man to protect her, an elderly woman has to confront her fears alone and unattended. The integration of Rosedale brought elderly white women face-to-face with deeply held beliefs about the "black menace." This confrontation took many forms.

Residential Integration and the Violation of Racial Etiquette

The views of many elderly whites concerning proper social relations between the races are consistent with historical accounts of southern segregationist philosophy. An elderly woman clarified how the integration of Rosedale violated established racial traditions:

> Well, you let a few of them get in and then it seems like all of them want to move. There's still that old white flight. You want to move when they come in. Maybe they're next door to you, and they're not taking care of their property, and they don't have the sense of pride and achievement in that they have to earn what they have. It was given to them so it has very little value. A loan was made to them and sometimes the payment was paid for them and they don't really add to the community. I know I'm coming off like I don't like blacks and that's not true. But still, I don't want to live next door to them either. It's just that simple.
>
> No, I don't want to have anything to do with them. They're lurking and sneaking around. They have made so many attacks. You can talk to anybody. All of them have had a bad experience with them. One lady was out watering her yard. She was out between the sidewalk and the curb, and turned around and there was a nigger sneaking up and trying to get in her house. And we had one go in our home not long ago. They had gotten in and turned the house upside down. They got a little money. They found it and took it. When you come home and know one of them has been in your own house, it really takes something out of you.

Racial etiquette in the South has historically been based on a highly specified system of rules and regulations that define proper contact between blacks and whites. In Rosedale, one of the most frequent and serious violations of traditional racial etiquette is involuntary physical contact and the invasion of personal space.

Residential integration, by definition, is a process that contradicts established racial practices. Black invasion into previously white neighborhoods forces closer and more intimate forms of personal and physical contact.

Psychological and social prisoners of their own attitudes, many of the elderly unwittingly revealed how racial rules and traditions restricted their own behavior in the neighborhood. Their comments also explain why their former friends and neighborhoods thought it necessary to leave Rosedale.

One woman usually very active in door-to-door fund-raising for local charities said: "They call me and want me to walk our block for different things, you know. Why, I couldn't walk that block and knock on those Negroes' doors for anything. I just couldn't do it."

Many of Rosedale's elderly were distraught over the invasion of personal and private space that accompanied the racial transformation of the neighborhood. Greater interracial contact in the stores and shops was forced by residential integration, but most of the elderly carefully regulated their personal associations with blacks. One lady explained:

> A family that just moved in over here is white, and the young couple that lives right here and a nigger family lives directly across the street. Three Negro families right in a row there. They don't bother us. I don't have anything to do with them. A Negro family moved out of this house right here, and no, I don't associate with them at all. A Negro family lives over there and has six kids and they come over here all the time and I give them candy and popcorn. She came to my house one time and stayed about three hours, and they're uneducated and ignorant and, no, I don't have anything to do with them.

Another woman commented: "Well, in front of me is Negroes and to the side of me would be Negroes. They have been in there and they have had to make the house over now. They are working on it. Nobody else but Negroes would rent it, and the house next to me belongs to my husband's parents, and we don't rent it because we couldn't rent it to anybody but Negroes."

The woman explained that she preferred to withdraw the house from the rental market altogether rather than rent it to "niggers." The thought of "Negroes" being in the house of her husband's parents was just too inconsistent with her sense of proper relations between the races.

Lamenting the intrusion of blacks into all facets of neighborhood life, one woman grieved over the fact that even her church was no longer safe from the invasion: "They have ruined our church. The elders and such wouldn't like me saying this, but they are trying to get the black people to come to church and they tried to get us to go along with it. Well, I'm just not that sold on the blacks."

Another man reported that when elderly blacks came to the Senior Citizen's Center, he just ignored them: "I don't associate with them. They come up here, but I don't associate with them. I don't shake hands with them. It's a different world."

The perception of and preoccupation with the wholesale invasion of personal space by African Americans was frequently expressed by the elderly

of Rosedale. One lady explained that black children were a special problem. Many children played too close to her home and yard. She had tried to
keep them out by fencing her yard, but the effort to constantly monitor her
private space was becoming overwhelming: "They play out in the street
and play all over everybody's car. And so I told them one time, they had a
great big nice yard to play in over there and I said to them, they get all over
my car and I didn't want to have to put it up because I wanted to use it
again. You see? But they run across my yard, across my porch a lot of times
in the front. I just think every day that I'm going to have to move out of
there, but I don't know where I would move because they are trying to get
in everywhere else."

Of special significance in the minds of many elderly was the need to up-
hold racial norms that prohibit sexual contact between blacks and whites.
One woman related a story that revealed her feelings toward whites who
violated the sexual codes of racial etiquette. One evening she was forced to
call the police because

> there was a white woman trying to get into my house. It was about 2:00 in the
> morning and she almost knocked the door down trying to get in. She didn't
> talk nice at all. She said, "Open the door, I want to talk to you." And I said,
> "What do you want?" and she said, "I want to talk to you" and kept raising
> her voice. And I said, "No, you're not coming in my house, you leave," and
> she went away and came back three times.
>
> In the meantime, I called the police. When the young man came, he came up
> on the porch and she was gone and he couldn't see a soul anywhere around.
> And I figured there was somebody else involved. So he went around my house
> and he didn't find anything and he said, "I'll be on this beat until 3:00 and I'll
> come around and watch for you." He hadn't been gone ten minutes until she
> came back to that door. And she went to my backdoor, so I went and got my
> gun and thought I've never shot this pistol before, but it looks like I'm going to
> have to shoot her. But she went away.
>
> She went next door. She went to the door and they wouldn't let her in either.
> What she wanted was she was living with a nigger man and he beat up on her
> and she wanted to get to a phone for help. Well she didn't tell me that. But I
> wouldn't have let her in anyway. No, I wouldn't. I should have opened the
> door and said "Look you low-down trash, you go back to him. If you don't
> have any better morals than to live with a Negro, you go back to him and live
> with him. I don't care if he beats you to death."
>
> The next morning the man that lives next door was outside and I asked him
> if he heard her, and he said, "Yes, she came to my door and was trying to get
> me to come to your house and get you to let her use the phone." I said, "She
> would *never* get in my house, *ever*."

Many of the elderly subscribe to traditional notions of racial purity when
it comes to sex and reproduction: "Well, I just don't want to have anything
to do with them. I don't believe in mixing the races and I think that they

should be proud of their race and keep it pure. And I think the white people should do the same thing, and the Mexicans the same thing. All the marriages that I know of with Mexicans have not turned out successfully. I think it is the best thing to keep the races pure."

Not only are black and white adults who violate racial norms subjected to the personal scorn of the elderly but special contempt is reserved for young blacks who transgress established social practices that regulate social relations between the sexes. One man explained how young blacks had insulted both him and his wife by behaving in an overly familiar and casual manner:

And they seem to come in on my property. One time they came in, two of them up around sixteen to eighteen years old, came through my little gateway there and they wanted to see the chickens. Well, my wife was out there hanging out clothes and I just politely told those boys, I said, "Now boys let's look at this thing like you would look at it. Would you appreciate me walking down through your property and pass upon your wife like you did on my wife?" I said, "I don't appreciate it. You just coming up like this and just asking me to look at the chickens. That's no way to ask. If you want permission, if I wanted permission to go on your property, I would go to your front door and ask for permission. I wouldn't go past the front door." They sniggled and looked at me. But I had them setting on the picnic table before I approached them. And then I told them. Of course they got up and left and I haven't seen them around.

The man just couldn't believe that young blacks would behave in such an arrogant manner, especially in front of his wife. He asked me several times, shaking his head in disbelief, "Can you believe they did that?"

Black children and adults, especially African American males, who behaved in an "uppity" and "disrespectful" manner were frequently mentioned as a serious concern of the elderly:

In the stores, the kids just run. They think the grocery store is a place to play. They just run down the aisles and knock into you and everything else. They seem to have the right of way everywhere. One Negro down the street, down Binkley, that was on the right-hand side as I go up towards Rosedale, he had cars parked out there and never would park close to the curb. They will park three or four feet out and then he had his door open on the car and he was standing outside of that door. Well, when I got there, I saw that if I went around, and I would have to go in the incoming lane, and I honked. Well he refused to even move. Now that's the things that have happened that makes you feel like that niggers don't want to be equal to you. They want to put you out completely.

To the extent that traditional stereotypic images of blacks shape the behavior of the elderly whites in Rosedale, their racial orientations and attitudes are partially inconsistent with their present life circumstances. In the sense that they are living relics from a prior era of extreme racial segregation, their personal orientations toward Rosedale and its new residents constitute a form of personality disorder. The social conditions of life have changed so rapidly that their personal and behavioral repertoire no longer corresponds to the actual conditions of neighborhood life and culture.

The racial views of the elderly no longer provide an adaptive or practical cognitive map of their social world. Reflecting this personal dissonance and obviously uncertain about her racial views and confused about how to believe and act, one lady explained:

> You know, I just wonder if they're any worse than the whites. And you know what I think about it? Now I don't mean the people they are hurting now, but I'll bet you if you go to those colored people that are doing these things, their people have been slaves way back and they've been hurt by being slaves. And you know, lots of people just can't stand a Negro. If they call them a nigger, then that's bad. You know when I was growing up that's what you called them and you didn't mean anything by it. You just meant they were dark skinned. And that's what I mean today when I say Negro, the dark-skinned people.

The deep-seated prejudice held by many elderly whites in Rosedale has contributed to the destruction of neighborhood life and culture. Because many of the elderly are so strongly committed to traditional racial ideologies and because these ideas shape their behavior, neighborhood institutions and organizations have been undermined. Social relationships have been transformed, as have informal patterns of neighboring. Informal support systems have broken down as the elderly no longer nurture the children of the community or assist their neighbors. In addition to the powerful economic and political forces contributing to the ghettoization of Rosedale, the elderly themselves have been a party to the destructive set of forces transforming Rosedale's sense of community.

The Erosion of Mental and Physical Health

The racial views of Rosedale's elderly have also contributed to an erosion of their own emotional and physical health. The terror felt by many elderly women compels them to withdraw from community and neighborhood life and severely limits their social contacts. Many fail to go outside their house, to exercise, or to purchase food that might contribute to a healthy diet. The widely held belief that black males are violent criminals harboring wanton sexual desires for white women preoccupies the minds of many women and directly limits their physical mobility.

Most elderly white women believe that in the presence of black males they risk violent attack or rape. One woman, recounting a recent experience with black men, expressed these concerns through frequent proclamations of safety, presumably designed to provide self-assurance. Describing her visit to a house being remodeled by two black men, she said:

> Anyhow, he wanted me to go in and I felt very safe. You know the girl here at the center, she's very nice and just jolly, and she passed by. I went back up to the center to pick up Mrs. Stickney and she wanted to know why I was standing on the corner talking to those two black men.
>
> And I said, "Well, I wasn't scared," and I wasn't. And she told some of the others and they said, "And what were you doing down there?" And I said, "Well, that's my house and it's still my house; we built it and we sold it to them and I'm still holding the note on it and I felt very, very safe."
>
> And I did, I felt safe. Of course, I went in the house with them and looked around and they showed me different things in the house and we were out there in the yard talking and she passed by. Yes, I felt very, very safe. I'm not scared, as I say, but it isn't as safe as it used to be.

The emotional stability and self-esteem of elderly white men are also negatively affected by fear of potential sexual misconduct among black males. Norms of southern masculinity require that women be protected from the sexual advances and basal urges inherent in all black males. For the elderly men of Rosedale, the inability to protect their women has produced feelings of emasculation and simultaneously reinforced racial prejudice.

In order to describe further the psychological magnitude of racial fear in Rosedale, it will be useful to examine some of the survey findings. The elderly of Rosedale were asked to indicate how safe they felt moving around the neighborhood during the daytime as well as during the evening hours. I was able to compare their responses with a citizen survey administered to all residents of the greater metropolitan area during the same period.

Table 4.1 shows the comparison among the elderly of Rosedale, the elderly who live in the greater metropolitan area, and city residents as a whole. As can be seen, the elderly citywide generally do not feel as safe as most residents of the city. At the same time, it is clear that Rosedale's elderly perceive and express concern over their safety much more frequently than their counterparts living in other parts of the city.

Only 5.6 percent of the elderly in Rosedale feel completely safe moving about the neighborhood during the daylight hours, as compared to 38.2 percent of the city's elderly and 47.3 percent of the city as a whole. The most striking differences appear in the responses to the question dealing with safety during the evening hours.

Over 70 percent of Rosedale's elderly express varying degrees of concern about their safety during the evening hours. The interview data provide much more vivid insights into the extent to which fear dominates the lives of Rosedale's elderly.

TABLE 4.1 Perceived Safety During Daylight and Evening Hours (percent)

	Citywide	Citywide Elderly	Rosedale's Elderly
Daytime safety			
Very safe	47.3	38.2	5.6
Reasonably safe	35.0	39.8	45.6
Somewhat safe	10.5	13.5	12.0
Somewhat unsafe	5.2	6.1	20.8
Very unsafe	1.8	2.4	13.6
No response	.2	.0	2.4
	N = 2,945	884	125
Evening safety			
Very safe	14.7	10.7	4.0
Reasonably safe	34.5	29.1	16.0
Somewhat safe	12.2	10.1	6.4
Somewhat unsafe	19.2	19.7	24.8
Very unsafe	19.5	30.4	46.4
No response	.4	.0	.2
	N = 2,944	884	125

The sense of entrapment and powerlessness experienced by elderly women is pervasive. Their fear of black males paralyzes them emotionally and severely limits their desire to move about the neighborhood. They perceive danger everywhere. One woman's feelings summarized the concerns of other senior citizens in Rosedale:

Oh, it was a marvelous place. It really was. But I can't say that anymore. Well, it's so different and I've heard it so much, so many purse snatchings and knocking people in the head and now I'm afraid even to walk those two blocks. I still go to church when I'm able and I'm afraid to get out after I had my heart attack last Christmas. My doctor told me I had to get out and walk a mile everyday. Well, I started but I got afraid and it's just not safe, I feel. I just walk in my house. That's the only exercise I get in that way.

Young black males in particular elicit intensely emotional and hysterical responses from elderly women. The most terrifying experiences are those that confirm the suspicions and fears of the elderly, exemplified by one woman's premonition that became a reality:

I called the police three times recently. The last time was Monday morning. It was strange the way it happened to me. Last Sunday night, when I went to retire, I went to sleep in the den. I just slept on the couch in the den that night. Between 12:00 and 12:30 I heard a lot of loud talking. It happens that way all the time up and down the alley and I didn't get up to see. I just waited. And I couldn't go to sleep that night. I had a premonition, and I didn't get up to follow up the loud talking.

In a little bit, I had to go to the bathroom and I was in there quite a little while and when I came out and laid back down the loud talking began again. It was closer and it was at my backdoor. When I went to my backdoor in my den, I raised the curtain to look on my back porch and there they stood at the door that goes into the side of the house. And they saw me and they broke and ran just as hard as they could.

Since the elderly are convinced that danger constantly awaits them, terror can overwhelm them at any moment, at any place. Many elderly women, especially those living alone, spend their nights overcome with dread. Sleep for many of Rosedale's elderly is always a tentative proposition.

One elderly woman explained: "I've got all my windows nailed down. I have two dead-bolt locks and I still take my little stick and my can of Raid under my cover in bed. Sometimes I wish I had a fence in back because the people that live on the last lot don't have a fence either. They [blacks] can come right through the yard. It's pretty well lit up and I have two little dogs next door and when they bark, up I come."

In the evening, suspicion and fear dominate the range of emotional responses among the elderly. All blacks are seen as potentially threatening during the evening hours. What might have been perceived earlier in Rosedale's history as a routine event in neighborhood nightlife is now viewed by the elderly as an occasion rife with potential danger.

At night, neighbors become strangers and potential predators:

One night about 1:30 I was here and someone knocked on the door. I looked through the door and it was a woman, a Negro woman. She wanted to come in to use the phone and I said that I couldn't open the door but I would call for her. She said, "Well, no," and she'd had a drink of something. But she said, "Look, I'm just a woman like you, I couldn't hurt you." But I didn't know who she was and wasn't going to open that door. There could have been a man stashed around either corner, staying out there waiting.

Some of the most frightening and anxious moments for the elderly involve encounters with young males. For the most part, these encounters take place while the elderly are moving or walking about the streets of Rosedale. Because these events are so frightening, many of the elderly simply stop walking, a decision that affects their physical well-being: "I would like to walk. I used to, but I don't anymore. It's been about four or five years since I walked. Once when I was walking, there was a bunch of them [black youths] coming down the street. Some of them were on the sidewalk, and a bunch of them were on the street. And I jumped in a car real quick and locked the doors."

Another lady said: "I'm supposed to walk for my health. I haven't walked for several years. All those years that I walked, about two miles a day, I was never accosted. In fact, the white youth that I would meet would speak and talk. That was true when the first few blacks came in. But now, I'm afraid. I don't walk anymore."

The simple act of walking around the neighborhood has become, for the elderly, a risky form of exercise. Among the most intimidating experiences are those involving isolated, one-on-one encounters with black males:

> I went around the building one day to check on the back entrance to the center. I was walking by myself. And just as I turned the corner, there was this big, broad mass of muscle with a great big stick in his hand. He was about fifteen or sixteen. And when I saw that big chest, a wave of fear went right through me. It just scared me because I didn't know if he was going to hit me with that stick or what he was going to do. It turned out that he didn't do anything, but for that instant there was that eye-to-eye threat. It was there and it frightened me.

Crime, Isolation, and Withdrawal

Over and above the fear triggered by negative images of blacks, especially young males, the elderly of Rosedale are intensely anxious about being the victims of crime. Whereas fear of blacks and of crime are closely related, our field experiences suggest very strongly that fear of criminal victimization is the single most important concern dominating the lives of the elderly.

During our initial interviews, news of criminal victimization in Rosedale was widely covered by local radio and television stations as well as by the metropolitan newspapers, a fact that probably fed the high level of fear among the elderly. The police had told the elderly of Rosedale to be wary of strangers and to take precautions against being potential victims of crime. News of a robbery or assault spread throughout the elderly community like wildfire. Systematic networks of communication, primarily filtered through the Rosedale Senior Citizens' Center, informed the elderly about the details of neighborhood assaults and robberies.

One of the most visible manifestations of fear of crime was the physical transformation of homes into armed fortresses. Once havens, places of peace and traditional domestic activities, many homes were like forts situated in a hostile urban frontier. In all of our interviews, the elderly consistently stressed the belief that their homes were their only buffers against criminal intrusion and victimization. On the streets, they were vulnerable. In their houses, they were at least partly protected from those committed to harming them.

A minister said: "I don't know whether you cruised the neighborhood very much, but they have bars on their windows, bars on their doors, a dead-bolt lock on their front and back doors. If they had a fire, I don't know how they'd get out of there."

Once inside their houses, the elderly felt that all outsiders became potential enemies: "Oh, I keep my doors locked day and night. I don't leave my house open. Someone pulled on my door yesterday and wanted to know if that house next door was vacant. I said, 'You just go next door and they can tell you if the house is vacant,' or whatever he asked about it. No one gets in here once I'm in."

The dangers perceived by the elderly compel them to take extreme steps to seal off the outside world once inside their houses. The measures taken to prevent crime compound their sense of isolation and alienation from community life and increase their feelings of loneliness and psychological deprivation.

Crime-prevention measures also increase the financial strains experienced by most of Rosedale's elderly. One woman explained:

> I feel like the rising cost of utilities is killing us, too. You know this is one of the things that is hurting us so bad, so I want to use as little as I can to keep my bills down. Rather than keep the windows closed all the time, it's nice to have them open. I remember when we didn't have air conditioning. If I can just get a cross-ventilation, I can save on my electric bill. I used to rarely ever close my windows. I never turned on the air until the sun is really hot in the west. Then, I'd put it on for the evening. But if you don't have guards on your windows, you really don't feel safe raising those windows. I've put in the bolts and the locks, the best I could find. I'd love to replace some of these hollow doors that I have in the front because I don't feel they are safe as they should be.

The lady told me that she just couldn't afford to do the things that might keep her safe from intruders. But if she didn't open the windows or turn on the air conditioner, the house became unbearably hot, a fact appreciated by anyone who has weathered a Texas summer. By and large, there was no solution to her dilemma. She was forced to choose among rising levels of fear, an unhealthy home environment, and an unacceptable depletion of financial resources.

Others reported similar experiences and problems: "I have my windows nailed where they [blacks] can't raise them. In the summertime, I like fresh air and all, and that hampers my way of living if I can't raise the windows and open the doors. In my bathroom, I do raise them to a certain distance. But I used to sleep with the doors open and the screens fastened. I haven't done that in about three to four years."

During my fieldwork, I encountered numerous houses that were literally boarded up from the inside. Many of the elderly had nailed their windows shut. Doors within the house were locked. One woman had a neighbor nail boards over all her doors except the one in front. She had only one exit and entrance to the house. Another elderly lady had not only nailed her windows shut but also barred them and covered many with plywood. It was nearly impossible to see daylight from inside the house. She had no air-conditioning, and the house was unbearably hot and uncomfortable.

Many of the elderly are literally prisoners in their own homes, individuals under "house arrest." The emotional impact that accompanies the transformation of one's home into a fortress was revealed to me by an elderly woman living alone. As she described her plight, her voice changed from strong resolution to tearful resignation:

> I've slept in this house when I first moved here with all the windows up. We didn't used to have air conditioners, you know. And I didn't think a thing of it. But now we just don't take those chances. The times have just changed. I don't know what it is. But I don't think things will ever change back to the way they were. It just gets harder and harder for people like me to get by. I haven't told anybody, but I have a gun. I don't want to hurt anybody, but I don't like window peepers and people cutting through my yard. My life's mine and when I think they're [blacks] coming in through the window, well, they better just back up, because it is not a child that comes to your house in the middle of the night [with strong resolution].
>
> I even make my son call before he comes to see me. When he's at the edge of town, he calls and says when he'll be there. He says to me: "Mother, when I get there, don't open the door or unlock it until I get around to it." When he gets to the front porch, he calls, "Mother, Mother," and I open it. This is all I got is myself, and it's like there's nobody else [with sadness].
>
> I know the Lord and the law tells you not to shoot anybody until they're inside your house. But law or no law, do you think I'd be dumb enough to let them come in? Not me. When they start tearing at the screen or messin' with it in some way or another, that's the time to protect yourself. I've stayed up at nights and cried and prayed trying to figure out what to do. I could leave here but you go anywhere and it can happen. The woman who got killed, she didn't live but a few blocks from here.
>
> My son-in-law, he's a policeman, told me: "Mother, we'll get you out of here. Get you a mobile home or something. The city won't say a word if we put one right next to my house for a while." But I said I really don't want to leave. Do you see my door with all these locks? I still don't like the idea of the door being like it is, but I have to [weeping softly].

Not only has the relationship between the elderly and their homes been altered by fear of crime but nearly all other aspects of their daily lives have changed. Small events, activities that most people take for granted, such as attending church, shopping, or going for a drive, have been touched in some way by fear of crime.

One woman would not even leave her house to pick up a newspaper left by a tardy delivery boy: "Oh, no, goodness. I'm even afraid to go out when they are late throwing my paper. A lot of times I think I will just leave that paper out there until morning, but I turn on my porch light and go out there, but it's not the safe thing to do. Most of the time, I just leave it there."

Routine social events are no longer viewed in a casual manner. "No, I don't go out at night now. The neighbor that lives right across the street, about the second or third house down, one night she wanted to bring me a box of goodies, fudge and divinity, and cookies. She didn't walk across the street like she used to. She took the car. She got in under a light. They watched her get in the car and kept the outside lights on until she got in her house."

Religious activities among the elderly have been largely discontinued. Once highly active in church affairs, many of the elderly now rarely participate. According to an elderly minister who had served in the Rosedale area for three decades, services had "simply declined" over the past couple of years: "Many are not fearful for themselves, but I am fearful for them. Women by themselves are not actually safe by themselves in Rosedale. They are afraid to go to church by themselves at night, which is right. I'm not sure it is right, but we don't have services here at this church on Sunday night on that account. They cut out their Sunday night services because of the environment in Rosedale."

One of the parishioners elaborated on the minister's observations: "Yes, I used to get up and go anytime I wanted to, even at nighttime. I'd go to church at night and come in. I don't get out of the house anymore. I stay in at night because I am afraid. I wouldn't get out and go by myself. I wouldn't get out and walk the streets with a purse in my hand."

Shopping is also thought to be a potentially dangerous activity for the elderly. One lady said to us: "When I walk to the center, I don't carry a purse. There's a lady up there on South Littlefield. She went to the grocery store, and she was walking back and they knocked her down and stole her purse and her groceries. The police came and there was a big knot on her head."

A man explained the kinds of precautions he took when shopping. He found it necessary to mentally and physically prepare himself to go to the grocery store:

> Well, I insist on watching my wife's purse when we go to the shopping centers. A woman will put her purse in the shopping cart, and I think she should hold onto it. It doesn't matter where you are if people think you have money. And I think there is somebody who more or less has an eye on you this day and time. Has an eye on your purse. If you turn your back, regardless of where you are, down at Dillard's or Monnig's, there is somebody there who might grab your purse in this day and time we are living in.

All forms of recreation for the elderly have become defined as potentially dangerous. The traditional Sunday drive around the neighborhood is viewed with caution. The elderly feel they might become trapped in their car, or the car might break down. If it breaks down, they are vulnerable. If they encounter trouble while driving, the car is their only defense against danger. But the car itself can be broken into, and they can be pulled out of it and robbed: "Well, I don't go anywhere at night, and if we stop our car out here, and there are some of them [black youth] out there, we wait until they get by before we get out of the cars to come in if we are alone."

And another man said he was afraid to drive in the neighborhood at all anymore: "Yes, I am afraid. I keep my doors locked at all times I am in the car. Because they would just as soon walk up to a car and jerk it open and pull you out as not."

Other forms of social activity have been deleted from the lives of the elderly as well. One gentleman explained: "There aren't many organizations out here anymore. I used to belong to a lodge. It was kinda like the Masons and I used to get out and go to church at night. But now I don't even get out to let my dog out. I just don't get out. I'm too scared. There's just so many teenagers going up and down the street all the time and they are prowling."

Another man said:

> There is no place to go that a man and wife can go that is safe. I drank beer all my life, but I had rather go without than to go to one of these beer joints [black clubs]. The simple reason is that you might get shot, knocked off a stool or something. It is absolutely unsafe. I think if we had a safe place to go where we could have a night activity and different things for people to do, it would be good. If we had a safe place to go, whether we participated in the activities or not, we would go just to mix and mingle with the people. But there's no place to go anymore.

Fear has transformed the lives of Rosedale's elderly. Fear dominates them emotionally and spiritually. Fear shapes their everyday activities and life choices. As a result of fear, neighborhood life and culture have changed. The elderly have discontinued various routine social events in which they used to engage. They have converted their homes into fortresses and withdrawn from social contact.

Many of their fears, however, are rooted in real events. Their perceptions of danger are partly accurate; the dangers they see are real. Despite their belief in traditional racial stereotypes, their fears can't be dismissed as fabrications of racist imaginations. Their subscription to racist ideas exists simultaneously with high rates of crime in the neighborhood. Violence against the elderly is a crime of epidemic proportions in many American cities. Crime directed against Rosedale's elderly is part of this epidemic, and it is toward that subject that attention will now be focused.

5

THE ADOLESCENT MENACE: BEYOND RACIAL STEREOTYPES

You would like to get a little pleasantness in your community. Not this fear and hassle that you never know when you go home: Is it going to be me today? And I can't replace anything. I've worked hard for everything I've got, and if they steal my television, I don't know how I could replace it. I'd have to do without, which I don't think is fair.

There's a whole lot of this purse snatching going on, and several of our friends have lost their purses at shopping centers. A fellow went down to make a deposit on a Sunday afternoon and they shot him and took his money away from him—killed him. Of course that wasn't a shopping center, it was a bank, but it was a public place.

CONVENTIONAL WISDOM ALLEGES that time heals most wounds. Most criminologists concede, however, that violent assault significantly alters the victim's personal orientation toward life. Only those who have been the victims of violent crime can truly understand its impact on the human personality. Many of us have experienced the anger and resentment that immediately follow the discovery of a household break-in; it is probably more difficult to fathom and appreciate the sense of loss that overwhelms an elderly woman after her home has been ransacked. Most of her possessions transcend functional and utilitarian considerations.

Old china and earthen dishes have symbolic meaning. A timeworn chair has special significance. A sturdy wooden rocker in the den might have been her husband's favorite place to sit. They may have sat together in that room over the years, until he died a few summers ago. She still hears the chair rock when she muses over past memories and remembers their conversations. There are special places in her home—the mantel where she keeps old photographs, an old wooden chest where she stores treasures from the past such as love letters and souvenirs from trips she took to visit her son in Colorado.

In the living room there is a special spot where she displays important possessions. Like an altar, these little areas enshrine pictures of her family, the sacred icons of her life. Her grandchildren are on display along with high school graduation pictures of sons and daughters. Wedding photographs, hallowed with time, need to be reattached to the well-turned pages of a scrapbook. Knickknacks are carefully placed among the pictures. The pictures and ornaments have been carefully positioned upon white linen or embroidered doilies.

In her bedroom, old jewelry boxes are filled with baubles, necklaces, and rings. They have little monetary value. She keeps them there for her grandchildren to play with. But she knows when she received each little spangle and bead in the tarnished box and who gave each one to her. When vandals and thieves enter the house, all of her precious objects are crushed and torn, randomly and maliciously smashed, desecrated. If she happens to be at home when the thieves enter the house, she is totally defenseless. Weakened by the ravages of age, she is unable to protect herself or her treasured possessions. If she resists the intruders, she will be beaten, raped, or murdered. She can do nothing but pray the horrors of criminal victimization will pass by her door.

Besides emotional and psychological trauma, there are other side effects accompanying the experience of criminal victimization. Two of the most immediate consequences are lost resources and damaged property. Crime is costly to everyone involved. It is the victim, however, who shoulders the direct financial costs of criminal activity.

Over the past two decades, the costs of insurance premiums and replacement of lost property and the fees for psychological counseling, medical treatment, and legal services have steeply escalated. Many insurance firms either are reluctant to extend coverage to urban neighborhoods with high rates of crime or offer policies only at premium prices.

The community of Rosedale and its elderly residents are burdened by the personal and social costs of crime. Rosedale is considered a high-crime area by the police department and city officials. Residents have low to moderate incomes and inadequate home insurance coverage and medical care. Should they require medical or psychological treatment because of criminal assault, most are simply not covered by comprehensive health insurance plans. As a result, they are less able both physically and financially than other groups in the city to recover from the side effects of criminal victimization.

Crime transforms the lives of the elderly found in its path and alters their enthusiasm for daily life. In addition to fear, numerous other psychological consequences plague the elderly victims of crime. Victims suffer from depression and anger, conversion reactions, and related physiological disorders. Many experience a consuming desire for retaliation and revenge and feel irrational and emotionally unstable. They are burdened with fatigue and loss of sleep, paranoia and nightmares, and a deepening sense of racial hatred. During our research, we found all of these pathological symptoms present, in varying degrees of intensity, among the elderly of Rosedale.

Crime in Rosedale

The criminal acts involving Rosedale's elderly are distinguished by their bold and brazen nature. Victimization in Rosedale is characterized by aggressive and blatant acts of street confrontation. Neighborhood street crime is unsophisticated. It is not disguised or camouflaged. It is not clever or well conceived. There are no ingenious or shrewd schemes to swindle or flimflam the elderly. There are no nimble-fingered pickpockets or cunning extortionists in Rosedale. Crime simply consists of forcibly taking what belongs to the elderly. The face-to-face rip-off is the modus operandi among the thieves of Rosedale.

Crime against the elderly is conspicuous, noted by an exaggerated display of lawlessness, an open defiance of the elderly's personal and property rights. Street crime is perpetrated in a manner that flagrantly disregards established institutions and sanctions. It is careless and indiscreet. Those who victimize the elderly assume the role of bully: the strong taking from the weak. On the streets, black adolescents seize the personal possessions of the elderly. Like predators, they forcibly overwhelm them and steal bags of groceries, wristwatches, purses, wallets, cash, and social security checks. The elderly are pushed down, shoved, and beaten. Some have been pulled out of cars, assaulted, and robbed.

Anything owned by the elderly is fair game for the predators of Rosedale: their possessions, their dignity, their lives. Household break-ins take place in broad daylight and in the dead of night. In some cases, household robberies are executed while the residents are away. In other instances, adolescents simply break down the doors, ransack the house, and, if resistance emerges, they assault or kill their victims. Groups of six to ten adolescents have been known to knock at the back and front doors simultaneously. Before the elderly person in the house has had a chance to determine who is outside, one of the doors is broken down and the terror of robbery is unleashed.

Many robberies are accompanied by violent assault, rape, or murder. During the first four years of this study, victimization had become so rampant in the community that news media frequently used terms such as "crime wave," "paralysis of fear," "terrorization," and "prisoners of crime" to describe the surges of lawlessness that periodically swept Rosedale.

Between June 1 and September 30, 1980, 4 homicides occurred in Rosedale, along with 3 rapes, 14 street robberies, and 63 residential burglaries. The chief of police in the city was quoted as saying that the young people who perpetrated the crimes had the "morals of wild animals." For the most part, the victims were elderly whites. Of the rape victims, all were elderly white women. Among the 63 homes burglarized, all were occupied by white retirees. And 14 of those who experienced household robberies were also violently assaulted. The average age of the victims was between 70 and 75. The chief of police also said it appeared that members of a gang were terrorizing the elderly of Rosedale. He added that if they were caught during the act of robbery, "they didn't hesitate to kill."

Rosedale is a dangerous place to live. One woman who worked at the Rosedale Senior Citizens' Center said:

> There's not anything that makes it safe; it is just plain not safe. Anybody that would get out around here after dark is just taking their life in their hands; that's all there is to it. Of course what makes it unsafe is these roving bands that just rove up the streets with nothing else to do. Not going to school, rove in the daytime and rove at night. Anytime you look out, they're just roving around. Instead of going to school and being taught something useful, they're out looking for some damage to do.

A local minister thought that Rosedale was probably the most dangerous area in the city:

> I don't know whether crime is any higher than in some other areas or not. I talk to policemen and none of them are real sure. They just say I don't know whether it's the highest or not, but it ranks close to the top is the only answer I get. But I know there is a definite attitude of fear. And ever since I've been in this church, I tell you it's been amazing what a percentage of my congregation has in some way been the victim of some kind of robbery. I've had one rape, a seventy-nine-year-old woman about seven years ago. But the rest of it has been knocking them down, beating them up, and taking their money, and so forth.

The police themselves, off the record, did not hesitate to express their opinions of the Rosedale area. One officer who had worked the Rosedale beat for over two years told me that he preferred to patrol the area during the daylight hours because "you can at least see the shit before you step in it." He explained that the area was populated with "junkies, punks, and scumbags; the place is filled with garbage."

He stated that adolescents and juvenile delinquents in the area were among the most dangerous of criminal elements in the city: "You can't take your eyes off them for a second; you can't tell what they're going to do; they'll kill you quicker than a heartbeat." Official police records confirm what residents of the metropolitan area already know about Rosedale.

There are four "bad areas" in Fort Worth: Northside, Southside, Rosedale, and Freetown. Southside and Freetown bound Rosedale geographically and are predominately African American in racial composition. For all practical purposes, the three areas are merging racially, socioeconomically, and spatially. At the same time, they have historically constituted separate urban neighborhoods. Northside is a predominately Chicano community with small clusters of black and working-class white settlements.

In spring 1983, the city released official crime statistics. The data were reported for the first time by city council districts. Although the formal council districts do not exactly correspond to the natural boundaries of Rosedale, they nonetheless revealed the magnitude of the crime problem in the community. In 1982, the council district corresponding roughly to the Rosedale area reported 18 murders, a figure that placed it third highest in the city. The Northside district reported 23 murders, and in Southside 22 people lost their lives.

Rosedale ranked second in rapes with 79 sexual attacks being committed there in 1982. In the Southside district, 112 rapes were reported, and in Northside 56 women were raped. The Rosedale council district accounted for 12 percent of all crimes reported in the city. Freetown reported the highest proportion of crime with 15 percent of the total, followed closely by the Northside and Southside districts, each accounting for about 14 percent of all reported crimes in the city. Over 55 percent of all reported crimes in 1982 were committed in these four districts.

In order to convey to the reader just how much crime was being committed in the community during the initial phases of the study, police reporting districts were broken down in a manner more closely corresponding to the natural boundaries of Rosedale. Complete data were available from the police department for 1981. During that time, 116 robberies were reported to the police along with 105 aggravated assaults. Also during 1981, 766 burglaries, 643 property and 127 automobile thefts were reported in the Rosedale area. These data must be interpreted in light of the fact that they represent only crimes that were actually reported to the police.

A comparable survey commissioned by the police department showed that Rosedale also had one of the highest rates of unreported crimes in the city. Especially high rates of unreported crime were found among the elderly. Fear was the primary reason behind their reluctance to report crime. Elderly respondents also reported they were convinced that the police simply didn't care about their problems. Living in Rosedale is a hazardous experience and is especially dangerous for the elderly because they are singled out as special victims.

When our first set of research activities were initiated in 1979, there was little official response to our survey findings or public presentations on the part of the police or social agencies responsible for delivering services to the elderly. By spring 1983, however, both the press and the police publicly acknowledged the nature and gravity of the crime wave that had existed in Rosedale for at least five years.

The news media eventually gave front-page attention to the problems there. Efforts at objective journalism ultimately fell victim to sensational headlines vividly portraying the gravity of the situation: "Thugs Victimize Aged in Rosedale" and "Punks Prey on Rosedale Elderly." The sergeant eventually assigned to the Rosedale area—his beat also included part of Southside and the western edge of Freetown—by 1983 was well aware of the problems faced by the elderly. A streetwise and hardened professional, he was responsible for deploying more police to the Rosedale area, but only after the plight of the white elderly had become a major political issue in the city.

When I asked him in 1983 why the police had failed to respond sooner to the situation there, he stated candidly that the police were doing the best they could, but it was simply not possible to invest a disproportionate amount of resources in the area: "Well, you know, sometimes I think that I was not paying as much attention as I should have been. I could have possibly caught it sooner than what I did. But up until about June 1982 there was not a real problem. You know, one maybe a month, of some incident. But then, shit, it got like every couple or two to three days. That's when I went in and talked with the lieutenant and said this area just flat doesn't have enough patrols. We need to do something."

Our survey findings partially clarified the type and amount of crimes directed toward Rosedale's elderly. Through the surveys, it was possible to compare rates of victimization among Rosedale's elderly, senior citizens living in other neighborhoods within the metropolitan area, and those who had experienced theft or robberies in the city as a whole. Five types of criminal activities appear in Table 5.1: (l) theft or destruction of outside equipment or furniture, (2) theft of a car or car parts, (3) attempted home break-ins, (4) actual home break-ins, and (5) street thefts and muggings.

The survey findings clearly indicated that the elderly of Rosedale were victimized at rates several times higher than other senior citizens or citywide residents generally. In the area of outside equipment, nearly 30 percent of Rosedale's elderly reported loss of property. Among those reporting loss of outside property, over 44 percent had been robbed twice or more. In comparison, only 2.8 percent of the citywide elderly reported loss of outside property, and about 5 percent of citywide residents lost outside equipment or furniture.

Twenty percent of Rosedale's elderly lost car parts or the car itself. About 27 percent of these victims were robbed twice or more. The comparative data show that approximately 3 percent of the citywide elderly lost cars or car parts and about 7 percent of citywide residents. In the area of at-

TABLE 5.1   Rate of Criminal Victimization Among the Elderly of Rosedale

	Rosedale's Elderly		Citywide Elderly		Citywide	
Theft of outside property	28.8%	(125)	2.8%	(884)	5.2%	(2,495)
Car or car-part theft	20.0	(125)	3.3	(884)	7.1	(2,495)
Attempted home break-ins	17.6	(125)	1.0	(884)	1.6	(2,495)
Actual home break-ins	17.6	(125)	4.3	(884)	6.1	(2,495)
Street thefts or muggings	16.0	(125)	0.6	(884)	0.4	(2,495)

tempted break-ins, similarly large differences were found. Nearly 18 percent of Rosedale's elderly found evidence of attempted household break-
ins. Among the citywide elderly and citywide residents generally, the figures
were approximately 1 percent and 2 percent, respectively. About 18 percent
of Rosedale's elderly also reported actual break-ins and household robberies. And about 27 percent of these persons reported to us that they had
been broken into twice or more. At the citywide level, about 4 percent of
senior citizens had experienced break-ins and about 6 percent of residents
generally. Last, 16 percent of Rosedale's elderly residents had been mugged
or been the victims of a purse snatching or street confrontation. Over 14
percent had been victimized twice or more. Comparable data at the citywide level were much lower; less than 1 percent of senior citizens and other
residents had been victims of street crimes.

The Subjective Side of Criminal Victimization

Formal crime statistics and survey reports, although very useful, do not reveal the subjective dimensions of criminal victimization. The field interviews provided a much better understanding of the emotional and physiological consequences produced by victimization. Many of the elderly
women trembled or cried when they spoke about crime. Many asked for
help that neither I nor members of the research team could extend to them.
The field research and interviews dealing with the criminal victimization of
Rosedale's elderly were exhausting and emotionally draining.

In order to report the subjective elements of victimization among the elderly, the interview material is organized according to different types of
crime. This will provide the reader with a clearer idea of how crimes are
perpetrated and their effect upon elderly victims. The relationship of crime
to neighborhood transition and change will also be clarified through these
personalized accounts.

Cars and Outside Equipment

Much of the property loss that occurred outside homes was simple vandalism, deliberate acts of destruction. The elderly felt strongly that they were

being singled out by adolescents and systematically harassed for no specific reasons: "Well, they molest my property. I had big sand rocks that go from my porch to where the curb would be and they have broken those rocks and ruined them. They just tear my flowers up when they go across my yard. They are disrespectful in every way. And they want me to move. Night and day, they throw rocks at my house. I don't know who does it. I have never caught one of them doing it. I think it's boys and they have been instructed to harm me in any way they can."

By and large, the theft of outside property involved breaking into garages or stripping parts from automobiles: "Well, I was robbed. Not a person or physical crime. I was lucky. They stole my radiator out of my car and they stole about $500 worth of equipment out of my garage. Mostly that compressor that I used to paint my house with."

The theft of car parts and the loss of equipment stored in garages were mentioned frequently by the elderly of Rosedale. The themes and the mode of operation were always the same, as were the psychological consequences—a deepening of racial suspicion and further alienation from neighborhood life and culture: "Well, for one thing, my garage was broken into and they stole about $500 worth of property. And my car was sitting right out there in the driveway. They stole the radiator right off it. My wife's sister a few doors down, her house has been broken into twice—vandals; they just vandalize besides stealing. Nearly every house in this block has been broken into at least one time."

Cars can be stolen or vandalized at any time, at any place. "I've had tires cut on my old car. They couldn't get the hubcaps out so they cut them. They took some of this rough cement and rubbed it all over the car. That old car out there has a good motor so I've gone and had it painted. Lonnie over here, they stole his wife's new car. Well, I've known Lonnie since we've been out here. He bought his wife a new Chevrolet, and they stole it."

Local garages and gas stations are apparently good places to steal cars in Rosedale. Several elderly residents have had their automobiles stolen in less than ten seconds. One senior citizen pulled up to the pumps, left his car running, and stepped out to pay the cashier inside the station before filling his tank. In the time it took to walk across the station yard to the cashier's booth, an adolescent had jumped into his car and driven off.

Household Robberies

The more serious and personally threatening crimes involved household robberies. The elderly were always concerned about the presence of adolescent males. Many maintained, however, that black males of any age needed to be watched carefully. All black males were seen as potential predators. The elderly felt that crime had become a way of life for most young blacks in Rosedale: "Oh yeah, we hear continually about the thefts. I heard a lady just yesterday. She came home unexpectedly and she looked around the corner of the house and there was a little nigger just tearing out. He jumped over the fence like a dog and kept going. He had been trying to break in her house. Just yesterday. It happens all the time. I don't know how they are gonna stop it."

Even preadolescent black males are viewed with suspicion. One woman explained:

There is one lady here. They went into her house and she had a little old music box with some costume jewelry that she had for her grandchildren to play with. She had some nice things in there, and the little old box she had it in was worth more than all the jewelry. And the jewelry was all they took. They didn't mess up her house; they didn't go through the drawers or anything. They went to her refrigerator and ate some of her food and of course that indicates children. It was old costume jewelry that her grandchildren played with, and she put it in that little box to save it until they came back. And that's all in the world they took.

And another lady said:

Whoever broke into our house must have been a child. The window was open not much more than eight inches. I had made the mistake of going off and leaving my window up as far as it could be raised. When I came back it was broken. They came over the chain-link fence and ruined my aluminum screen. They came in through the window, and over the coffee table. They got my clock radio. There was a used glass right there on the table. They just sat there at the kitchen table and drank my soft drinks and had ice water and listened to the radio. The only other thing taken was a cigar box with some silver dollars in it.

Most of the elderly victims were not nearly as fortunate. More often than not, major property losses accompanied household robbery. Additionally, most of those who engaged in serious victimization were not children. Some adolescents didn't even bother to break into the house. One lady told us that black adolescents had been known to simply appear at the front door and aggressively demand money for services never requested or provided:

A short black boy and a tall black boy came one day. I imagine they were sixteen or eighteen years old and they were not even paperboys; I was sure of that. They didn't have any credentials or anything so I had my door locked and I wasn't especially scared. The smaller boy, he got angry and he kicked the door and I was afraid he was going to kick it in. So I just turned around and called the police while they were there. And I called my neighbor across the street and he grabbed his gun and he was going to come across. They saw him come and they ran. So when the police came, I told them and they said they didn't know whether they could do anything about it or not. They were doing this all over the area and some of the older people get scared and go ahead and pay them.

This type of extortion involved small amounts of money; many of the elderly reported more serious forms of criminal intimidation by young males. One of the more brazen robberies involved a midday encounter in which two black males simply arrived at the home of an elderly man, loaded his possessions in their pickup truck, and drove to the next block. A woman at the Rosedale Senior Citizen's Center described what took place:

> I know an elderly man on my block. He's in his eighties. He lives in a nice brick house. We noticed that he kept standing around in his yard. Someone went over and asked him if he needed help in crossing the street, and he said, "My furniture's over there in that pick-up truck." They found out that a big black man across the way and another young man had just backed their pickup truck over here in that man's driveway and went into his house and took his furniture and told him to keep his mouth shut. The man never did get his stuff back.

An equally bold theft was reported by an elderly woman. The black family living next to her robbed electricity on a regular basis. They simply plugged their extension cord into an outlet beside her garage. She responded by disconnecting the plug and asking the family to stop using her electricity. Her requests were countered by verbal abuse and threats. After two months of higher utility bills, confrontations, and threats, she hired an electrician to remove the outside receptacle.

In addition to TVs, radios, furniture, and jewelry, the elderly often lost social security checks. Since many of the elderly depended on social security benefits, this kind of theft constituted a serious disruption in their daily lives:

> I had my social security check stolen out of my house. I was working out there in the yard, raking, and they came in and took the check and just closed the door there. And of course I left my backdoor unlocked and parked my old car down there and I just kept working. I'm sure they came into the back. The little one saw me put that check in there because their grandfather was living on social security or welfare. Now that I get social security, I hadn't been getting it long enough to know better. But that taught me a lesson and well, I was the fifth one. I felt so embarrassed that I was so dumb, but I was the fifth one in this neighborhood to lose their social security check. Back on the next street is a house facing this way, back of the TV shop; her husband was in the rest home and they went into her house and got her social security check and cashed it at a grocery store. They cashed that check without any ID card or anything.

Not only were the elderly angry about the ease with which their own checks could be cashed by those who stole them but they were also frustrated by the lack of responsiveness to their situation on the part of the criminal justice system. Many of the elderly contended that the police seemed to respond to their fears and concerns in a very casual and cavalier manner. Many elderly didn't even bother to report crimes anymore even if they were the victims.

Explaining that she had called the police after being robbed, one lady complained: "Well, the policeman that came, he didn't seem too concerned. All he said was he'd try to find them. He didn't even come in and see where the screen had been torn. He didn't seem very interested. The next one that came, he at least took down the license plate that we took. But we never did hear if they caught them."

Another elderly gentleman had been robbed twice. He had utterly given up on the criminal justice system and accepted as fate being permanently vulnerable to criminal victimization:

> They went into my house the first time. I was away for a while. And when I got back, why the place was all tore up. I called the police, and the first time they came out they caught the boy that same evening. But they said that I'd have to get me an attorney to get the stuff back that he took. They found it right down there in the 100 block in the pawnshop. Well, I was going to have to pay the attorney more than what the stuff was worth so I just let it go. The second time they came in they got most of my clothes and things like that. A tape recorder too. I don't think the police can do very much. They even caught the boy that robbed me and told me where the stuff was pawned at. And they still can't go down there to get the stuff for me. I don't feel like they can do very much. I just let that go too.

Many of the victims interviewed were personally shaken by the act of household intrusion itself. For many, the psychological impact of robbery was more severe than the actual loss of property. One lady expressed her sense of personal violation when she returned home and saw that her house and private possessions had been "turned upside down":

> Two or three months ago I came over to the center about 11:15 and got back about 11:30 and my house had been broken into and robbed. You never saw such a mess in your life. They had pried a window and they just turned things upside down. They got several things, my TV, my radio, and a gun and different things. They took them out to the alley and came back and got a valuable locket that I would liked to have kept, and they got my husband's coin collection, and they got my watch. That's all that I have missed that they got, because I got the other stuff back. The inconvenience, though. They just tore my house up. If I would have been well, I could have cleaned it up. But you can imagine taking things in a sewing box and putting them on the rug. And getting all that stuff and all your thread and things and every paper that you had in your desk turned upside down. Your bed's torn up and your clothes all out of the drawers. You can't imagine.

Some of the household break-ins and subsequent activities are intentionally designed to instill in the victims a sense of personal degradation and debasement. Whereas a thief obviously finds it necessary to ransack a house in search of valuable items, many of the acts perpetrated in the homes of the elderly suggest that other forces besides criminal rationality are at work. Several of the victims reported that their personal belongings had been strewn all over the house. All of the drawers had been dumped on the floor, cupboards emptied, and furniture overturned. Many personal items were simply broken, crushed, or torn.

One lady said: "They broke into Mrs. Williamson's, and they tore everything out and broke it. They even nastied in both beds. They pulled down the covers and got right in the middle of it." When asked to explain what she meant, she said: "Why, they just messed in the bed. They shit in it."

The actual loss of property and the embarrassment and humiliation that accompany victimization are insignificant in comparison to the terror produced when an elderly person is present during a household robbery. One man recounted the experiences of his neighbor: "Mrs. Quigley, she's ninety-five years old, her house has been broken into twice. A black boy tore the screen off the door and tried to get in with her standing right there. She slammed her door and she was calling to her husband screaming, 'Clarence, shoot him! Go, shoot him!' Her husband's kind of crippled and very slow to get around. The boy ran fast and got into a car and drove off."

Others who have been present during a household robbery have not been as fortunate:

And there's an old man that's feeble. They broke in his house one night and he's deaf and couldn't hear and they ransacked the house and couldn't find anything. They woke him up and beat him up cause he didn't have any money. That happened last summer sometime. The man goes to the Senior Citizen's Center. And there's another woman right up here on Collard Street, three blocks maybe from me. She had gone to the beauty parlor. She had her purse and she's real thin and sickly looking. She got to the alley right by her house and was getting her key out to unlock the house and two teenage boys passed in the car and saw her and got out and each one of them got ahold of her and knocked her down and stomped her and took her purse. She was in the hospital about a week.

Other stories were even more frightening. A lady described what happened to her neighbor's daughter:

One night a man got in her bedroom. I think he broke a window glass. But that's not the first time that somebody had come into her house. One night she said that two colored boys got in. She and her sister was back in the back room, a den or something, watching TV and they heard somebody turn the front room light on and the porch light on. And they went and called the police. The boys took their time about leaving, but left. Them being women, they knew they couldn't probably hold them or overpower them. Then the second time they came in the bedroom and she said when she awoke it was about midnight or early morning. And she said he was right over with a pillow mashing down on her face and he was going to smother her. She said she jumped up . . . and he had put his hands all over her . . . she started fighting him. She said they fought and turned over the TV, the radio, and I don't know what all else. But finally one of the neighbors heard her screaming and called the police and he left without harming her anymore, other than her nerves. Well, she didn't live too much longer after that.

At the Senior Citizen's Center, a woman told a story about an acquaintance who let someone in to use the phone:

Well, her husband was working at night then, and she was there by herself. One night they broke into the house next door to her and she was afraid. I know she was. She thought it was her house. She told the police she was by herself and they came out. But it was the house next door to her. So she started to call me at night. But they came in one night. They cut her. She threw up her arms. The Negro was in her bedroom. They always come in through the bedroom. He didn't have anything on him but his pants. And she had a cyclone fence, a six-foot one with barbed wire all around it. And he got in her house. She said that she thought perhaps he got in through a window. They called her to go to work late in the evening and she went to work. She said she thought she left her window over the sink open. She said she just fought him and fought him every way she could. He pulled a knife then, and she knew he was going to cut her. She raised up her arm and he cut her arm and her throat. She could just whisper after that. They had to take stitches, and now she wears a high-neck dress.

Street Crimes

When the elderly of Rosedale were victimized on the streets or in the stores, some type of personal assault or violence was nearly always involved. Many of the elderly considered themselves fortunate if they lost a purse or their groceries and escaped without being personally assaulted. A lady's purse was a common and easy target for the youth of Rosedale. Unfortunately, carrying a purse was a habit many elderly women found hard to break. All too often, a familiar story was told:

They do get your purses. You have to be careful. I know the policemen have very muchly warned us to not carry shoulder purses. But we will do it. We do. I don't, but most do. And they said to hold your purses. At Piggly Wiggly, our pastor and his wife was up there to buy groceries. She had just got out and here came two fifteen-year-old colored boys and snatched her purse. She yelled at them and somebody else ran after them and they throwed the purse down. She got it back but she had $60 to buy groceries and they got it.

Another lady said: "It's happened in broad daylight sometimes. One of my friends, she crippled. She has an artificial leg and she was up there at Safeway grocery store and she was putting her groceries in her car and a couple took her purse away from her." Elderly women lost their purses and groceries in the parking lot or right at their front door. A lady at the Senior Citizen's Center related the following incident:

> The lady right across the street from me came home from shopping a few weeks ago. She went to that little grocery store off Feagin Street. She got up in her yard, and she just stooped over to straighten the rug. She has a rug that goes up to her steps. And she was just leaning over to straighten the rug, and a black boy went to grabbing her groceries out of this cart that she had. But he knocked her down and took one sack and her purse. And that happened right across the street from me.

Nearly everyone interviewed in Rosedale either had been a victim of street crime or knew a close friend or acquaintance who had been assaulted or robbed. One lady interviewed at the center told about her friend. Since the two women spent considerable time together, the lady was very upset by her friend's experiences. She had been victimized twice during the past month:

> Mrs. Carney, the woman that comes with me most every day, she didn't come today. I came early because the craft class was gonna meet, and her house was broken into. They caught them, though. She got there, and I think they were still in the house when she got there. The police came right out and they found all the stuff out in the alley. Her colored television and everything. All she lost was her watch. And then she got knocked down over at Montgomery Wards. She was with her son-in-law and daughter. And they went to get in the car and these two kids just came up and swept her right down, and she hit her head on the concrete. They took her purse, her keys to her car and her door were in her purse.

Among the victims of street crime, it is clear that the experience leaves a lasting and detailed impression:

> I had been over to Piggly Wiggly's to get groceries. And then I had to go over to Buddies to get something. So I drove over to Buddies and parked out front. I got out and went in, and they had plants just outside the front door. I wanted a bunch of tomato plants, and I was walking along the wall with one hand on the wall, stooping over to look at the plants. They had the prices and things on the plants. I saw a nigger boy coming down the street. I didn't pay any attention though. I felt something tugging on my purse. I had my purse on the hand that I was holding onto the wall with. I thought it was somebody teasing me, cause people would always tease me when I'm walking and things. I just got a tighter grip on it. And so he jerked it again. Jerked real hard. Jerked my hand off that wall, and I fell.
>
> He got my purse and he ran. So I started screaming and a package boy came out of the store and took off after him. And there was a man that jumped out of his car, and he left his motor running, and they both took after him. They chased him down to Thackery Street, and he got in a car and they run off. They got the license plate. I had about $19 in my purse and a charge plate from Sticklers and Montgomery Wards and different places, and BankAmeri-

card. I got on the telephone at Buddies and called these places and told them what happened. The police came and took me home. They never did catch them. They found my purse on the playground at school. The principal called. They just took the money and left all the cards in it.

The lady explained that she no longer went shopping because of this experience. She was simply too afraid to enter the stores anymore. Because street crimes are so prevalent in Rosedale, some women feel they may be inviting crime by the simple act of carrying a purse. Many realize too late that they should have left their purse at home. One lady confessed that she almost became hysterical on the street when she remembered that her purse was on her shoulder:

I used to carry my purse on my arm all the time. Had my purse on my arm when I went to church. But now I'm just afraid someone will reach up and grab it. There was a black man on the corner when I was coming by on my way to church. And the man didn't pay me no mind. But I got a glimpse of him, and by the time I got to my front door I was scared to death, afraid that he was going to grab me. Just a big imagination that's all that was. When I finally got to where I could look back, I didn't see the man. It was me, then. I put bars on my doors and windows last year. And I feel a lot safer now. I sold some of my furniture to get the money and I don't ever buy any clothes. When I go to church I feel kind of embarrassed in a way because I don't get anything new, but I think the peace of mind is worth more than anything else.

Many of the street crimes in Rosedale combine violence and theft. But in some cases, the violence appears to be more important to the perpetrators than the theft. Two women described an incident involving several of their friends at the Senior Citizen's Center:

We've had two or three who have had brand new cars stolen. We just never know when the batteries may be gone from the car. And then we have had two women attacked at 5:30 in the evening. Punched out. And here they were back at the center, crying and all clawed up. The car just drove up by the side of her. They jerked her down and took her purse. She had her arms full of mail to take up to the post office. And she came back, of course, just hysterical. And the other woman is about sixty-five. She is retired, but she works in the center. And she lives right down here on Mallory Street. She is the one that moved out of Rosedale recently. She was attacked by three men in the parking area at 5:30, and they were after her purse. She said there were three and one was driving the car. They jumped out and grabbed her arm and her purse and she told them she would give them the purse. But a customer saw the incident and he tried to run over them, deliberately run over them in his car. And they jumped in their car with her purse and took off.

Other victims of street crime have not been rescued by gallant bystanders. Many of the more severe forms of violence are committed on the streets of Rosedale, in full public view. Some of the most violent street assaults involve elderly white men. A woman explained what happened to her neighbor:

> Mr. Casey, bless his little old heart, he was sick and he's a widower. It was up there in the vicinity of Skaggs Albertson's, and he was there and he was walking home. He doesn't have a car, you know. Some Negroes knocked him down and robbed him. Stomped him and nearly killed him. And he had just went to help somebody else and they did that on his way home. He lives over there close to Skaggs Albertson's. I don't know just exactly where he lives. I was there and he went back and went home and he just nearly died before he got there. But he was able to be back at the center. About two weeks ago they broke in his house again, broke the window out and got a lot of things out of his house, clothes and things.

Some of the street assaults do not even involve acts of theft. One elderly man who had been stabbed on the streets of Rosedale explained in a bewildered tone: "There was a black man that stabbed me. April the first, that would be two years ago that it happened. I was here on Thackery and I was shopping. And there was a colored man there. I turned to see where he was at, and the next thing I knew, why he was coming right up behind me. And I still got scars. Why, I was in the hospital for about five weeks. He didn't take a thing from me."

When asked why he thought he was attacked, he said: "It doesn't add up, you know. He didn't take my watch. He didn't take my change, my billfold or anything. I feel like he was afraid of something. I don't know what. I finally walked across the street, to a light. I walked in a store and fell down. They never caught him, you know. They asked me to identify him, but all I know is that he was a black man. He just come up behind me and stabbed me."

A man in his mid-seventies was nearly killed by the same kind of unexplainable aggression. He was painting his house one afternoon. While he was standing on his aluminum ladder, reaching up to paint under the eaves of his brick home in which he had lived for nearly thirty years, three adolescents appeared on his front lawn. They asked him if he needed help: "You got work for us old man?"

When he said he had no work for them, they shook the ladder violently. He tumbled off the ladder, injuring his leg and back. The adolescents then proceeded to beat him brutally with a two-by-four that was lying on the ground. He nearly died as a result of injuries sustained.

These random acts of violence were mild in comparison to the waves of terror that swept Rosedale during the summers of 1977 and 1982. During summer 1977, several rapists terrorized the elderly women of Rosedale. During summer 1982, a series of wilding incidents brought the city to the brink of race riots.

6

SEXUAL VIOLENCE
IN ROSEDALE

*Rape was an insurrectionary act. It delighted me that I was defiling and tram-
pling upon the white man's law, upon his system of values, and that I was defiling his women—and this point, I believe, was the most satisfying to me because
I was very resentful over the historical fact of how the white man used the black
woman. I felt I was getting revenge. From the site of the act of rape, consterna-
tion spreads outwardly in concentric circles. I wanted to send shock waves
throughout the white race.*

—Eldridge Cleaver, Soul on Ice, 1968

DURING THE SPRING AND SUMMER OF 1977, a series of rapes occurred
in Rosedale. Hysteria ravaged the elderly community. Between April and
August 1977, over forty rapes were committed in Rosedale. The age of the
victims ranged from thirty-three to eighty-five; the attacks directed against
elderly white women were especially malicious and violent. Media coverage
of the rapes increased dramatically in May and June, and by midsummer
local reporters had created the name "Rosedale rapist" to describe the person who was terrorizing local women.

By the time the police sifted through various descriptions of the rapist, it
was apparent that media terminology was incorrect. The Rosedale rapist was
not a single individual. In fact, several rapists appeared to be at large in
Rosedale. A young African American rapist was apprehended and arraigned
during May. Police suspected that he had committed over fifteen rapes, although he was actually tried and convicted of raping three elderly women.

Preoccupied with the television series *Roots*, the rapist would converse
with his victims while molesting them. He talked randomly about events
that occurred during the various *Roots* episodes. Apparently intent on ex-
tracting some type of revenge for the humiliations depicted on the show, he

asked his elderly white victims if they were aware of "all the bad things done to blacks on *Roots*."

Feeling confident that apprehension and conviction of this suspect would dissipate public concern over the rape spree, the police prematurely closed the file on the Rosedale rapist. The months of June and July, however, revealed that a violent rapist was still at large in Rosedale. By mid-June it was obvious to the police that at least two rapists were still victimizing the women of Rosedale at regular intervals. The accumulated descriptions provided by rape victims revealed two distinct styles in the rapists' mode of operation. One individual, described as a young black man with a beard and closely cropped Afro hairstyle, gained entrance to his victims' homes either forcibly or by false pretenses.

The other rapist, also a young black man of slender build, attacked his victims between midnight and dawn. Always partially clothed or naked, he would usually enter the woman's home through the window and stand beside the bed until the victim awoke. Descriptions of the rapists included a young man with a strong and offensive body odor, a man in his mid-twenties to early thirties, a middle-aged man, and a tall person with an Afro hairstyle.

By mid-July, police surmised that these latter two descriptions were related to isolated rape incidents in the area and concentrated their activities on the two young males who seemed to account for the vast majority of attacks. From the elderly's point of view, it made little difference if one or two rapists accounted for all or most of the assaults in Rosedale. The combined impact of both isolated rape incidents and the frequent assaults attributed to the Rosedale rapist had already transformed the emotional lives of the elderly.

Most everyone with whom we talked during our field research either knew a rape victim or had been touched in some way by the assaults. "One of my neighbors was a victim at ten o'clock in the morning. A colored man just came in her house and raped her." Another woman said: "What makes it unsafe is the bad elements that has come out in the last ten years. We used to never have that. Maybe you know about this girl that was raped, murdered, cut up in broad daylight. I'd known that girl ever since she was a little child. I knew her parents; they are both dead now. She was in the yard working. She never suspected anything, you know."

Personal knowledge of rape incidents, including the details of the assault, was pervasive among the elderly. The personalization of rape incidents increased the elderly's sense of terror, often to the point of personal instability. "The lady that lived next door to this place, right across in front of me, when she first moved there last summer, well she was molested. Then he [the rapist] would come back at night. She said something woke her up, and she looked again and she said it was one of the largest men's feet she ever saw. He was standing at the window laughing at her. And he was a black man. She's had that happen two or three times. He just comes back and laughs at her in the window." It was not clear if this event was real or imagined. The reality of the event, however, made little difference to the victim.

One lady explained what happened to a friend after taking her home from a shopping trip:

> This lady was almost raped, but she got out of it. After that, her family moved her out. She had been right in Rosedale and we came home about 4:00 in the afternoon. We let her out and she went in. When she got in, there was a nigger boy about seventeen, and he told her that he was going to rape her. He started in clawing at her clothes, and she had on a real tight girdle and he couldn't get her girdle off. She was begging him to leave her alone and she said she couldn't get her clothes off. He said alright, "you can just suck it." And she said, "Oh my God, no, I'm going to pray for you." For some reason the man across the street realized that she was in trouble and came in and the boy ran off.

Other women had friends who were not so fortunate.

> One woman here at the center was let off the bus one evening. She was a very popular person here at the center. She walked in her house and she was raped by three colored boys. She was also stabbed countless times. She survived but was unable to ever come back to the center. A friend lived down here in the third house from the corner. Miss Stone. She was raped and killed. Right here on my block. And another person, Mrs. Bensen, she was out in her backyard and she was attacked. She's way up in years. There was a nigger man, he walked up behind her and held her and threw her down. He was unfastening her clothes and pulling her dress up, and she was screaming just as loud as she could. He got scared and ran and went across the street. He went right to another woman's house right across the street. It was right next door to Mrs. Brown's house. He raped the woman across the street. After that, her son moved her out. I don't know if they're going to sell the house or what. It's just vacant now.

One rapist seemed to direct his attacks exclusively toward the elderly. More often than not, he violently assaulted the elderly victim during the attack. Among the rapes committed during April 1977, all were believed to have been committed by a slender black man about five feet, eight inches tall. Police reported that the man usually carried a knife and removed part or all of his clothing before entering the victim's home.

Between April and July, about sixteen attempted rapes and robberies, all perpetrated by a man fitting this description, were reported in Rosedale. In some instances, the police said that the man had struck three times on the same street. The first few weeks of April 1977 were especially terrifying for the elderly of Rosedale. By April 12, police were searching for one suspect who raped a sixty-five-year-old woman and two men who beat and robbed a ninety-three-year-old white man who was partially blind. The elderly man was violently beaten by two young black men before they stole his food stamps.

The elderly woman returned home from church early Sunday evening and found a slender black man in her bedroom. The man was nude and threatened her with a rubber hose and butcher knife. The man struck her across the face with the hose and stomped on her feet and legs before raping her. Police reported that the woman's eyes were black and swollen, as were her legs and feet. In the other incident, the elderly man reported that two young men attacked and beat him after he returned home from Easter services. The adolescents were waiting inside the house when he returned from church. They ransacked the house, took food from the icebox, and stole about $40 worth of food stamps. They also took the only money the man had in his pocket, a $1 bill.

By the last week of July, the entire community of Rosedale was in panic over the rape spree. Police publicly admitted that they were puzzled by the rapist's style of operation and were becoming concerned over the rising levels of violence that accompanied the attacks. A police official stated, "He seems to be getting more violent." Earlier rapes were characterized by polite admonitions to the victims to keep their windows and doors locked if they wanted to avoid getting raped in the future. The rapist even lectured his victims about home security while sexually abusing them.

One such victim, a seventy-six-year-old woman, awoke about 3:00 A.M. to find a shirtless, barefooted man in her bathroom. When the woman attempted to run out the front door, the man grabbed her, tied her wrists, and dragged her to the bedroom. The rapist wielded a knife and forced the woman into acts of sodomy. While raping the elderly victim, the assailant said: "I could get into your doors anytime; you should have chains and latches. This is my business. I know." The rapist left with $2 removed from the victim's billfold.

The July victims, however, were violently raped. One was stabbed and the other shot in the head. A sixty-five-year-old woman furiously struggled with the rapist. She suffered a slashed arm and multiple bruises in the face before managing to scare off the rapist with a barrage of gunfire from her pistol. Another July victim, seventy-four years old, awoke with a sharp pain in her head. She found a knife beside her bed. She got up and encountered the rapist, wearing only a pair of pants, in her living room. She demanded to know what the man was doing in her house. Offering no answer, the man simply turned and fired one shot. The bullet struck the woman in the head. She died several days after the incident.

Police later found out that the man entered the victim's home through a window. A police spokesman said, "He must take his clothes off outside and pick them up on his way out." During the first week of August, another violent rape took place. The victim was a sixty-nine-year-old woman. As in previous patterns, she was raped in her home and savagely beaten. The woman told police that she awoke in her bed and found a man standing beside her. During the struggle that ensued, she was beaten, stabbed, and struck on the head with a hammer. She remained in critical condition for several weeks at a local hospital before succumbing to the wounds inflicted during the attack.

During this same period, the private hysteria in Rosedale was fueled by other rape incidents not consistent with the nude or partially clothed style of the so-called Rosedale rapist. Several women reported being raped by men whose description and style differed from those of other reported rapists. By August, it was apparent that several rapists were terrorizing Rosedale. Some rapists were gaining entry to homes on false pretenses. Police reported that certain rapists would tell the victim that their car had broken down and they needed to make a phone call. The rapist would sometimes pose as a repair or utility man. In other instances, he would simply knock at the door and force his way into the house once the door was partially opened.

The ages of the victims attacked by this person ranged from early thirties to mid-eighties. The attacks were not only violent but also designed to humiliate the victim. In one instance, the rapist forced a woman's eight-year-old son to witness the violation of his mother. In addition to what appeared to be two active rapists on the loose in Rosedale, an alarming increase in random rape incidents and rape threats were reported by police. Obviously concerned about media coverage of the violence and the widespread use of the term "Rosedale rapist," a police detective investigating the case told the media that notoriety of the rapist may have spawned other rape attempts by young men seeking publicity. He said, "We can get too many rapists out there if we're not careful."

In support of his observation, he cited two incidents that occurred during the first week of August. In one situation, a man claiming to be the Rosedale rapist tried to rape a seventeen-year-old pregnant woman outside her home. In another incident, a woman was chased down a major thoroughfare in Rosedale by a man claiming to be the Rosedale rapist. The man threatened to rape the woman while chasing her. It seemed apparent that copycat rapists had been spawned by media coverage of the Rosedale assaults.

By mid-July, the police had increased street patrols in Rosedale. Additionally, police cars were added to the Rosedale beat, as were K-9 units. The city's minority leadership responded aggressively to the rape spree overwhelming Rosedale. Several African American community organizations, outraged and humiliated by the attacks on elderly whites, put up reward money for capture of the Rosedale rapist. The Black Chamber of Commerce offered a $1,000 reward. The East Side Lions Club followed suit. By the latter part of July, the reward bounty for the rapist totaled $5,000, all raised by Afro-American organizations.

A spokesperson for the black Lions Club was quoted as saying, "I've never seen our group so upset; most of the $1,000 price on the head of the rapist was gathered right at the meeting." The Black Chamber of Commerce announced that it was planning "a moratorium on crime in the black community." Police sketchings of the rapist were widely publicized in the local media. "Face readers" attempted to interpret the character of the rapist on the basis of the sketches. Psychics rendered their predictions and attempted to assist in the apprehension of the rapist. The police department announced to the press that the Rosedale situation was their "number-one priority."

By August 1, 1977, many of Rosedale's elderly had armed themselves. Irrespective of additional police controls or escalating levels of reward money, the elderly were more insecure than ever. Their fears appeared justified. The Friday paper ran a whole-page composite drawing of the suspected Rosedale rapist. At that time, the man in question was suspected of seven rapes, five attempted rapes, and five robberies. Over the weekend, the rapist struck again. The intended victims were a fifty-eight-year-old widow and her daughter.

The daughter awoke to find someone standing near her bed. The person left the room, and she thought it must have been her mother. But sensing that something was wrong, she got up and went to the kitchen. The man was standing there. He looked at her and fired a pistol in her direction. The bullet ricocheted off the kitchen walls and cabinets. The man calmly turned, left the house, and disappeared into the night. During the first week of August, the local press reported that Rosedale had become an armed camp.

In fact, the widow and her daughter were now heavily armed and prepared for a possible return of the rapist. The women were later reported as having acquired three guns, all loaded and "easy to put our hands on." The widow confessed to local news media that she "didn't have a gun at the time, but now we're loaded for bear. My son brought his .22 pistol over, and I've also got a .38 and a rifle by my bed."

Other elderly residents in Rosedale reported similar feelings. One elderly man said: "I've been keeping up with that Rosedale rapist case sharply. We've got three guns in there, and they are clean and ready to go. If I catch anybody peeping in my window, they won't be peeping anymore." Many of the elderly reported to me that their attitudes toward guns had significantly changed because of the Rosedale rapist. An elderly woman said that guns used to scare her, "but they don't anymore." Referring to the rapist, she said, "If I could get him for what he's been doing, I'd be glad to go to jail for it."

Our early survey data showed that by 1979, over 35 percent of Rosedale's elderly had armed themselves. Some elderly women carried pistols in their purses and slept with guns under their pillows. Gunfire had already been exchanged between elderly victims and what they assumed was the Rosedale rapist. In one incident, an elderly woman answered her door, opening it just enough to identify who was on her back porch. A young black man attempted to force his way into the kitchen. The woman managed to close the door. She then pumped two rounds of ammunition from a .22 caliber pistol through the closed door. She claimed that the man was still trying to break the door down as she emptied the first round into the wooden door. The door and screen were riddled with bullet holes.

About mid-July, the police reported that two Rosedale residents had fired shots at a man who broke into their homes. A police captain was quoted as saying that local authorities were gravely concerned about the vigilante actions occurring in Rosedale. He said so many residents had armed themselves that either the suspect or some innocent person "was gonna get killed."

Some suspects were arrested and later released. On June 19, 1977, a young black man was apprehended and charged with two counts of aggravated rape, two counts of burglary of a habitat with intent to commit rape, and one count of aggravated robbery with a deadly weapon. The man was held without bond because of prior convictions and the fact that he was presently on probation. About two weeks after the man was arrested, he was identified by several rape victims as their attacker. The man behaved belligerently in lineups and aggressively maintained his innocence. He was eventually released. Several other suspects were arrested during June and July.

A nineteen-year-old man who resembled the composite picture of the Rosedale rapist was arrested during the first week of August. Because the man failed a lie detector test, police interest in the suspect increased. It was later disclosed that the man had deliberately lied when questioned because he feared for the safety of both himself and his wife. The suspect's wife told police that her husband was "quiet and shy" and spent his nights at home with her. She also said that her husband had never had a white girlfriend because he found them "unattractive." He was also eventually released.

A twenty-nine-year-old black man was arrested because he fit the description of the rapist who had been attacking elderly white women. After detectives questioned him and victims failed to identify him as the attacker in police lineups, he was released. Feeling community pressure, police spokespersons reassured the neighborhood that they were going to catch the rapist: "We're going to put him in jail. We're still biting at every lead we get. We consider it [the leads] the gospel truth until we can prove it one way or the other."

The police confessed that they still lacked conclusive threads of evidence that would enable them to move toward prosecution of the various suspects arrested. The district attorney's office and police officials thought that the nineteen-year-old suspect could have been involved in some of the rapes. They again stressed, however, that several rapists seemed to be loose in Rosedale. Their assessment did little to ease tension in the neighborhood or reduce the growing possibility of vigilante action.

One of the major reasons for suspecting more than one person, maintained a detective working on the case, was body odor. "For the first several rapes, no mention was made of body odor. However, all of a sudden, it seemed these women had a buffalo run at them. All they could talk about was his strong body odor." Further, it was clear that one of the rapists seemed to prey almost exclusively on elderly white women. His mode of attack was violent and brutal. Another rapist was more mild mannered, almost polite in his style of operation. Still others showed no consistent style or pattern.

A major break in the case developed during the second week of July. Interestingly, the lead developed because the elderly had armed themselves, an outcome about which the police were seriously concerned. In mid-June, one of the rapists attempted to attack an elderly woman. The woman reported that she awoke to find a half-naked man standing over her while she slept. She said she struggled with the man, who slashed her with a knife during the attack. She somehow managed to grab a pistol, which she kept close to her bed, and fired several times at the assailant. She did not know if any of her shots actually struck the rapist.

One of the bullets did find its mark and eventually led to the apprehension of a seventeen-year-old suspect. The police pieced the threads of evidence together after the suspect's supervisor told authorities that he reported to work on June 13 with a bullet wound in his leg. The rapist worked for the Texas Highway Department. He told his supervisor that he was cutting weeds while on the job and a moving vehicle sniped at him as it passed. Implying a racial motive to the sniping, the explanation initially seemed plausible to the supervisor.

The rapist sought treatment from a physician and was later transferred to a local hospital. The man became a serious suspect during the latter part of July and was eventually arrested in the first part of August. By the second week of August, the police were confident that they had captured one of the rapists. A search of the suspect's home produced enough evidence to confirm their suspicions. Several items of jewelry and a pair of blood-stained blue jeans were found. The jeans were probably worn during the unsuccessful June rape attempt.

The man was eventually identified as the rapist by several victims in police lineups, and the bullet removed from his leg in June was matched ballistically with the gun fired by the elderly victim. All the items found in the suspect's home were ultimately related to actual or attempted rapes: a woman's gold ring with missing stones, a woman's silver bracelet, a necklace of wooden beads on a leather string, two silver crucifixes, several items of army fatigue apparel, and a holster for a .32 caliber pistol and a black starter pistol. Additionally, magazines with sex pictures and sex ads were found. During one rape, a crucifix was ripped from the victim's neck. The clothes found also matched various descriptions given by victims.

There was little doubt that the police had one of their men. The rapist was indicted in September. He was formally charged with two burglaries with intent to commit rape and one aggravated rape at knifepoint. During August and September, the suspect confessed to having committed numerous rapes in Rosedale. He pleaded guilty to the formal charges at the October 1977 trial and eventually confessed to another twenty-five attacks in the Rosedale area.

The jury deliberated thirty minutes before handing down three consecutive life sentences. The district attorney's office made it clear from the outset that it was seeking the maximum sentence. The rapist's attorney begged the jury to consider probation. Attorneys for the defendant argued that he should be given the opportunity to pursue probation. Citing selected aspects of his background, the defense attorney said, "These are the makings of a man who could make it on probation. The man has confessed. There's no question of him walking out of here a free man. The only issue at this point is what should be his punishment. He made three mistakes and he's asking for the jury's mercy. He wants a second opportunity."

Prosecuting attorneys minced no words in their closing arguments. They referred to the rapist as a "pervert" and a "vicious animal who could turn killer at any second." Turning to the jury, the assistant district attorney asked: "Can you afford to put him on the streets and gamble that he won't do it again? I'm asking you to give him a life sentence because that's the longest you can keep him off the streets in Rosedale and away from the women of Rosedale."

The jury's verdict left little doubt that mercy was a quality not present in the courtroom that day. The rapist, who turned nineteen while in jail, expressed no emotion throughout the trial. He did not look at any of the jurors or any of those present in the courtroom during the deliberations. The only people that received his attention were three victims who testified against him and an eight-year-old boy who had been forced to witness the rape of his mother.

Even though the person labeled the Rosedale rapist had been caught and convicted, police were certain that others were still at large in the community. And although the neighborhood and the city generally sighed with collective relief with the arrest and conviction of the person everyone assumed was the Rosedale rapist, the police had good reason to remain apprehensive. In mid-September, police were confident in saying to the press that the Rosedale rapist was in custody and behind bars: "I believe we're down to isolated cases out there." The chief of police said that beefed-up patrols in the Rosedale area were working and that no more rapes had been reported there, at least no more than in any other part of the city. In fact, no rapes were reported in Rosedale between late July and October 1977.

The police were also quick to point out, however, that at least ten to fifteen rapes were still unsolved. This fact reinforced their suspicion that more than one rapist had been terrorizing the women of Rosedale. A police spokesperson told the media: "I never did think there was one Rosedale rapist. We've had rapes all over town. We've had a number of rapes on the West side, and God knows how many we've had that haven't been reported."

Worse yet, the officer said, "We still have the mystery of the old ladies." He was referring to the cases where the victims were very old and that always involved extreme violence and sometimes death. The last victim, a sixty-nine-year-old woman who was brutally beaten and stabbed, died before police could question her thoroughly. "We don't know much about her case," said a police detective. "We certainly still have some open cases out there," he continued. "I think the man who had done the slashing and raping of the elderly is still at large."

Although numerous attacks against the elderly were pinned to the rapists who were caught and convicted, the most brutal attacks remain unsolved. In fact, those cases have remained open for more than a decade. Curiously, however, the violent rape attacks ceased.

Two young rapists were eventually apprehended, tried, and convicted. One clearly fit the description of the infamous Rosedale rapist. The other came to be known by local law enforcement officials and attorneys as the *Roots* rapist. Analysis of their backgrounds and personal characteristics provide clues to their violent behavior and additional insights into why racial animosity continues to undermine the integration of urban communities.

The Roots *Rapist*

The victims of the *Roots* rapist were nearly all white; most were elderly. Juvenile parole officers, attorneys, and police familiar with the case all commented about his preoccupation with the television series *Roots*. The content of the series apparently triggered underlying hostilities and resentment toward whites. While committing various rapes, he lectured victims about various incidents portrayed during the series, especially those depicting degrading treatment of slaves or abuse of the major characters in the script.

Seventeen at the time of his arrest, Clarence Boyd Henderson had a fairly long juvenile record. He was first referred to the Juvenile Department at age fifteen for burglary. Pending the adjudicatory hearing for that offense and less than a week later, he was again arrested for theft. He failed to appear for the later hearings scheduled and was formally reported as a runaway. He was later apprehended and ordered detained.

While awaiting a dispositional hearing dealing with possible placement in a juvenile detention center, he was arrested for attempted rape by the police department. All of these events occurred in September and October 1975.

Henderson was allegedly seen following into her yard the woman who filed the attempted-rape complaint. She maintained he attempted to pull at her clothing and force her to the ground. After questioning Henderson and the victim, the authorities adjusted the case. In November 1975, he was placed on probation for a period not to exceed one year.

While on probation, he was again arrested for burglary. As a result of this latter charge, he was placed in the custody of the Texas Youth Council. In December 1975, he was placed in a juvenile detention center and then released to his mother's care in June 1976. One month after his release, he was arrested for burglary of a habitat. One month later, he was again arrested for burglary of a habitat. No revocation hearings were scheduled in response to his new violations.

He was arrested for attempted rape in April 1977. Further investigation resulted in additional allegations of rape and burglary of a habitat. Attorneys familiar with the case thought that he may have been responsible for an additional twenty to twenty-five rapes in Rosedale, primarily involving elderly white women.

Elements of Henderson's family background revealed additional clues about his consistent drift into criminal behavior. His father had been involved in a common-law relationship with Clarence's mother. The relationship ended in 1962. He remarried in 1963. His father had three children from a prior marriage, had completed five years of formal education, and earned about $6,000 a year as a janitor. He was living in Dallas at the time of his son's arrest for rape.

His mother was married once before establishing the relationship with Henderson's father. Three children were born before their separation in 1962. She remarried in 1962 and bore two more children prior to her last husband's death in 1974. His mother was not employed at the time of his arrest and supported her family with an estimated $4,000 annual income from social security benefits.

Henderson's two brothers also experienced trouble with juvenile authorities. One brother was charged with robbery in 1973. The other was referred to the Juvenile Department on runaway charges on four separate occasions. He enlisted in the marines in August 1976.

According to Clarence's mother, he was seldom home and had minimal involvement in family activities. Her relationship with him was "inconsistent," according to juvenile records, and she reported "minimal communication and no shared activity." According to social work records, "There were frequent situations of argumentation and a resentful response to supervision." According to his mother, Clarence spent little time within the home: "He frequently leaves early in the morning and does not return until late evening." During the year prior to his arrest she had little or no idea of his whereabouts or activities.

Clarence was described by his mother as not particularly close to either parent. He rarely expressed emotion other than anger. According to his mother, her son was a loner who had few friends or companions. He had last attended school at Rosedale High School. Before dropping out in November 1976, he was failing nearly all subjects and had a record of excessive absences. No church attendance or activities were apparent in his personal biography.

Henderson created a uniform impression among his family, juvenile officials, probation officers, and court psychologists as an angry and brooding personality. In October 1976, he was shot in the neck during a neighborhood confrontation. His condition was serious and surgery was required. The bullet was not removed but lodged near the spine in an irretrievable position. According to psychologists who interviewed him, "This event fueled his sense of anger and reinforced the belief that life was being unfair to him because of his race." After interviewing Henderson, a psychiatrist reported:

> He tends to collect resentments and grudges and uses them to justify his behavior. He says he began to steal only after being shot. He thinks he has been unfairly treated in numerous instances, feels that he has been given more severe punishment than others who have committed worse offenses because of his race. Throughout all of this is an angry tone and a desire to get even. He has had homicidal fantasies, but has never lost control or carried out a plan to hurt someone else and, when in fights, may seize a weapon impulsively as a equalizer. . . . Another recurring theme has to do with his wish to amount to something, be known for something good, and an underlying trend that he views himself in many ways as a bad person.

Psychiatrists and psychologists examining Henderson noted that he minimized sexual problems and that exploration of this facet of his personality was essentially unproductive. Reports from victims, however, suggest that Henderson's behavior was consistent with the kind of racial anger described by Eldridge Cleaver in *Soul on Ice*.[1] Just as Cleaver had embraced the poetry of Leroi Jones, Henderson had identified with the television drama *Roots*. But it did not cause Henderson to rape. Rather it provided a cover, a justification, for acting out deeply embedded feelings of racial animosity.

Clinicians studying various forms of rape behavior maintain that in all types of rape, three elements are typically present: power, anger, and sexuality. In certain types of rape, anger is the predominant emotion. Psychiatrists who study sexual violence contend that "anger rapes" are found in situations where

> the offender expresses anger, rage, contempt, and hatred for his victim by beating her, sexually assaulting her, and forcing her to perform or submit to additional degrading acts. He uses more force than would be necessary simply to subdue his victim. The assault is one of physical violence to all parts of the body: the rapist often approaches his victim by striking and beating her, tears her clothing, and uses profane and abusive language. The aim of this type of rapist is

to vent his rage on his victim and to retaliate for perceived wrongs or rejections he has suffered at the hands of women. Sex becomes a weapon, and rape is the means by which he can use this weapon to hurt and degrade his victim."[2]

They go on to explain that the discharge of anger rather than sexual gratification is how the anger rapist achieves satisfaction. Pleasure is derived from degrading and humiliating his victim. According to the researchers, "Older or elderly women are a particular target for this type of rapist. ... His motive is revenge and his aim is degradation and humiliation."

At the trial of Clarence Boyd Henderson, three victims testified. All were elderly white females, aged eighty-five, seventy-six, and eighty-four, respectively. The first victim indicated that Henderson ordered her to remove her clothes while pushing and shoving her toward the bedroom. With his trousers down and his genitals pushed against her stomach, he asked the terrified, elderly victim if she had seen or read *Roots*. The elderly woman responded: "I kept begging him to take the money. I had my purse lying there on the table. I kept begging him, 'Go on, take the money and go.'"

According to the victim, Henderson responded: "Money is not what I want." He pushed her into the bedroom and worked feverishly and aggressively to pull her clothes off, repeatedly saying, "Don't call the police. If you call the police, I'll kill you. I'll kill you." While raping the woman, he made frequent and rambling references to the *Roots* series.

The second rape victim testified that she was raped by Henderson at 8:00 in the morning after finding him in her bathroom. Wielding a knife and gun, the rapist shoved her into the bedroom and pulled off her night clothes. Right before the actual rape, the victim reported that Henderson talked incessantly "about *Roots*, and how white people hated them, and old roots and all that stuff."

During the actual rape, he asked the victim repeatedly to hold him and attempted to push her legs around his feet. The elderly woman suffered serious genital bruises, an outcome consistent with the style of anger rapists. She told the court: "He talked all the time nearly. ... He asked me if I saw *Roots*. I said that I saw part of it. He said 'How come you didn't see it all?' He said the white people hated them. That's the way it was in *Roots*."

When he was finished, he said: "If I called the fuzz, he'd kill me. He'd come back and kill me and burn the house down just like he did the other white women. He said, 'So help me God, I'll do it' over and over, some twenty times."

The last victim reported similar events. Upon entering the house, Henderson physically assaulted the woman: "He had hold of my hair, pulling my hair, and he picked me up and threw me on the bed ... and then he hurt me, pushed on me here on my chest, and then, he reached down and pulled my nightie off over my head. He said, 'I'm going to get a piece of this.'"

The victim reported that while being raped, she remembered him talking "about a book or story or something." During the assault, the phone rang and the woman was able to grab it and scream for help. Henderson eventually left the house as a result of the phone call but not before violently shaking the victim, injuring her neck and shoulder. While shaking her he yelled: "'I'll be back and I'm going to kill you and burn your house down.' ... He kept talking about *Roots*, and he said, 'You know what roots are?' I said, 'No, I don't. What was it, a story, a picture show? What is roots?'"

Apparently infuriated by her response, Henderson shook her even more aggressively and stated: "You know what it is." The woman testified: "That is when he shook me because I wouldn't talk about it. I didn't know about it. That is when he hurt me."

The Rosedale Rapist

David Allen Gillman, the convicted Rosedale rapist, appeared driven by similar levels of anger. Although he did not confine his attacks exclusively to elderly women, most of his victims were white. During the rapes he did not express racial motives. He did, however, reveal high levels of anger and rage. In comparison to Henderson, Gillman was more violent and physically aggressive.

Gillman was indicted on September 6, 1977, on one count of rape and two counts of burglary with intent to commit rape. He signed statements confessing to charges. The three victims eventually testified at his trial. Police thought that at least thirty other counts of rape could be attributed to Gillman, although they had insufficient evidence to close the books on these other cases. Their conclusion was based upon similarities in the type and style of rape behaviors reported by victims.

Gillman lived with his father and mother. Unlike the family situation of Henderson, the home environment of the Rosedale rapist was somewhat more stable. Both parents were present in the home; each noted that their son kept late hours and was frequently absent from the household. Doing poorly in school and frequently absent, he withdrew at the end of his eleventh year. There were three other children present in Gillman's household, two sisters aged sixteen and thirteen and a younger brother who was eight years old.

During the two years prior to his arrest, he developed a reputation in the community as constantly on the edge of the law and headed for serious trouble. During those two years, he was arrested for burglary and referred to the Juvenile Department on several occasions. At the time of his arrest, he was employed in a summer job with the Texas Highway Department.

Gillman signed three statements detailing one rape and two burglaries with intent to rape. Each explained how he entered the victims' houses and how they were assaulted. Of particular significance are the similarities between his style of forced entry and the numerous reports by residents of Rosedale describing their fear of criminal victimization.

Statement One

I went to a house located on _____ Street and found a front door on this house that had a broken out door pane on it. I reached thru this broken window door pane and was able to unlock this front door and go into the house. On this morning I was wearing my blue jeans which are light blue and my white tennis shoes. I found a ladies purse in the living room of this house and I went through it but it did not have any money in it. I then found a small dog in this house that I think was a puppy and I put it in a small room right off the living room and shut the door to this room. I then went into the bedroom of this house which has a bathroom leading off it and I turned the light on in this bathroom. At this time I observed a woman asleep in a bed in this bedroom that appeared to be about 21 years old.

This woman woke up after I turned the bathroom light on and I put one of my hands around her mouth. I told this lady not to say a word or I would kill her. This woman then kicked me and I noticed that this lady had a gun in bed with her and I turned and ran out of the house. I had my tennis shoes in my hand as I had taken them off in the living room and I dropped one of them as I was going out of the front door and as I turned around to pick this shoe up the lady shot me in the front of my left thigh. I was able to get away and I made it to my house at _____ Avenue. A couple of hours later I reported to work at 8:00 AM for the Texas Highway Department. At about 8:30 AM after I had gotten out to our work area for that day I reported to my boss that a motorist had driven by and called me a mother fuckin' nigger and had shot me. An ambulance was called for me and the bullet in my leg was taken out at _____ Hospital.

The other two confessions showed more clearly the consistent style of forced entry and provided some indication of the degree of violence directed toward victims.

Statement Two

On Sunday . . . in the early hours of this morning I went to a house located on _____ Street and took a window screen off a rear window to this house with a screwdriver I had with me. I then crawled thru this window because the window itself was already opened all the way up. I then went into the kitchen of this house and found a kitchen knife about seven inches long. I took this knife into the living room of this house where I found a woman asleep on a couch and a small boy about 7 or 8 years old asleep on another couch. A television set was on in this room but there was nothing showing on it. The woman that was asleep on the couch looked about 25 years old and I woke her up and threatened her with the knife and told her to take her clothes off. The small boy woke up at this time and I pointed the knife at him and told him to shut up. I then raped this woman and after I got thru with this I asked her if she had any money. She said she had some money in the bedroom and we went to the bedroom and she gave me her money.

Statement Three

On Saturday _____ in the early hours of the morning while it was still dark I went into a house located at _____ Street. I entered this house by taking a window screen off of a rear window with a screwdriver and then raised a window that was already unlocked. I then crawled thru this window and prowled around in the house and found a ladies purse that I took about $40 or $50 dollars out of. I found this purse in a bedroom of this house and there was a lady sleeping in a bed in this room. This lady seemed to be about 23 or 24 years old and I shook her on the face with my hand and woke her up. I told this lady to shut up or I would kill her baby. This lady began to struggle with me as I was bending over the bed; this lady snatched a necklace off of my neck that I was wearing. . . . For some reason while I was struggling with this woman I decided to leave and I ran out of the house and left through the same window that I had come in at.

Actual testimony provided at the trial by the three victims provided more insight into the level of violence directed at victims by the Rosedale rapist. The woman who shot Gillman testified that he entered her home around four or five o'clock in the morning: "The bathroom light came on and the defendant was standing in my bedroom. He grabbed ahold of me. He grabbed me around the throat and tried to force me, keep me down on the bed. He said he'd kill me if I screamed." The woman explained that she struggled with the rapist and kicked him and hit him with her fists. During the struggle, Gillman "pulled a knife out of his pocket."

She explained to the court that she was able to retrieve a ".22 caliber H and R nine shot" from her nightstand. The rapist ran out of the bedroom, but she pursued and shot him in the leg. After the incident, she went to her mother's room and called the police.

The victim whose son was also attacked was not as fortunate. She testified that she lived in Rosedale with her parents and her three children. On the night of the rape, her parents were not at home. She and her eight-year-old son had watched television until quite late. Both had fallen asleep in the living room. She awoke and "there was a black man. He jumped over the coffee table and raped me and stuck a knife to my eight-year-old boy's throat. He told me if I didn't shut up that he was going to kill me and then my eight-year-old boy started screaming and he jumped off me and stuck the knife at his throat and told him if he didn't shut up he was going to kill him."

After raping the mother and confronting the boy, Gillman returned to the victim: "He got off him and jumped back on me and tried to get me to perform oral sex on him. I scratched him. On his face. My fingernail broke into his face." The rapist then violently slapped the victim and demanded money.

"I told him that I didn't have any and my eight-year-old boy said, 'Mom, you got your check yesterday; give it to him.' Then he took us to the bedroom, had the knife at my eight-year-old boy's back and I handed him the money, the envelope the money was in. He took the money and threw the envelope on the floor. Then he took us to the kitchen where he put his clothes back on. He got to the backdoor and he told me if I called the police that he was going to have my house watched and have me killed."

During the actual rape, Gillman violently assaulted the victim. She testified that he pulled and ripped her clothes off and held the knife "to my throat; he never did lay it down." Explaining her efforts to resist the rape, the victim stated: "I put my legs together and when I put my legs together he tried to pull them apart and he hit me right here and right here [indicating]. He pulled my legs apart with the knife and cut me right here [indicating]." The eight-year-old son also testified, corroborating that he and his mother were assaulted with a knife and that he had been forced to watch his mother's rape and related demands to perform oral sex.

The third victim who testified also stated that her child was threatened by the rapist. She awoke at approximately 5:00 A.M. to find "a black man standing over my bed. He had hold of my shoulder and told me that if I said anything that he would kill me. I grabbed ahold of him and he came down on my bed and then my bed broke and my little girl started to scream. I grabbed hold of his—I don't know if it was his neck but it slid off and his necklace—I got his necklace and it broke."

The testimony and confessions were sufficient to convict Gillman. As stated earlier, he was sentenced to three consecutive life sentences. It was widely assumed that he was responsible for numerous other rapes occurring in Rosedale, many closely resembling the level of violence displayed in the case of the mother with the eight-year-old son.

While awaiting trial, Gillman sent a letter to his attorneys. The letter revealed partial recognition of the sexual pathologies that drove him to rape and the mounting fear over facing the consequences of his actions. Similar to others in comparable circumstances, he claimed to have discovered the error of his ways and had found religious inspiration.

Dear _____:

Please try and get me probation. I pray to God and I talk to Him every day and night. Please do it for me, sir. Please try and give me a chance to start all over again. God in heaven have save me. Now I am a child of God. Please don't let them take none of my life away. I want to go back to school and make something out of myself. I can't do it in prison. Prison just makes it worser.

I didn't do does things because I wanted to do them. I have a serious problem. I had it since I was about 11. I use to play with my sister when they was asleep. I was very scared of girls and shy. Ask my mother and tell her about it. Mr. _____ I need your help and I want help. I'm not saying this just to keep me out of prison. I know Mr. _____ lock up behind bars isn't going to solve it. I would have told you this before but I was so shock in side when you told me about the years. I was trying to keep calm. I pray to God and ask him to save me. Mr. _____ and Mr. _____ please pray for me and save me and get me help so I can live a normal life. I didn't want to do those things. Please believe me. I just had the problem for so long that it just got worser. I'm telling you the holy truth. Please don't let me go to prison. Please don't. I'm sorry I don't tell you this before. I was so shock when you tell me about those years. I'll tell you the rest of my problem when you come and see me. It's so much to tell that I can't write it all. Please help me and save me from going down.

David Gillman

7

THE WILDING
INCIDENTS OF 1982

Mrs. Ethel Marlow, a retired bookkeeper, was found dead in her ransacked home. A 14-inch wooden dowel had been stuck down her throat and her body was riddled with stab wounds. (June 10, 1982)

Mary Bradley, 74, lay in bed at Metropolitan Hospital Friday, the bruises that covered her body and the cuts above her left eye reminders of the beating she suffered in her home of more than 50 years. One or more intruders entered her Rosedale-area home early Thursday, waking her from a nap by jamming a pencil-like object up her nose and demanding money. . . . She was discovered two hours later in a pool of blood when her husband returned home. The booty had been $40.00, some jewelry and a wristwatch that didn't work. (September 11, 1982)

Ralph Johnson was stabbed to death at 3493 Avenue East at about 9:00 P.M., Thursday. Two suspects broke down the front door, ransacked the house, killed Johnson and beat his 79-year old wife, Marie. (September 30, 1982)

LIFE IN ROSEDALE RETURNED TO NORMAL with the arrest of the infamous rapists. But normal for the elderly simply meant that their fear of being raped lessened. High levels of street crime, thefts, and burglaries continued. With the capture of the Rosedale rapist, publicity and media attention directed toward Rosedale waned. Extra police units assigned to the area were curtailed. The plight of Rosedale's elderly gradually faded from public attention. During the spring and summer of 1982, however, the violence returned. The violence took the form of gang murders and wilding attacks.

The term "wilding" became part of the popular vocabulary in 1989 after a gang of New York youths attacked and nearly killed a female jogger in Central Park. The teenagers told police that wilding was a pastime well known to the city's youth. As used by the New York youth involved, the term means to run around like a pack of wild animals, acting out the most basic and violent inclinations. The youth of Rosedale were engaged in wilding violence long before the New York City incident shocked the nation. As with public reactions in New York, the Rosedale summer wildings racially polarized the city.

By September 1982, Rosedale was again an armed camp. The anguish of the elderly again captured the media's attention, and threats of race riots again confronted public officials. Appearing on the front page of the city's largest newspaper, the *Fort Worth Star Telegram,* on Saturday, September 11, 1982, was the following bold print: "Thugs Victimize Aged in Rosedale." The latest victim of the violence was a seventy-four-year-old woman.

She had lived in Rosedale for more than fifty years. As a result of the attack, she was confined to one of the local hospitals, hovering near death. Her face was severely battered from a beating suffered at the hands of two or more black adolescents. They had broken into her home earlier in the week, waking her from a nap by jamming a pencil-like object up her nose and demanding money. When the woman did not respond immediately, she was brutally beaten and kicked.

She was discovered several hours later when her husband returned home from an errand. He found her on the floor, unconscious in a pool of blood. The only items missing from the house were $40 and an old wristwatch that no longer worked. She eventually died in the hospital.

The woman was the forty-sixth elderly victim attacked between June and September 1982. Three rapes were also perpetrated during that time. The ages of the victims were seventy-seven, eighty, and ninety-four.

On September 13, the local paper announced that the Guardian Angels planned to patrol Rosedale. A former resident of Rosedale whose mother had been recently attacked announced his wholesale support for the Angels or whatever other vigilante group was willing to rid the neighborhood of the "animals" who were attacking the elderly: "Apparently, this has gone on too long. I'm sure the police are doing what they can, with the laws and the manpower they've got. I'm getting down on the public. We've let this go on too long. I'll cool off when the Rosedale area straightens out."

Fearing racially inspired vigilante action, several African American pastors called for restraint: "I think especially in black neighborhoods, it would remind them of what happened in the past." Another declared: "Anything of that nature [vigilante action] would probably be more trouble. It would just add fuel to the fire. It would leave a bad taste because of the racial overtones." A local civil rights leader agreed with the clergy: "I like to work within the framework we have. We need to talk with City Hall and bring pressure to bear there. We don't need to come up with some renegade group."

The first serious assault leveled against the elderly was perpetrated in March. The number of incidents grew steadily after that. Ten violent crimes were perpetrated in July, twenty-two in August, and eight during the first nine days of September. In response to public pressure, the police again were pressed to devote more units, time, and special patrols to the Rosedale area. A police spokesperson said that most of the crimes had been committed between the hours of six and midnight. Nearly all the crimes were directed against older white women living alone.

Young males ranging in number between one and five and between fourteen and twenty years old were forcibly entering the homes of elderly women. They were robbing and violently beating their victims. The police suspected that gangs of black youth were systematically terrorizing the elderly of Rosedale. The deputy chief told the press: "In my opinion, it's not two or three. It's more like 15 or 20. I'm taking this very personally because I have an elderly mother who lives alone. And I'm very much offended by people who victimize old people, and we're going to stop it."

Three violent murders during the summer pushed the elderly of Rosedale to the brink of collective hysteria and the city toward political and racial crisis. On June 10, Mrs. Ethel Marlow was found dead in her home. She was a retired bookkeeper, eighty-eight years old, and had lived in Rosedale for years. Three or more young black males broke into her house and dragged her from room to room. The attackers eventually killed her by jamming a broom handle down her throat and stabbing her more than thirty times. The house was ransacked. The discovery of her nude, stab-riddled body, the dowel protruding from her mouth, served notice to the elderly community that the violence had returned.

On July 15, another violent murder occurred. The brazen nature of this attack shocked the community as well. Mr. Clyde Robbins, a fifty-seven-year-old resident of Rosedale, had pulled alongside a car wash. Four youths jumped in front of his moving car, opened the door on the driver's side, and pulled Robinson out of the car. The four teens kicked the man brutally and eventually beat him to death with his own cane, which was lying beside him in the car. The four assailants took his wallet and disappeared into the early evening.

On September 3, two teens broke into the home of Mr. and Mrs. Ralph Johnson. About nine o'clock, they broke down the door of the seventy-seven-year-old man's home. They ransacked the house and stabbed Johnson to death. His seventy-nine-year-old wife, Marie, was severely beaten. She remained in fair condition at a local hospital with multiple bruises covering her chest, face, and stomach. The intruders escaped in the couple's 1978 Pontiac, later found about five blocks from the murder.

By October 1, a $1,000 reward had been posted for any information leading to the arrest and apprehension of those responsible for the summer crimes. More than forty city firefighters volunteered to walk the Rosedale area door-to-door and distribute reward information and posters. Numerous community leaders and local officials publicly pleaded with those responsible to end the terror. Residents were exhorted to step forward with any information useful to the police.

Frustrated and impatient, a police spokesperson told the press: "The roots of the problem are deeper than the police department can attack. We have no control over social problems or social change."

In the second week of October, the violence ended as quickly as it had begun. An informant told police that several young blacks she knew might be involved in the attacks. The lead proved accurate and eventually led to the arrest and indictment of five young residents of Rosedale. Two of the youngsters were sixteen, one was fifteen, one seventeen, and the other twenty. The press described the adolescents as a "loose-knit gang" that had terrorized the neighborhood for over a year. Two of the men were brothers; two were uncle and nephew.

They were charged with burglary and the beating deaths of Mrs. Ethel Marlow, Mr. Clyde Robinson, and Mr. Ralph Johnson. All were certified to stand trial as adults. In April 1983, the first youth was prosecuted and found guilty of capital murder. During the course of the trial, prosecuting attorneys showed pictures of the violated and brutalized bodies to the jury. The youth, Johnny Lee Brown, was found guilty on three counts of murder and sentenced to life in prison.

By December 1983, the remaining four adolescents had been prosecuted and sentenced. Because of plea bargaining, lesser charges were leveled against other members of the "gang." Two other adolescents were eventually arrested and charged. One was tried as a juvenile; the other was eventually released because of insufficient evidence. The latter suspect was not prosecuted even though he was linked to the crimes by gang members.

During February 1983, I interviewed each of the five adolescents involved in the murders, their attorneys, and police officials involved in their apprehension. The information gathered from these interviews provided a clearer understanding of the violence directed toward the elderly and the events leading to the arrest of the adolescents. Additionally, I spent time riding with the officers assigned to the Rosedale beat. They described how the adolescents were eventually captured.

The evidence obtained during my interviews illustrates the magnitude of the barriers posed by minority adolescents that undermine the successful integration of many urban neighborhoods. Of particular significance are the problems created by the growing number of minority adolescents who drift toward drugs, violence, and illegal enterprise in response to the absence of opportunities in the urban labor market. The biographies and life circumstances of the Rosedale wilders are all too typical of a growing number of minority youngsters in American cities. Adolescent crime is as great a deterrent to the stability of interracial neighborhoods as are traditional forms of racism.

One evening in February I rode with the sergeant responsible for increasing police patrols in Rosedale during the summer wilding attacks; we drove to each of the three murder locations. It was dusk as we pulled in front of

Mrs. Marlow's brick home. The house was dark, vacant, and lifeless. The trees cast eerie shadows on the walls and roof. The yard was overgrown. I felt strong apprehension because I knew too many details of the elderly woman's murder, having read her autopsy report and talked with those who found her body.

Earlier that week I had talked for several hours with one of the adolescents awaiting trial for the murder of Mrs. Marlow. His attorney was trying to cut a deal for his youthful client if he testified for the prosecution. The young man was present during two of the murders but allegedly did not actively participate. I asked the youngster to tell me what took place the night Mrs. Marlow was killed. I recalled his words in particular as I looked at her vacant home.

A slender, clean-cut young man of only fifteen, he seemed honest and bright. I had difficulty comprehending what he told me and even more trouble accepting the fact that he was actually involved in the murder. But he was. Multiple emotions flashed in his sad brown eyes as he related what "went down" that night. His eyes blinked rapidly as visions of the violence moved across his memory.

Well, we got together one night, just talking and jiving. We were playing some video games. We were lookin' for a house to burglarize, and we picked that house because nobody was there. One or two of us was in front, and the other fellows went around back. And then all of a sudden, you know, I heard the window break. And by the time we got back there—me and this other guy— the door was kicked in and the glass was busted. We got inside through the kitchen and went into the living room.

I saw they was holdin' this old lady by the arms, and they was pickin' her up by the chin. And they started draggin' her around the house and slapping her and stuff. And askin' her where the money was and stuff like that. And she kept tellin' them just quit hittin' me and I'll show you where the money is. But they just kept hittin' her and draggin' her around and stuff and hittin' her.

The other fellows were searching the house to look for something of value. But we didn't find much there, nothin' really. And they was still hittin' her when we didn't find nothin'. And they were hittin' on her and she fell. When she fell, they started stompin' on her. They just stomped on her real hard. They started stompin' on her head. They just kept stompin' on her real hard, upside the head.

Then me and —— left and went down the street to this place called the Video Room. We played some video games and we left. You know, he left. He went his way and I went mine. I went over to a friend's house and we talked, you know, and jived, and the other fellows came back. There were two other fellows that came up and told me, you know, that they shoved a stick down that lady's throat. We just laughed when they said it.

I went on to their house and met up with my brother [also involved in the killing], and he said, "Boy, we killed that old lady," and after he said that, we decided that we didn't want to talk about it no more.

Mrs. Marlow was a popular woman at the Senior Citizen's Center. She was simply known as a kind old lady by her neighbors. As I sat in the police car outside her house, the captain involved in the investigation said: "I've never seen anybody around here since it occurred."

I asked him if he was here when they found her body. He said he didn't go inside the house that night. It is standard practice for only the homicide detective or criminal investigator to enter the scene of a crime so that potential evidence will not be disturbed. "The homicide officers called me to the scene and while I was parked outside the house, they went inside and found her. I never went in the house. I never saw her, and from what I was told, I'm glad I didn't. Now Mrs. Marlow, she worked her yard every day. Of course, she couldn't cut her own grass. But she was out pullin' weeds and clippin' here and there. That's what the neighbors told me. She'd give anybody anything. She was an extremely active woman for someone of her age."

Police records revealed that Mrs. Marlow suffered more than thirty stab wounds, a fractured skull, and numerous bruises and contusions. The intruders initially found her in the bathtub. Her genitals and breasts were spraypainted. In fact, fingerprints on the spray can eventually led to the arrest and prosecution of one of the wilding suspects.

Mr. Robinson was murdered outside a car wash in an equally violent manner. The sergeant drove me to the scene where Robinson had been killed. The main thoroughfare in Rosedale takes a sharp turn north shortly after the small central business district. A shopping center was built there in the 1960s. A small car wash is located adjacent to the shopping center:

> This is where Mr. Robinson was killed. When I got here, his car was sitting right here. He was headed this-a-way [pointing north] toward the Kroger store. His car was pulled straight into the curb. There was blood on the other side of the street where they drug him out and dragged him across the street. They beat him with, I guess, a two-by-four or something. He was awake and talking when the officer was here, and then he died in the hospital. It was about 10:30 at night. Four or five kids just got out in the middle of the street and blocked his way. They ran up and jerked the car open and drug him out.

I had difficulty imagining what took place. I asked the officer, with some degree of skepticism: "This place is reasonably well-lighted at ten o'clock at night, and they just beat him, killed him right here in the road?"

He looked at me and replied: "Several people saw it. Nobody did anything. They called us though. And of course, by the time we got there, it was all over with and they were gone." The account given to me by the officer was identical to that reported by one of the adolescents who participated in the murder. The same young man who described the Marlow killing related to me the details of how Mr. Robinson was murdered.

Sitting behind a metal table in a small conference room in the county jail, he matter-of-factly said:

> We were up at Kroger's, you know, playing videos. And the guys spotted an old man, and we started pickin' with him and stuff. And then one of the guys tried to grab his wallet. And, you know, the old man tried to swat his hand away, and the old man cursed him out. And he got in his car and drove up there by the car wash. And two guys got up behind him and when he stopped, why they opened his door and started pokin' him in the face with something. They took his wallet. We just left him there. We got a little money off the dude. And we spent the rest of the night just jiving around, you know.

The brutal beating and stabbing of Mr. and Mrs. Johnson eventually led to the apprehension of the five adolescents. The sergeant in charge of the area told me that the Johnson murder was a "tough one" because by September the police had more patrol units in Rosedale than in any other part of the city. "Mr. Johnson, he was killed on Thursday night, which is my day off. He was stabbed to death. I was asked what occurred that night that was different than any other night. You know, why could it occur and not be seen? You know, we had an average of eight to ten officers assigned to this one beat. And I had no idea what to say."

By mid-September, the evidence had already begun to pile up, but not in time to prevent the final attack. The police had narrowed the suspects to several adolescents. Most important, Mrs. Johnson survived the beatings, and her story enabled the police to eliminate some suspects and concentrate on others.

During the break-in, the Johnson's television set was stolen, a fact that Mrs. Johnson reported to the police. The robbery, assault, and murder made front-page news and received widespread local television coverage. In the news accounts, Mrs. Johnson was quoted as saying that her television set was the only thing stolen. Later, a shotgun was also reported missing. The press used the television theft to emphasize the brutal and senseless nature of the attack, and this concern over the TV proved to be a blessing in disguise for local police investigators.

A person in the neighborhood called the police a few days later and reported that she had personally witnessed a man buying a television set from two kids. She said that the purchase was negotiated the same night that the murder took place. She said the person buying the TV was driving a black or maroon Lincoln Continental with port windows in the side.

For the next few days, the police stopped every Continental in the district that halfway met the description given by the eyewitness informant. One officer told me: "We made every car that we could, and we put everyone in jail that we could put in jail. On whatever charge. If they committed a traffic violation, instead of giving them a ticket, we cash bonded them. We gave them a ticket and we took them down to the jail and made them put up a cash bond."

The intensified effort to round up potential suspects enabled the police to get fingerprints, pictures, and further information about the car in question. A few days later, it became obvious to everyone in Rosedale that the police had launched a major crackdown and were tenaciously and single-mindedly looking for the Continental that fit the description given by the informant. Concerned over the crackdown, even those involved in illegal enterprise in Rosedale were willing to assist police apprehend the wilding gang.

Two days passed before the police actually found the car. A female caller told the police that she knew where the car was parked and that it was the one they were looking for. When police arrived at the address of the caller, the car was parked right next to the house from where the women had phoned. The officer got out of his car and walked toward the house. A woman came out the front door and said: "I need to talk to you, but I can't do it here. I'm being watched. Drive down the street two blocks."

The officer met the woman on the next block. The woman and her husband had purchased the stolen television and were also the owners of the Continental. They lived very close to the residence of one of the kids who had sold them the TV. They were frightened. The woman told the police that her husband bought the TV the night of the murder. After they pieced together what had taken place, they called the homicide detective.

A few hours after the street meeting, the police met with the couple and got the television. They got a clear series of prints from it. Through the information the police had obtained from various informants in Rosedale—from other adolescents, those in pawnshops, and other streetwise people who wanted an end to the violence—they were able to narrow the list of suspects even further. They obtained a court order to obtain fingerprints on several of their prime suspects. And as fate would have it, the prints of their number-one suspect matched those found on the television.

He was immediately picked up and booked. Initially, the sixteen-year-old suspect denied everything. Eventually, the police were able to extract a confession from the youngster. Based on his statement and the evidence gathered by prosecuting attorneys, a clear picture of the Johnson robbery and murder emerged.

Three youths were actually involved. They made a decision to break into the Johnson home because it was dark and occupied by an elderly person. The house had bars on the windows and dead-bolt locks on the doors. One youth stood outside as a lookout; the other two entered the house by breaking a window in the door and opening it. The recipient of a pacemaker, Mrs. Johnson had returned home from the hospital only a few days earlier. The two youths encountered the couple in their bedroom.

Mr. Johnson, at eighty-seven, attempted in vain to ward off the intruders. During the furious struggle that ensued, he was stabbed in the chest with a knife apparently picked up by one of the attackers as he walked through the Johnsons' kitchen. According to the autopsy report, Johnson's face was grotesquely slashed several times, many of the cuts measuring ten to twelve inches in length. His arms and hands were also badly cut, undoubtedly from attempts to protect his face and vital organs from the knife-wielding attacker.

Mrs. Johnson, watching in horror as her husband struggled unsuccessfully to keep his life, was beaten by the other intruders. The couple were found a few hours later by their grandson. The body of Mr. Johnson was slumped against the bedroom wall in a pool of blood. Mrs. Johnson was lying in her bed, obviously in shock, praying to Jesus for someone to help her. The house had been ransacked. While Johnson was bleeding to death on his bedroom floor, one of the attackers had taken the cash from his wallet. Having obtained the booty, one teen said to the other: "Let's get out of here . . . the old man's gonna die."

On their way out, the assailants took a television and a shotgun and then left the scene in the Johnsons' family automobile. One of the officers involved in solving the Johnson case explained how a confession was ultimately obtained from the prime suspect: "The only way they finally got him to tell the truth was when his mother came down and she wanted to make a deal. We said no deal. This one's too big. This is capital murder, and we're not making any deals. We did tell her, though, that it would be better for him if he told the truth. She talked to him, and even then he still lied." Eventually, however, he confessed to committing the crime.

Continued interrogation produced more leads. The young suspect would mention one or two names, and the police would immediately pick up those persons. They would be interrogated, and another name would surface. That person would be arrested and interrogated and so forth. One suspect eventually turned himself in to the police. The police concluded from the evidence and the arrests that six to seven adolescents hung around together.

Informants in the community, including other street kids, known drug dealers, and prostitutes, fingered this group as responsible for most of the violence. Although nobody actually told the police that these kids actually committed the murders, they were identified as the ones "doing the bad things in Rosedale."

By spring 1983, the police felt reasonably comfortable about the job they had done in the community. Five suspects were in jail either awaiting trial or convicted of capital murder. One suspect was still at large, a fourteen-year-old whose street name was Bug. An officer told me: "He's still running around out there. We don't have a picture of him; nobody over there carries identification."

In mid-November 1983, the sixth suspect was apprehended. About 8:00 A.M. on a Friday, an informant called the police and told them where the suspect could be found. Detectives and patrol officers sealed off the area about 11:30 A.M. and approached the house. One officer explained: "We knocked on the door and nobody answered, but we heard somebody scuffling around inside." After kicking the door in, the police realized the youth had slipped away.

"Bug" had slid through a hole cut in the floor and was hiding on the premises. He kicked through the wooden siding covering the crawl space and ran down the street. Realizing what had happened, the police chased after him and eventually apprehended the suspect hiding under the bed in a house two blocks away. They also found a loaded .38-caliber pistol in the house where the sixth youth was captured. He was eventually tried as a juvenile. His fingerprints were found on the spray can obtained at the site of the Marlow killing.

In retrospect, the efforts on the part of the police to apprehend the wilding gang were substantial. At the prodding of the sergeant responsible for the Rosedale beat, the police launched an eight-month effort to curb violence in the neighborhood. Beginning in April 1982, recognition of a sustained pattern of victimization against the elderly gradually registered in the consciousness of the police. At first, the crimes seemed random. Examination of the offense reports and data on the complaints, however, showed systematic and consistent regularities.

It was obvious that those being victimized on a regular basis were elderly whites. These observations were confirmed by the crime-analysis section of the city police department. By July, it was apparent to the sergeant, the precinct captain, and those few officers assigned to the Rosedale beat that the elderly were being systematically harassed and victimized. By that time as well, some of the violent murders perpetrated had received widespread press coverage. Community pressures to nab those responsible escalated.

In August, the Rosedale sergeant approached the precinct captain and asked to start a special detail. The request was granted, and several extra units were assigned to the Rosedale beat. Eventually, all of the city's reserves were allocated to the area. At one point, over twenty people were given special assignments in the community, a number far exceeding the attention given to other areas in the city. The special units went door-to-door, gathering information on where the elderly lived. One officer noted, "We stopped anything that walked or drove through Rosedale."

The police attended community meetings. They met neighborhood leaders and merchants. The crackdown in Rosedale produced a short-term reevaluation of police-community relations. One officer confessed: "They just didn't think we cared, you know. It really tore me up. I wish we had done something sooner, but there's just no way we could watch every house. There's just too many of them."

But by the beginning of summer 1983, the police were ready to close the curtain on the gothic tale of horror that had overwhelmed Rosedale. The special units were reassigned to other areas of the city. Crime in the area was no longer a big news item. Community pressure relaxed. Prosecuting attorneys prepared their case against the adolescent wilders of Rosedale.

As the summer months of 1983 passed by, many of the elderly expressed hope that "things will get better and go back to the way Rosedale used to be." During fall 1983, however, their fantasies were exploded by reports that some of the adolescent murderers might be set free on legal technicalities and plea bargains. One of the adolescents, Johnny Lee Brown, was sentenced to life in prison. He was fingered by the other four as the "leader" and the "real killer."

Brown, a tough street kid, apparently delivered the actual blows, stabs, and slashes leading to the deaths of Mrs. Marlow, Clyde Robinson, and Ralph Johnson. Billy Hardin, at twenty-one the eldest of the gang members, received a twenty-five-year sentence in a plea bargain negotiated between prosecutors and defense attorneys. Like Hardin, Lawrence and Earl Coleman also pleaded guilty to the lesser charge of burglary. Lawrence, at seventeen the elder of the two brothers, was sentenced to serve a thirty-five-year prison term. His younger brother, fifteen at the time of the killings, was given a consecutive thirty-five-year sentence in return for a plea of aggravated burglary.

The last Rosedale defendant, Charles Raymond Roosevelt, pleaded guilty to robbery and received only a five-year term. Apparently Roosevelt was present when Clyde Robinson was beaten to death in front of the car wash, but he was not involved in any of the other attacks. Whereas Roosevelt did not participate in the actual murder, he did receive and spend some of the money stolen from the victim. Testimony also established that he was a peripheral member of the "gang."

Another peripheral member of the gang was released due to insufficient evidence. Unlike other defendants, he confessed to no crimes and therefore avoided prosecution. Several weeks earlier, attorneys representing the Coleman brothers had argued that crucial evidence against them should not be admitted into the courtroom. Detectives had initially questioned the teenagers in the fourth-floor homicide division room rather than in the fifth-floor juvenile division, as stipulated in the Texas Family Code. After dismissing the argument, the judge evaluating the technicality told reporters: "It just gets down to questions of are we going to throw out a confession because they went to the wrong room. I'm not going to do it. A statement is a statement, and he voluntarily gave it."

Determined to bring the Rosedale defendants to trial and in recognition of rigid community sentiment about the cases, Judge Benson assumed a tough posture: "These cases have been dragging too long. We're not going to quit until we've tried everything." Despite the judge's no-nonsense approach to the Rosedale defendants, the elderly and their families were still not satisfied with the results of the trial.

While handing down the consecutive thirty-five-year prison term for Earl Coleman, Judge Benson said to the defendant: "You're awfully young for 35 years, but you made your own doings. It was your problem; you're a grown man under the law." In the wake of the press coverage surrounding the trial, residents of Rosedale were told repeatedly that young Coleman would be eligible for parole in less than eleven years. Residents were also reminded by the local media that attorneys for the Coleman brothers planned to appeal the verdict on the grounds that statements from the juveniles were taken in an improper setting.

Despite the judge's tough ruling on the matter, the defense attorneys planned to push their case to a higher level. One level of appeal upheld the initial verdict, and a second appeal was in the process of being implemented. Angry and discouraged, many residents of Rosedale felt cheated by the "fancy shenanigans" in the criminal justice system. One elderly man said: "They are getting off pretty light. They should have been given life because they will be out in little or no time and they won't be worth a thing when they get out."

Many of Rosedale's elderly were outraged by the plea bargains and felt that since "they took a life," the young murderers should at least be sentenced to life in prison. Prosecutors, however, thought the bargains were fair because evidence and testimony clearly established that Johnny Lee Brown was the one responsible for the actual deaths: "It appears from everything we've been able to determine that Johnny Lee Brown is the real killer."

Hardin and the younger Coleman brother were initially charged with the murder of Ralph Johnson and the beating of his wife. They testified, however, that they had waited outside and did not enter the premises until after the murder had already been committed. Upon entering the Johnson household, according to their statements, they found Mr. Johnson propped against the wall, bleeding to death and unconscious. Similar arguments and statements eventually led to a plea bargain for the older Coleman brother.

One of the dead man's daughters was present at the trials and watched the plea bargains unfold. She later told the press that the punishments were insufficient. She questioned the prosecuting attorneys and asked them why they let the Rosedale murderers off so easily. The attorneys responded that they had done their best, and the verdict was reasonable under the circumstances. The victim's daughter, however, was not compelled by the logic of their response: "I really would hate to see any of them turned out on the streets on parole to do the same thing over again."

She explained that her mother was now bound to a wheelchair as a result of the beatings and had lost her sight and hearing. The elderly victim was not satisfied with the plea bargains either. Her daughter explained that her mother moved into deep depression and trauma when discussion of the trial and plea bargains emerged: "It upsets her because it brings back all those bad memories."

One of Mr. Robinson's sons, also angered by the plea bargains, bitterly accepted the verdicts: "Since they say that Brown was the one who actually killed my father and he got life, I guess we can't expect more." The elderly community of Rosedale, philosophical in their waning years, resolved to accept the peculiar machinations of the criminal justice system.

As the curtain closed on the wilding attacks of 1982, however, it was obvious to everyone that the social conditions producing the violence had not been addressed or mediated by the criminal justice system. The root causes of hatred and violence in the community remained untouched by the crime-prevention efforts of the police. The high levels of psychological and economic deprivation compelling black teenagers to murder and rape remained embedded within the institutional structure of neighborhood life. The grinding and degrading residue of racism and poverty, like the white elderly themselves, were left behind in Rosedale.

Criminologists maintain the breakdown between socially approved goals and the means to obtain them push lower-class youths to create delinquent subcultures.[1] The alternative values found within these subcultures reinforce delinquent modes of obtaining status, material rewards, and the resources necessary to maintain a criminal lifestyle. Delinquents must choose among many behaviors, only a few of which actually violate established rules.[2] As a result, delinquents often drift between criminal and conformity behavior and are seldom totally committed to a life of crime. Their lives are often characterized by deliberate movement between the deviant and the straight world.

The economic dilemmas facing Rosedale's youth and their drift in and out of crime are best illustrated by case study profiles of the six teenagers convicted of robbery and murder in 1983. Members of a loose-knit gang, they systematically terrorized elderly households in the neighborhood. Case histories reveal the relationship between societal forces and individual biographies. Each of the case histories presented illustrates the social factors that nurtured and sustained criminal behavior among the adolescents of Rosedale. Although the case histories are limited to those apprehended and convicted of criminal behavior, they probably represent the consistent patterns in the lives of many other black youngsters caught up in the hopeless maze of drugs and street crime.

Billy Hardin was twenty years old when he turned himself in for the murder of Clyde Robinson. He had lived in Rosedale for four years, having resided in other parts of the city before moving there. He was employed part-time at the time of his arrest, making about $4 an hour. His longest tenure in a job situation spanned only two months. He had one child, nearly three years old at the time of his arrest; she lived with her mother in Kansas. He had never married and paid no child support to the mother of the child.

He had a prior arrest record for burglary and a history of drug use and heavy drinking. He was described to me by a paralegal assistant assigned to the case as a prototypical "loser," as someone who was just "nowhere." Billy was "just lost; there's no way to get through to him." There were six siblings in his immediate family, three older brothers and two sisters. Both of his parents were absent from his household, having left during his early years. He lived with his sister at the time of his arrest. She was the head of his immediate family unit. His sister and her husband worked and were seldom present in the home. He had never met his father and knew him by name only. Some of his brothers and sisters had been fathered by different men.

Hardin dropped out of school in the seventh grade and worked at various short-term jobs. He pumped gas, washed dishes, peeled vegetables, and worked briefly in a battery shop. He had a marginal attachment to the economy for four years prior to his arrest and "earned" money primarily through short-term work, petty theft, and burglary. He did not appear highly intelligent, an opinion sustained by psychological profiles, and appeared to have great difficulty understanding even the most elementary concepts used by his attorney.

He boasted of having a strong attraction to white and Oriental women. He told me that he liked "white" and Oriental "pussy" and that he didn't "much like being around my own color." Court psychologists described him as a moderately "dysfunctional personality" but capable of standing trial for his crimes.

Before moving in with his sister, he lived with an older brother. His brother tried to serve as the head of the household since both parents were absent from the home. Hardin started to lose interest in school in the fifth grade: "The first time I missed school was about the fifth or sixth grade. Me and this girl just went off [to have sex] and I just got used to it. I just started doing it all the time. Then I started getting expelled. I used to get two whippings a day from my oldest brother for missing school. In the seventh grade I missed and I knew I was gonna get a whipping. I ran away then and left for about three years. I went to live with my sister."

Billy said that he "just skipped school and growed up." He was raised on the streets with little or no guidance from established social institutions. His older brother tried unsuccessfully to discipline him. Caught up in his own struggle to make a living and support a family, the brother failed in his attempt to be a surrogate parent. His sister tried to provide support and a place to stay; she too, however, had her own burdens to shoulder.

Hardin appeared totally alienated from religious institutions in the black community. He had attended church occasionally but was unimpressed by what he encountered. He had last participated in a church service four years prior to his arrest: "I always believed in God. I used to go to church off and on with my girlfriend. She really talked to me. Preachers don't have much to say to kids. Every time I got to church I see lots of kids get put out of church. They be playing and running around and yelling." Religion appeared irrelevant to his life, and it was apparent that he invested little or no mental energy in evaluating his behavior according to traditional codes of morality.

Most of the money he received from stolen goods was spent on drugs and alcohol. Goods were pawned at local shops: "You can sell it in a pawnshop. They usually have an older person that deals in stuff. They also give you grass for stuff. They sell dope, marijuana, all over school. The teachers, they be knowing about it, but they don't do nothing." Items that are easily pawned include televisions, stereos, guns, radios, and jewelry.

He was also involved in car theft. The actual theft of a car garnered only $20; he knew, however, that the adults got paid "a grand" for a car. Most of the kids who stole cars spent the money on drugs. Explaining the nature of street life in Rosedale, he said, "The kids I know, they'd rob me if they had a chance; if they know that I got something."

Hardin gave no explanations about why he participated in theft and ultimately murder. He had a limited vocabulary to describe his actions. He seemed to have no comprehension of the institutional forces that compelled him to drift in and out of crime. He simply stated that he took what he wanted and that the killing of the people "just happened."

Lawrence and Earl Coleman were raised in a similar family situation. Their father was not present in the home, and the mother of the two boys tried her best to raise a family of six children by working as a domestic and a short-order cook and by finding any other type of employment she could secure. The Coleman brothers were involved in church activities as preteens and achieved a reputation as potentially good athletes in grade school.

Despite a more stable socioeconomic environment within the family than Billy Hardin's, the Coleman brothers were exposed to violence within the household. They were known by neighbors and peers as tough "wise guys." A next-door neighbor remarked: "They were some of the most roguish fellows around. You can't tell them nothing. They thought they owned this world. When you see them one at a time, they were nice as you would want them to be. But when you got two or three of them together, there is no telling what they would do."

The next-door neighbor had gone to the Coleman brothers' home to complain about bottles and rocks being thrown at his house. The two Coleman brothers, with the assistance of four other teenagers, responded by beating the neighbor and his brother with sticks and rocks; they suffered head cuts and multiple bruises. The mother of the Coleman brothers did not intervene in the confrontation.

Ralph Coleman, the older brother of Earl and Lawrence, had plea-bargained on a murder charge in connection with the 1979 death of a Carswell Air Force Base serviceman. Then age fifteen, the older brother pleaded guilty to robbery with bodily injury. He served time in the state penitentiary from November 1979 until he was paroled three years later. Members of the Coleman family had a sustained history of being out of work, out of school, and in trouble. Their reputation in the community as violent, aggressive kids was widespread.

Several students from Rosedale High School said they feared the Coleman brothers and did not want "to cross them" in any way. A twelve-year-old boy who lived near the Coleman household said the Coleman kids terrorized the neighborhood with unprovoked attacks. On many occasions, he said, the Coleman brothers had tried to beat him and other kids on the street. Neighbors maintained that during the day, the Coleman brothers and other teenagers would drink beer in the alley between their house and other residences.

During the day, the boys would burglarize houses and try to sell stolen radios, televisions, and stereos. Neighbors reported to the police that the Coleman brothers had offered to sell them guns, jewelry, small appliances, and other items. They assumed the items were stolen because neither of the two brothers was employed. Both Earl and Lawrence Coleman had a history of periodic trips to juvenile detention centers.

Their school attendance was uneven to nonexistent. Earl was known as a very aggressive and "dirty" player by the coach of a grade school soccer team. The vice principal of Rosedale Middle School commented to me about the Coleman brothers: "I've never been able to get them to attend school. They may have been on the rolls, but they did not attend school. I can't say nothing good about them." The younger Coleman brother enrolled in Rosedale High School in September 1982 and withdrew in October. Lawrence, at the time of his arrest, was not enrolled in school at all. Before dropping out of school, both were chronically absent or tardy.

The two Coleman brothers, in association with two to four other teenagers, systematically prowled the streets of Rosedale. Their criminal activities were always perpetrated in a group; seldom was the act of theft carried out alone. Lawrence Coleman told me: "It was mostly just when we'd get together. Sometimes we'd plan it out. We'd check a house out to see if no car was there. Sometimes, you know, you can go up to the door and see if the screen is hooked and stuff. See if there are lights on and stuff like that."

In addition to petty theft and household robbery, the Coleman brothers also sold fake drugs: "There are a whole bunch of ways to get money. Like, one guy, you know, he make some of that fake, ah, hash, you know. Cook it up and sell it. Five dollars a block. Some people sell fake pills and stuff. They make money that way."

Charles Raymond Roosevelt was the most articulate member of the theft ring. Because of his marginal association with the Coleman brothers and other members of the gang that terrorized Rosedale, he was able to plea-bargain a five-year sentence. His socioeconomic and family profile, however, was consistent with that of his partners in crime.

Eighteen at the time of his arrest, he had lived in Rosedale for less than four years. Including himself and his mother, there were nine members in his immediate family, consisting of two brothers and five sisters. According to him, "Three of us got the same daddy; three more of us got a different daddy." Both his biological father and stepfather lived in Dallas, about forty miles away. They saw him infrequently.

His mother, the head of the household, worked as a maid and household worker in the white suburbs. She took the bus to her various places of work. Charles dropped out of school in the eleventh grade, a pattern similar to that of other members of his family. After dropping out of school, he spent most of his time on the streets of Rosedale: "Rosedale is like a club, you know, nothing but a disco club. You go there to get drunk, to look for girls. You know, to mess with the girls, to look for a date, to carry on, you know. Just a day's vacation. That's all it is."

Rosedale was considered a good place to "get high," to look for "pussy," to spend the day on the streets: "They got a certain person, you know, like someone who is running a drug house. You know, he goes to school and puts it out from there." Because drugs were costly, theft and the sale of stolen merchandise were the only ways to stay high: "There's different ways, you know, like most people get a car and get them a couple of batteries. You know, go sell it to a filling station or something. Steal some tools. Most people I know be smoking grass here and there. But if they want some stiffer drugs, like some cocaine or heroin, they go try to hold up something."

The drug traffic in Rosedale, according to Roosevelt, was extensive. One major source was a place called the Texas Nigger, a club located about two miles from the center of Rosedale. The locations of the "drug houses" were well known to the youth of Rosedale: "It's just a little old area, you know, where they have houses selling weed and stuff."

Roosevelt's drift in and out of crime was directly related to his marginal attachment to the local labor market. He had never held a full-time job. His employment history resembled that described by Elliot Liebow in *Tally's Corner*:[3] "You know, they got these little old centers, recreation centers, that they be hiring for little old part-time jobs out of school, summer jobs. They got grocery stores that hire people. If a person really wants a job, he can get it. There ain't no doubt about it. I was working at this Paris Coffee

Shop. I was working downtown at the Hilton Inn. Then I was working at Terry's Grill, downtown. I had a little old job on weekends, helping this dude set up fruits and stuff." He got most of these jobs by simply being on the street at the right time or by inquiring directly. Most of the jobs, however, were part-time or short term. Because work was uneven and unreliable, crime became much more lucrative than the "straight" labor market.

Roosevelt provided a fairly detailed description of how kids obtained money through theft, burglary, and street confrontation: "I guess they kind of have fun; it's easy money, you know, without getting a job. Most likely, they'll find somebody to deal with, you know, like a drug house. Trade this off for some weed or some money or something. You know, like a diamond ring, trade it for $15 or $20. He can probably make $200 in two or three hours. It depends on what he gets. You know, how he gets it and what he do with it."

The money earned from theft was spent on things that gave the thief pleasure and promoted a "cool" and comfortable lifestyle: "The average person, you know, he be liable to go buy him a pair of pants, shirts, some shoes. Go out to a little old dance. Just enjoy it, you know. Really, you know, just enjoy it."

Roosevelt, more so than any of the other subjects interviewed, seemed to understand clearly the forces that pulled him into crime. Not only did he seem to understand them, he was also able to articulate the sociological factors that generated and sustained criminal behavior in the neighborhood. Explaining that he tried to avoid groups of young people because trouble would soon follow, he said he preferred to be alone. "A crowd draws attention, so I just lay my way out of it really."

Many acts of theft and violence flowed from the challenges and dares issued in a group situation:

> It starts out just drinking and messing around. He's liable to do something. Go break in a store or something. His partner see that he stole something. I ought to go rob something to make myself look good, you know; all of them try to race to be the leader. It just keeps going and going just like a chain. I guess they figure out who's the toughest. It don't never stop, you know.
>
> Kids don't get in trouble by theyselves. It mostly happens in a crowd. Like one being encouraged by the other. Just to be top, like, you know, "You're a punk if you don't do that." Just little old names that they use to encourage it.

According to Roosevelt, the primary difference between kids who were in trouble and those who were not was the simple absence of money. Explaining the intersection between poverty and strain within the black family, he shared his own thinking about why certain kids were always involved in crime: "The average black dude, he wants to be standing out there, just pitchin' hisself. Mostly all black dudes I know want that."

But the kids who didn't get into trouble were the ones with

money. They have better clothes. It's a family matter. You know, like they ain't got no brothers and sisters, so they can ask for telephones and clothes and stuff. For them, it [the money] just goes further, you know; it's just two people when they ask for clothes. There may be five or six brothers and sisters in another family, and there be two in this other family, and they got to take it from the others. Two parents, you know, for two kids, but one parent trying to supply for five needs [makes things difficult].

Perceiving the advantages accruing to a small family with two working parents, he explained:

The father, he lets them drive and takes them places, and give them money. If a lady is trying to supply for five boys, she's having a hard time. It's just that she can't. The other kids complain if one gets something better. Two parents, they both be working and he's got a good job. The kid [in the bad situation], the dude just starts running with the crowd. He starts helping the mother, trying to take pressure off her. They get out there and try to make a fast dollar. You know, when kids ask mother for something, she can't give it to them because there's too many kids.

But many kids think that theft will help the family. Within some situations, theft is interpreted as the child's contribution to family welfare:

The average kid sees his mother struggling and [trying to] provide needs for him. He kind of thinks he's helping if he just leaves and goes about his business, stealing and stuff. He thinks he's helping but he ain't doing nothing but hurting 'cause she's got to worry about him, about him stealing to take pressure from her. The brother does it, and his brother is liable to see him, and he goes out to do the same thing. In the other house, you know, they got three bedrooms, just living the average life. The other kids have two or three in one room and he get tired and says, "I'm going out on my own." And he starts selling drugs, you know.

When asked to explain why kids in Rosedale stole from the old whites, he candidly observed that racial and class differences played a part in the street crimes with which he was so familiar:

The blacks figure, you know, that the world owes them something. They just take what they want. You know, the whites, they have a history and a background. They have their banks, and their doctors and lawyers and stuff, you know. Blacks come over to Rosedale and figure if they [the whites] done that, I'll just break into their house, and try to rule and take over. They figure that the whites that are there [in Rosedale] have something better that they want. But they don't know that the people who stayed in Rosedale are all older. They be of the same class. There ain't no color out there. They [the teenagers] didn't know that, but there ain't no color in Rosedale. Just everybody struggling, trying to do good. But most black people think that white people got more in their house. They try to see what they can take. But they ain't realizing that they be struggling just like they be doing.

Violence dominated the family and neighborhood environment of Johnny Lee Brown, considered by most to be the leader of the gang. He and his two brothers had a history of violent and aggressive confrontation with neighbors, peers, and teachers. His mother had had numerous confrontations with the police, school officials, and various other representatives of established institutions. She had a reputation of reaching quick conclusions about the racial motives of white school officials, police officers, juvenile caseworkers, and social welfare administrators. Police officers dispatched to investigate frequent complaints of neighborhood violence had been called "honky," "racist," and "white mother fuckers" by Johnny's mother or accused of treating her children poorly because they were "black."

She didn't hesitate to call whites "prejudiced" or "white bigot." It was apparent from police reports and interviews with social workers and neighbors that the mother of Johnny Lee harbored intensely negative feelings toward whites. It also appeared that her high levels of racial animosity encouraged and nurtured intensely negative and hostile feelings toward whites among her children. Sustained exposure to poverty and to their mother's attitudes toward whites, especially those in positions of authority or those who exercised some institutional influence over their lives, probably legitimated hostile feelings in the minds of her children toward the white world.

At the time of his arrest, Johnny Lee Brown was sixteen years old. His socioeconomic profile and family background were similar to those of the others involved in the summer murders of 1982. There were seven members of his family, including his mother. His father was absent from the home. He had two brothers and three sisters, his older siblings being the product of an earlier union. He seldom had contact with and had not established any lasting relationship with either his biological father or the man who fathered his stepsiblings.

His mother worked for a while at a Volkswagen supply plant but got laid off. She was employed as a clerk at Burger King at the time of his arrest. Her employment record reflects that she did her best to earn a living through whatever opportunities might be available.

Johnny Lee had never held a steady job and seldom worked part-time. He had attended a neighborhood school before moving to Rosedale. He grew up in another part of the city and moved to Rosedale during his sixth year of school. During the first two years of high school, he was bused to another part of the city. He seldom attended classes in high school and was constantly in trouble with teachers and administrators.

He stated that confrontations between teachers and students were a form of sport:

> When we get together before we come to school, we get full of that drink and smoking them weeds. When we get to school, we don't do nothing. They like to show off. They like to mellow people and mellow the teachers and things. Like say something smart to the teachers and everybody will laugh at that teacher. And they send you to the office. Kids are always beating teachers at Rosedale too. They get together and they outdo the other. I know that if I was at Rosedale, I'd get in trouble.

He was not involved in any school activities, although he briefly developed an interest in track during the seventh and eighth grades. He said he liked track and wanted to be a runner. He could beat people and it made him feel good to run fast and win. He wanted to be a car mechanic and have a family. He had a girlfriend at the time of his arrest. She was also sixteen. Johnny told me, "She's gonna' have a baby in June; I talk to her every time I get out of my cell."

Extensively involved in theft, burglary, and street crime, he developed an official record in juvenile detention centers and in formal police reports. He was known by social workers, teachers, and juvenile detention officers as an extremely violent and fearless kid. A police officer told me: "The kid will fight anything." During interview sessions in the county jail, I was warned by guards to be extremely careful. Both black and white guards said they could "see it in his eyes." They claimed to possess an ability to recognize certain traits associated with pathologically violent inmates.

He was confined to special facilities because of his violent history and was always given special treatment by juvenile caseworkers for fear that he might attack other adolescents. In the county jail, he was also isolated because other inmates often attacked or violently molested those accused of assaulting children and the elderly.

Despite a reputation for extreme violence, Johnny Lee was not an imposing or intimidating figure. He was only about five feet, five inches tall and had a small but muscular physique—somewhat inconsistent with his widespread reputation as a violent and pathological criminal. His face and arms, however, revealed clues about the anger lurking behind the improbable exterior. His face was chipped and knotted with small scars sustained from street fights. His knuckles, hands, and arms were etched with white and pink lines where the healing process could not conceal prior confrontations. Despite a diminutive stature, his face radiated anger. A scowl was permanently embossed on his forehead, and his nostrils flared when speaking.

His involvement in and knowledge about street crime in Rosedale were extensive. Like his associates, he said that car theft garnered only about $20 for each vehicle. To avoid "getting busted," he sold only the keys to stolen automobiles. The car key would be purchased and the buyer told where the stolen vehicle was located. Stolen televisions could be sold to a pawnshop for about $40 or to someone in the neighborhood for about the same price. Stereos, radios, guns, and rings were also easy to turn over in Rosedale. Drugs were easy to sell, but it was difficult to enter the substance market. Drugs were too expensive for most kids to buy in volume; consequently, it was not possible to make much money selling them. Individual "joints" could be purchased for $1 or $2, and "pills" cost about $4 or $5.

All of those arrested and convicted of the Rosedale summer murders viewed Johnny Lee as a tough kid. He was admired by other members of the gang, and most spoke reverently about his violent exploits and praised his reputation as someone "you don't mess with." When about thirteen years old, he bashed another kid's face with a brick and fists and threw him out of a second-story window in a neighbor's house:

> So, I pick up a brick, and he goes off in the house. And I say, "Hey man, tough man, get you out of that house." His friends say to me, "Get out of that house." And I say, "I'm going in there to get him." So, the dude that stayed there, he go around to the back of the house and I follow him. And my friends, they stay around front. I go to the back and go in. I see him running and I go upstairs and I catch him. I still have the brick in my hand and I beat him up with the brick [crushed the kid's face]. I'm beating him with my brick; then he ran and dived out the second-story window. He landed on the roof, right through the glass. So, they told him, "Don't mess with him if he's gonna mess with you like this." We don't have no trouble no more.

The police came and took pictures and interrogated those involved in the brick fight. Johnny Lee said that every time he passed the kid's house the boy's father would come out with a shotgun and say not to mess with his son.

Similar incidents were laced throughout his childhood and adolescent years, but the story of the second-story brick fight established the reputation of Johnny Lee in both police records and within the adolescent street culture of Rosedale. Other confrontations, however, were equally important in securing his family's reputation as aggressive and violent. A black woman who lived across the street from the Brown household said that she was forced to move after neighborhood violence, primarily initiated by Johnny and his brothers, became intolerable.

Another neighbor, a twenty-five-year-old white woman, Mrs. Sutton, lived two houses down from Johnny Lee. A working-class family that had moved to Rosedale in response to the drop in housing prices, the Suttons lived in the area for five months before leaving. Mrs. Sutton said that she carried a shotgun around the house for fear that she and her five-year-old son would be attacked when her husband was at work. She claimed that she and her husband worked in shifts to maintain a twenty-four-hour vigil over their lives and property. They kept written logs documenting the violence and rowdy activity initiated by Johnny Lee and eventually turned them over to police detectives in the hope of spurring arrests.

City police actually filed reports on two assaults during July and August 1982 in which Johnny Lee and his brothers were suspects. In a July 30 confrontation, Johnny Lee's mother called the police and reported that a man had fought with her boys and thrown a brick through her window. Official records reveal that about forty minutes after the call, police were dispatched to the Sutton home to discover that James Sutton and a friend, Michael Jeter, had been beaten by youths armed with sticks and pipes. Sutton told police that a band of teenagers had ringed his car and beat him and his friend with iron pipes and two-by-fours. A confrontation ensued between Johnny Lee's mother and the police as she verbally directed racial abuse at the police and victims. No arrests were made. Ironically, the police had ample prior contact with the leader of Rosedale's wilding gang.

About three weeks later, another incident occurred between the Suttons and Johnny Lee's mother. Mrs. Sutton was beaten by three teenagers who allegedly harassed her while she was playing with a puppy in her yard. Police records indicate that when she crossed the street to tell the boys to stop throwing rocks at her dog, she was attacked and beaten. One of the boys was charged with delinquent conduct in the attack. Johnny Lee and his stepbrother were listed as accomplices in the assault but not arrested and formally charged.

Albert George Lawson, given the street name Bug by gang members, was the sixth member of the gang to be prosecuted. His socioeconomic and family profiles were nearly identical to those of the other participants in the Rosedale murders. Additionally, his formal records displayed an extensive history of prior arrests and involvement in criminal activity.

In October 1980, he was referred to the Juvenile Department by the Fort Worth police department on the charge of burglary. He was placed on probation. A year later, he was again referred to juvenile detention on the charge of burglary of a coin-operated machine. Only one month later, in November 1981, he was apprehended and charged with aggravated robbery.

In June 1982, he was charged with theft of under $5. One month later, he was charged with burglary of a habitat. Like nearly all of his cohorts in the wilding gang, his activities were well known to the police before the infamous summer of 1982. His biological sister also displayed an extensive criminal record. She was referred to the Juvenile Department by city police on six different occasions between November 1981 and December 1982. The charges ranged from theft of under $5 to truancy to burglary to aggravated robbery.

Lawson's mother stated that she had not seen him for over a year prior to his arrest. He had simply left the household after dropping out of school. She had had no idea of his whereabouts during that time. She reported that she thought her son was "smarter" than her other children, but she also thought he was "off" or "mental." When asked to elaborate, she could not explain what she meant.

Before dropping out of school, Lawson was failing every subject. Records indicate that he enrolled in the local middle school in April 1982 and withdrew in September 1982. During that time his attendance was infrequent. He held various short-term jobs in the community, none lasting more than a few weeks.

His parents were engaged in a common-law marriage that produced two children. His father had six children by a prior marriage. He reported three years of formal education and was unemployed at the time of Lawson's arrest. Albert's mother had five children by a former marriage and had acquired eleven years of formal education. She was also unemployed at the time of her son's arrest.

Although Lawson aggressively denied his involvement in the Marlow murder, court psychologists reported that he appeared resigned to the possibility that he would be convicted. He allegedly instructed his attorneys to drop any possibility of appeal. One psychologist stated: "He expresses a sense of futility about the whole thing, since his parents are apparently very poor." Another reported: "His rather blasé manner about the whole affair is of considerable interest. If indeed he had nothing to do with it, he appears to have just given up and accepted the inevitable." His resignation proved appropriate as he was handed a sentence comparable to that received by the Coleman brothers in 1983.

The biographies of the wilding gang members and of the Rosedale and *Roots* rapists raise critically important questions about family breakdown among the urban underclass in American cities and the capabilities of those families to create and sustain viable urban communities. It is toward this issue that attention will now be focused.

8

THE UNDERCLASS OF ROSEDALE: COMMUNITY INSTITUTIONS IN CRISIS

Anyone near my age needs to take responsibility for why kids turn to the street. It's our fault, not the kids' fault. Tupak wasn't a crack addict, I was. . . . Tupak became what he was in spite of me.

—*Mother of slain rapper Tupak Shakur, 1997*

It costs more to lock up our youth than to lift them up. Prenatal care, Head Start, and day care on the front side lessen jail care and welfare on the back side.

—*Jesse Jackson, 1995*

ACCORDING TO THE 1990 CENSUS, the number of poor people living in American cities was higher in that year than in any other year since 1962.[1] Particularly high rates of poverty are found among urban children, especially those of African American descent. Approximately 25 percent of children under six years of age and 22 percent of those under eighteen are poor. Nearly 50 percent of African American children under eighteen years of age are now classified as poor. The changing economic conditions found within many cities have had a profound impact upon African American family life and culture, especially among women and children.

During the 1960s numerous social scientists examined the relationship between family structure and high rates of poverty among African Americans. William Wilson summarized this research in the following manner: "These writers emphasized that the rising rates of broken marriages, out-of-wedlock births, female-headed families, and welfare dependency among poor urban blacks were the products not only of race-specific experiences, but also of structural conditions in the larger society, including economic relations."[2]

During the 1980s, discussion and debate over the relationship between poverty and family structure among African Americans focused more on cycles of welfare dependency and the intergenerational nature of poverty brought about by this dependency. Charles Murray, in particular, blamed the liberal welfare state for creating monetary incentives that helped weaken already unstable family institutions among African Americans.[3] Irrespective of one's perspective on the relationship among the African American family, poverty, and the social welfare system, most policy analysts agree that the growing number of female-headed households within black communities has dire social and economic consequences for many African American youngsters. Wilson contends: "Female-headed families comprise a growing proportion of the poverty population. . . . These proportions [are] higher for metropolitan areas, particularly for central cities, where 60% of all poor families and 78% of all poor black families [are] headed by women. The proportion of poor black families headed by women increased steadily from 1959 to 1977, from less than 30 percent to 72 percent, and has remained slightly above 70% since then."[4]

Despite earlier controversy over the matter, Wilson argues that renewed scholarly interest in the 1960s perspective that the African American family is facing severe structural pressure is warranted. He finds little support for the theory that increasing rates of poverty among African Americans are related to cycles of welfare dependency or to the rising levels of family breakdown that is allegedly produced by that dependency. Rather, he contends, a more fruitful line of inquiry is to explore the connection between "the disintegration of poor families and black male prospects for stable employment."[5]

Consistent with national trends, rising levels of female-headed households and increasing proportions of children living in poverty characterized the racial transformation of Rosedale. As noted in Chapter 2, rates of poverty among women and children in Rosedale are several times higher than countywide averages and are among the highest in the city. The number of children living in poverty in Rosedale has steadily increased since 1960.

Over and above any other institution, the family, and its inability to control the behavior of Rosedale's youth, must be singled out for special attention. Because the racial transformation of Rosedale changed traditional patterns of community life, any sense of collective responsibility for childraising disappeared among those elderly residents who were left behind. Equally important, family institutions within the black community appeared to progressively weaken as Rosedale changed.

In a previous era, neighbors reinforced parental discipline on the streets of Rosedale. Social change in Rosedale altered not only the racial composition of the community but also the involvement of the white community in the administration of collective discipline. The disciplinary power of elderly whites, in particular, and the institutional practices to which they were committed were eradicated by the cultural and socioeconomic chasm created by racial change. For all practical purposes, the white elderly were rendered impotent agents of social control in the neighborhood. Their place as grandparents in the hierarchy of family discipline and in the maintenance of community standards was altered by white flight and by the associated shift in the age composition of neighborhood residents.

Their place as aged but respected members of the community vanished in the face of racial and cultural change. Although it is probably not reasonable to expect elderly whites to play a meaningful role in raising black children, it is important to stress that the racial transformation of Rosedale eradicated prior forms of social control that were essential to the maintenance of community standards. Much has been written about the impact of poverty on the structure of family life among urban blacks. Yet few accounts have elaborated on the relationship between family breakdown and the collapse of community institutions, which appear to accompany racial change. Urban poverty, racism, and employment discrimination have created disorganization and instability not only within the family but also in other important institutions within African American communities.

Since the infamous Moynihan report, debate over the black family has been constrained by what is considered "politically correct" in liberal intellectual circles.[6] Moynihan was strongly criticized for his contention that family breakdown was a major cause of poverty among African Americans and that family disorganization perpetuated economic marginality from one generation to the next.[7] Both black and white social scientists have appropriately argued that family life among urban blacks takes many institutional forms, the female-centered matriarchy being one of many sociological possibilities.[8] Many argue that a misplaced focus on the black family drew too much attention away from the more important issues of prejudice, discrimination, and the perpetuation of white racism.[9] Whatever one's ideological persuasion, there is little doubt that the combined impact of racial discrimination, unemployment, and poverty seriously affects the quality of family life among urban minorities and contributes to the creation of the type of delinquent youngsters who are profiled in the prior two chapters. As explained by Lasch, "those who argue that study of the black family diverts attention from poverty and racism fail to notice the ways in which poverty and racism reverberate in every area of life, embedding themselves in cultural patterns and personality, and thus perpetuating themselves from one generation to the next."[10]

Of special importance to the Rosedale case study is the fact that poverty and racial oppression combined to render the family an inadequate mechanism of social control in the neighborhood. Poverty and racism also combined to produce incompetent and ineffective parenting. Single black parents, like the police and the merchants, were unable to keep adolescents off the streets of Rosedale and out of trouble. An African American social worker with a high adolescent caseload from Rosedale described the typical household situation experienced by most of his clients.

According to him, the single-parent home was the biggest problem in the lives of his young clients. Most of the time, the single black parent in Rosedale was a woman. Many were gone throughout the day, and some were absent at night as well. Because of odd working hours, evening employment, or a desire to have some kind of social life at night, many women were just not present in the home. The father, in some cases, had never been present. "They're just never there. As a result, no one is home to make the kids go to school. The kid is basically, minimally, taken care of because either the mother is on welfare and she gets so little money that she can barely provide or because she makes so little money that she can't supply them with any of the things that they want."

The teenagers of Rosedale were really no different from young people everywhere, he explained:

> They want nice jeans and shirts. The shoes have to be Nike or Adidas. A trip to K-Mart or Target to purchase a $50 wardrobe is just not sufficient. They got to have a radio and it's got to be a big, ghetto box. Those things cost so much money. It's not just getting by. It's getting by with style. In a single-parent home, kids see these things advertised on television, and they know that they are out there someplace. They know that they don't have any and that their mama can't buy them any. And there's no one there to tell them not to get it if they want it. And before you know it, you got a mess on your hands.

Economic deprivation was clearly the single most important cause of the high rates of criminal behavior among the black adolescents of Rosedale. Urban poverty has also helped to erode traditional family patterns among the African American population not only in Rosedale but in other communities. Implicit in William Wilson's notion of an urban underclass is the idea that family life within the African American community has actually deteriorated over time. This idea can be illustrated in greater detail through examination of the experiences of Rosedale's elderly black population. The movement of blacks from the rural South to urban ghettos fragmented community and family institutions within black society. The migration of rural blacks to cities weakened established patterns of family life and altered the traditional division of labor in childraising. Of particular importance is the absence of an extended family network in the urban ghetto, especially grandmothers and grandfathers, aunts and uncles.

In the case of Rosedale, it was obvious that elderly whites were not able to serve as childraising surrogates in order to partially compensate for the absence of more complete family arrangements in the lives of young blacks. Although some elderly whites made token efforts to mentor minority children, racial antagonism prevented most from doing so. Yet in a racially harmonious community there is no reason that elderly whites and blacks and Hispanics could not contribute collectively to childraising in the neighborhood.

Unfortunately, the ghettoization of Rosedale rearranged established patterns of family life in both the black and white communities. Unable to rely on an extended family network for support in childraising or on transient neighbors, young African American mothers, like the white elderly, found their family lives fragmented and estranged from prior patterns and practices.

The job of raising children in the urban ghetto is often the sole responsibility of a single mother. Informal support networks are insufficient remedies for the absence of an extended family system.[11] Without adequate resources, access to relatives, or help from neighbors, the police, the clergy, or teachers, a single black parent is engaged in a lonely struggle to keep her kids off drugs or mute the siren sounds of street life. More tragically, current statistics indicate that rates of illegitimacy among young urban blacks are soaring. In many cities, rates have increased from 40 percent to over 70 percent.[12] This situation increases the structural strain upon an already unstable institution.

In the rural South, many black families relied heavily on the grandmother for childraising.[13] The grandmother or grandfather played a special role in the community, but especially in raising children. According to some accounts, black communities in the rural South were often characterized by the kind of stability and collectivism found in Rosedale before its ghettoization.[14] Despite the grinding poverty encountered by blacks in the rural South or in small towns, the existence of family support networks made childraising much more of a collective experience than in the city.

Explaining that many of his adolescent clients in Rosedale were raised "on the streets," a juvenile caseworker emphasized how the rural to urban migration had affected black families:

> We've [black people] always had the support of grandmothers. There's always been that extended family that was there who would help the mother. Most of the time, they lived in the country. Now, the people have moved to the city, and they've taken the job away from these grandmothers. The old people have more knowledge, more sense of what the family ought to be. The people in the city, they're trying to do it all on their own. In the meantime, you don't have that grandmother there, that extended family to pick up your slack. They're all

back down on the farm, and you're sitting here working and know that your kid is not going to school, not doing anything he should. And while he's not doing what he should, there's nobody there to tell him what to do.

The caseworker's experiences appear applicable to many of Rosedale's teenagers, especially those involved in criminal behavior. His observations illuminate the terrible predicament faced by single-parent families in the community. Having been raised in a small town in south Texas, he was continually stunned by the wide differences in child-rearing practices found in rural and urban black communities:

> When I did something wrong in my neighborhood, or anyplace in town, before night came my mother was going to know about it. "Ruby, your boy did this and I whipped him, and I just want you to know it." I, in turn, would get another whipping because she would have to whip me for what I did and because I embarrassed her for what I did out there.
> In other words, on the whole, in Rosedale, no one is responsible for the kids. These kids grow up on their own. If you manage to discipline them, you better do it before he starts talking because he learns to curse early. They learn to disrespect you early. It's a scary thing. I don't know where it's going; I really don't.

Social workers, attorneys, and counselors were all staggered by the careless attitudes of Rosedale's youth. I was stunned by the careless nature of the accounts given by those who murdered the elderly. After committing the murder of Ethel Marlowe, for example, the assailants engaged in a Pac-man video contest with the dollars taken from the dead woman. Without adequate social controls at home or within the neighborhood, they approached complete indifference toward violence and theft. On the streets of Rosedale, children saw violence on a daily basis. They saw people being hit with sticks and observed other children throwing rocks at each other or engaging in some form of violent confrontation.

A psychiatric social worker told me:

> I had a kid who lives in the projects. He told me about an old lady whose house caught on fire, and she was burned to a crisp. He saw that. It was a real traumatic thing. I saw in Rosedale just a few weeks ago a woman in a car and another on the sidewalk. At a red light, they started cursing one another, and one cursed a little too much. One jumped out of the car right there at the intersection and they had a fight with sticks and bottles. These kids see a lot of violent acts, and they must become hardened to them like people in war. Especially if you see your mom doing it or your dad, it must get to be a little bit normal.

Integrally related to increasing levels of family disorganization is the pervasive influence of poverty on incentives to commit crime. Economic deprivation compels adolescents to engage in crime. Once drawn to theft, family institutions are unable to prevent or control delinquent activities. Adolescents steal because they want things they can't afford. They steal in order to supplement the family income and help provide the simple necessities of family life.

In some cases, the breakdown of family institutions not only fails to control acts of theft among children but actually supports and encourages criminal behavior. A local attorney that I interviewed had defended indigent clients in Rosedale for several years. He had grown up in Rosedale during the time it was an all-white community. Over the previous few years, he had seen and defended numerous black adolescents from the neighborhood.

He observed that most of the crimes perpetrated by his clients were caused by a combination of drugs, alcohol, and simple economic deprivation. Among teenagers and younger kids, however, the problems were always economic in nature. At Christmastime it was not unusual for families to steal a tree, decorations, and presents for the entire family. The alternative was no Christmas at all: "If you can steal a package of baloney, that's one thing Mama won't have to buy. It works real good, you know. One kid steals some baloney; one steals a loaf of bread; one steals some cookies. They all come home that night and have supper together. It's fun. I don't think it's all malicious. A lot of it is fun, but most of it is just plain old economics."

According to social workers and attorneys, the profile of delinquent kids in Rosedale follows a consistent pattern. The family lives close to poverty conditions. Parents are employed in bad jobs within marginal industries. Parents tend to be either AFDC (Aid to Families with Dependent Children) recipients or are receiving some form of state assistance. The father is not educated and does not have the skills needed to secure a stable job. Neither the mother nor the father has the initiative or time to acquire skills to make them more competitive in the labor market. If they do get a reasonably good job, they try to hold on to it and do not seek advancement.

The kids have a tendency to be slower in school and quickly fall behind. They have poor attendance records. The kids have inadequate clothing and no spending money. They are not equipped for the job market but often drop out of school before graduation.

Most of the kids have tried various kinds of drugs and drink more than most other adolescents in their age group. They work odd jobs, mostly of short duration. If they do get steady part-time jobs in a place like McDonalds or Burger King, they have to travel to the suburbs, and most don't have bus fare. As a result, they lose the job or fall further behind in school. They are trapped. Crime is a rational response to the absence of economic opportunity.

The inability of elderly whites to influence the increasingly problematic behavior of Rosedale's adolescents has its counterpart in the black community. Elijah Anderson has described the intergenerational breakdown occurring within the black family.[15] Changing family institutions within the urban ghetto have reduced the stature and influence of elderly African Americans in child rearing. Anderson summarizes the nature of this change in the urban community he studied: "Older black residents remember better days when life was more orderly and civilized, when drugs and crime were almost unknown, when young people respected their elders, and when the men worked in good jobs and took care of their families. But now many of the older, decent people are gone."[16]

In the wake of unemployment, crime, and drug use, family life has been radically altered within contemporary black communities. According to Anderson, the sense of community within African American neighborhoods has been severely undermined within most American cities. Describing the magnitude of change affecting the area he studied, he contends: "The interpersonal trust and moral cohesion that once prevailed are undermined, and an atmosphere of distrust, alienation, and crime pervades the area, further disrupting its social organization."[17]

One of the most important institutions that has been undermined by these changes, according to Anderson, is the relationship between young men and elderly African American males. The "old heads" served as critically influential role models for young males growing up in the city. The "old head" was typically "a man of stable means who believed in hard work, family life, and the church."[18] He served as an interpreter of the larger society; his primary role was to teach young men about responsibility, work, and traditional family values.

The wisdom of the old heads is no longer valued by young people in contemporary African American communities. As opportunities for employment continue to erode and as the lure of drugs and illegal enterprise increases, the moral lessons of the elderly no longer appear relevant. The old heads have been replaced by new role models. The new role models are young street thugs who have money and style. The new role models are usually affiliated with gangs and appear to have achieved success in illegal enterprise.

The female old head also played an important role in the growth and development of African American youth in earlier times. Summarizing the importance of elderly females in the community, Anderson contends they were an instrumental source of social control and organization within black neighborhoods. These women had a definite and understood place in the community and operated through both kinship and friendship networks: "Like the male old head, her role is often played out in public places. Supportive of the family, she served as a third party to publicly augment the relationship between parent and child. Needing a good deal of wisdom, sensitivity, candor, and trust, she is an important source of instruction and social sanction within the community."[19]

Most important, the female old head often exercised discipline within the community and served as an important vehicle of social control. Her moral authority was widely acknowledged, and her right to mete out corporal punishment was seldom challenged. Like that of elderly males, the status of the female old head has dramatically changed in the contemporary black community.

During the course of my more recent fieldwork in the mid- to late 1980s, many elderly black residents of Rosedale were interviewed about the changes taking place in the community. During the 1980s, the racial composition of the Rosedale Senior Citizen's Center shifted in tandem with the changes occurring in the larger community. By the latter part of the 1980s, Ms. Rollins had retired as the director of the center and was replaced by an African American woman. Elderly blacks were by that time the most predominant group at the center.

During several visits I asked them numerous questions about life in Rosedale and how they felt about the increasingly serious problems posed by the young people of the community. On many issues, their attitudes and opinions were no different from those of their white counterparts interviewed ten years earlier. Their observations emphasized the importance of Anderson's contentions that the historical role of the old heads had significantly changed in African American urban neighborhoods.

They too were concerned about the negative changes occurring in the community and were extremely apprehensive about the careless and dangerous behavior exhibited by young people. They were consistently critical of the parenting skills of young mothers and believed that community standards had sadly deteriorated over the years. They frequently commented that family values had eroded and spoke with sadness and irritation about the way in which children were being raised in the neighborhood.

Most agreed that the people of Rosedale had little or no sense of community and that the neighborhood was filled with transients. They knew very few people in the community and seldom had kind words to say about their neighbors. One elderly woman explained to me: "Well, when I first moved here practically everybody owned their homes, and now there's a lot of people moving, you know, just moving to and from."

Not part of any larger family network or informal circle of friends, this woman was marginal to the small array of community institutions that still operated in Rosedale: "I don't have any family here. I don't get out very much, only when I go to church. I don't go out at night at all."

Another elderly black female explained that she knew very few people in Rosedale: "No, I don't know anyone here. I knew one family that moved out of my neighborhood. But I wasn't here very long when they moved out. People just don't associate much with other people. They generally don't get out and mingle among each other." An elderly gentleman agreed with her characterization of neighborhood life in Rosedale: "No, I told you, I don't know the people around here. There might be some that I know. Mostly, I see strangers. But I don't know if they are the people that live here because I don't know these people."

Rosedale was characterized as a transient community of strangers by nearly all of the black elderly with whom I talked. "There have been about five or six families that have stayed here since we've been here. About four stayed here, three stayed there; they don't stay long enough for you to get acquainted with. Never did know their name. They just moved in and moved out," explained an elderly couple.

In summer 1988, I had lunch at the Rosedale Senior Citizen's Center. Several elderly African American women explained to me how difficult it was to get acquainted with their neighbors in Rosedale. "Everybody's moving in and out all the time. It's hard to have any sense of community and know who's living next to you. You can't have a sense of community. It's so dangerous at night; you don't go out at night," explained one woman. Her friends agreed with her observations.

An elderly African American couple explained to me in their home: "That house up there [pointing out the kitchen window], it has been empty; we've got a house right there [pointing in the other direction] that's been empty for a long time. They just stay in there long enough to tear it up and move." When asked about a group of black adolescents who had just passed by the front of his house, the elderly man commented: "Oh, I don't know. I don't know where that bunch comes from. They were out there the other night, and, oh man, you talk about talk. It was getting so I never heard such talk. I was gonna call the police."

He continued: "In this area, there isn't a teenage boy that I know of. But where do they come from? I see them walk up and down this street and I don't understand. We got some of them that walks up and down here with that music and all them things. I think they just take the money that they're supposed to eat dinner with and buy them some dope." The man was not alone in his contempt for the behavior and morality of Rosedale's young people.

Nearly all of the elderly African American residents of Rosedale with whom I talked offered ample commentary about the child-rearing practices of young parents in the neighborhood. All of them spoke with great conviction; many also expressed anger and irritation: "You know, I think broken homes is a whole lot the problem of that. You know, separate and divorce and all that where the child is mixed up. He want to be with his mother and he want to be with his father. He just don't know which way to go. So, therefore, he usually goes the wrong way 'cause he need the counseling of the mother and the father too."

According to the elderly, discipline had broken down in the homes and on the streets of Rosedale. The children of the community showed little respect for others. But many of the elderly thought that the parents of the children were as disrespectful. One woman explained: "When I was coming up, they'd call up and say, 'Look, Ethel, your kid was being a real ass three blocks over and when he gets home I wants you to take care of him.' In my time, they'd take care of him any way they wants. But you can't do that now. Why, if I told someone's kid what to do out there, you be likely to get a brick upside your head."

Another woman said that although she would have liked to help discipline the children of Rosedale, it was simply dangerous to do so: "I've tried so hard with the neighbors. Some of them, when I've been around them, I've tried, you know. But you can't. They'll come over and say things to you about their kid and the kid is standing right there listening. So, you don't do anything. You can't do anything. I know I be afraid. That kid will hurt you. The parents will too. They will say you can't talk to my kid that way."

Explaining her own orientation toward the preservation of community standards, she stated:

> When we was coming up, my mother, now we had neighbors, so if we do anything that the other neighbors didn't like or if they see us do anything, they would tell her and some would give us a whippin' right there. And when we got home we would get another whippin'. But see, you can't do it now. Mmmm, yeah. That's the way it was and it's so different than raisin' them today. That's how my mama raised us and the way we raised our kids, black kids. You watch 'em grow up. One of my daughters said, "Mama, you hit my kid." My daughter said, "Mama, you hit her too hard," talking about her grandbaby. And I said, "I whooped you, and you still here." That's what I told her, and she couldn't say anything else.

Many of the elderly were convinced that young black parents, especially juvenile mothers, were just too lenient with their children and that community and neighborhood standards had suffered as a result. Immature, inexperienced, and without the support of family and community institutions, young parents were not competently raising their children: "No matter where they are, they have to be disciplined. I know the children from around here; I say that they don't discipline them or nothing. I don't see why he shouldn't be at home maybe at nine or ten, but he's out. And a lot of times he's out, well, the mother and the father is out too. Children don't know where the mother is and the mother don't know where the children is."

Another woman commented: "Well, I think they have too much time on their hands. Nobody to discipline because the parents ain't there and they are on their own. And then a lot of times there are kids who cannot bring their problems home. The parents won't listen to them and when they go wrong, then the parents blame the children when they are at fault too. I heard a lot of kids say, 'I can't talk to my parents,' and they go out and talk to others and get in more trouble."

Explaining how she was raised, the elderly lady stated with conviction:

Put a list on the wall and each time that they did that particular chore they'd check it off. And you know they'd want an allowance. Let them earn it. That'll teach them in later years that they have to work for what they get. My kids were raised military. We went from one place to another and they learned a lot that way. But you have to check it off. Say he had a dollar a week, he had ten things he had to do. And if he missed one, a dime was cut off. It learned him responsibility.

Others agreed that important moral lessons were not being learned in the home and that parents were failing to do their jobs in the household:

Well, see, most of them, they don't have any homework to do. No, they have no cleaning, no yard cleaning or anything. Children don't have nothing to do now. When we was raised up we would have prayer at night instead of being in the streets. We would come in and have prayer with our kids. Counseling for the children, you know, when they're growing up. Sit down and talk to them. I counseled my children. I counseled my grandchildren before I would get the switch. But I would still get the switch if they needed it. But now, they don't have the parents at home like they used to. Most parents have to work to keep the home fires going, just to make it. And when a child comes home and the mother or father is not there, that's hard on them.

One elderly man summarized the sentiments of nearly all of the old heads with whom we spoke:

Kids shouldn't have to make the kinds of decisions that these kids make. That's just overwhelming. Kids need someone to tell them no. No, you have to go to bed at eight. No, you be at school this time. No to certain things, and someone should be there to enforce that no. Kids have to have it. When they jump the gun, that's when they get confused. When nobody tells them no, they go ahead and do this stuff. You have these unwanted pregnancies. You have kids ruining people's homes. You have all this. Kids don't know how to structure their time. They don't think about consequences. They don't know things. They have to be told. They have to be taught the principles behind things.

Irrespective of their causes, it is clear that the problems of African American youth in cities have reached crisis proportions. According to the Black Community Crusade for Children, African American youth face a greater likelihood of encountering violence than at any other time in recent history: (1) every ten minutes a black child is arrested for a violent crime; (2) every four hours a black child is murdered; (3) every four hours a young black person (20–24) is murdered; (4) more black children are poorer today than in 1948, and more are likely to live in extreme poverty than at any other time since these types of statistics have been collected; (5) black children face a greater infant mortality rate in comparison to whites than in any other year since 1940; and (6) blacks are generally less safe than at any other time since slavery.[20]

It would not be accurate, however, to single out the family as the only institution in Rosedale incapable of influencing the behavior of Rosedale's adolescents. Other institutions also failed as mechanisms of social control. Criminologists contend that when the institutions and groups to which people belong become drastically disorganized, they exert less and less influence over individual behavior.[21] In a situation where traditional institutional arrangements are in a state of chaos and chronic breakdown and economic deprivation is present, individuals typically recognize no established rules of conduct other than those rooted in basal self-interest. Émile Durkheim calls such a situation anomic, or normless.[22]

Traditional rules of behavior are ambiguous or nonexistent under conditions of anomie. Some criminologists contend that juvenile delinquency occurs when traditional mechanisms of social control are either weakened or break down altogether. Drawing from his analysis of urban delinquents, Travis Hirschi observed that criminal behavior becomes more probable when the individual's bond to society weakens. He posits that an individual's relationship to a social group is at its lowest point when that person ceases (1) to care about the opinions and evaluations of the larger collectivity, (2) to invest time and emotional energy in conventional behavior, (3) to become involved in established institutions and practices, and (4) to believe in the legitimacy of community traditions.[23] Similar arguments have been developed by those studying gang violence in American cities. Lewis Yablonsky observed that children, more so than adults, often experience intense forms of conflict over appropriate forms of behavior in rapidly changing situations: "Conflicts may arise between the different norms supported by parents, the school, and those operative in the neighborhood."[24]

During Rosedale's decade of rapid social change, 1975 to 1985, its traditional institutions were demolished. During the chaos accompanying racial transition, the traditional sources of social energy driving established institutions were removed from the community. White flight removed from Rosedale those elements with a stake, a vested interest, in traditional neighborhood institutions: young couples, families with children ready to start school, families with children enrolled in middle and high school, middle-aged couples with the potential to serve as community leaders. All these elements gave the community of Rosedale its civic energy. They sustained neighborhood businesses, staffed the PTA, coached the Little League teams, and served as den mothers for scouting organizations. But they simply abandoned Rosedale. The elderly who were left behind, drained of energy and resources, were just not capable of stabilizing neighborhood life and culture. In the face of such dramatic migration, it is surely not reasonable to expect newly arriving black residents to provide continuity to white social and cultural institutions.

In other American cities, newly arriving Jewish immigrants did not promulgate Irish Catholic neighborhood institutions when the control of urban space changed from one group to another. New urban immigrants will create and sustain institutions consistent with their historical and cultural traditions. At the same time, it is not realistic to assume that stable African American community institutions can be created rapidly enough to replace those in the process of decline and decay. The ghettoization of Rosedale occurred too quickly to be mediated by any federal scheme to promote urban redevelopment or rebuild community institutions. Levels of socioeconomic status dropped too fast to convince merchants to stay in the area or to compel financial establishments to continue the extension of credit to residents. Churches were abandoned too soon to ask ministers to consider building an integrated congregation. The black middle class passed through Rosedale too hastily to make any lasting contributions to sustain or modify existing institutions or build new ones. The geographic base of the area's black population expanded too swiftly for any permanent sense of community to take root. In the wake of those profound changes, traditional forms of social control simply lost their ability to shape the behavior of Rosedale's youth.

That the youth of the community were out of control was common knowledge among the adolescent population. The youth with whom we talked were brazen about the lawless free-for-all that characterized life on Rosedale's streets. My field research underscored the importance of declining police protection to the spiraling crime rates found among Rosedale's adolescents. By and large, the elderly were robbed by teenagers because it was lucrative and there was almost no chance of getting caught. We interviewed over 100 black youngsters attending special education programs between 1980 and 1984. For the most part, they were from low-income families and had been identified by the local school system as having learning difficulties or manifesting attendance or deportment problems. All of those interviewed knew that the elderly of Rosedale were victimized by teenagers. Moreover, most admitted that elderly whites were selected for special attention by those who preyed upon them.

Elderly whites were easier to rob than elderly blacks because "they ain't as strong as old black people. Old black people will probably shoot you or something like that. The white people, they gonna be too scared to do anything. Cause, you know, they ain't strong. They just weak and you can take anything you want."

That the elderly are easy marks was common knowledge among the streetwise teenagers of Rosedale: "They're old. They're more fragile and scared. You can hit them and the cops won't come. They're [old whites] afraid they'll get killed." A boy of fourteen told me how easy it was to rob old white people: "You can get away with more. You know you can get away with it because they're old. They can't run after you and catch anyone. You can hit them with something and knock them out easy. They hardly ever fight back." He explained that most kids knew where the old people lived because they "got bars on the windows."

A girl of fifteen told me that old people were easy targets because "they can't run as fast as other people" and that old white people "were up for grabs" in Rosedale. Those whom we interviewed consistently reported that the elderly were robbed and harassed because "they have more, and cause they can't do nothin' back." "They can't protect themselves. Old people be scared because they ain't used to no one else in their house like that. If someone breaks in they be scared. They probably have a heart attack." "Old people are helpless. They can't help themselves. Young people have their youth with them, and they're a lot stronger," boasted one teenager. "Old whites get things taken from them because most blacks think white people have everything. They have more than blacks, so whites get took," said another. "'Cause it's easy to get away with," claimed another.

Interview data made it clear that police protection was perceived as uneven to nonexistent among the teenagers of Rosedale. As explained by one youngster: "There's cops in Rolling Hills, but there ain't no police in Rosedale." His observation was not entirely accurate. The police obviously patrolled the neighborhood. In fact, a police substation was located one block from Main Street. At the same time, it is important to stress that only two to four cars were typically deployed, primarily to be seen and establish a presence in the large geographic area composing Rosedale. Additionally, those assigned to cover the area were also responsible for Southside and parts of Freetown and Hammond. With the exception of the intensive investment of resources to apprehend those responsible for the 1982 summer murders and to apprehend the Rosedale rapists, there had never been enough available police units to cover the myriad crimes occurring in those three neighborhoods.

When asked to respond to the widespread perception that they neglected the Rosedale neighborhood, many of those in the criminal justice system told me that the police were simply not equipped to prevent crime. At best, they contended, their presence in the community could only deter crime. Nonetheless, an attorney who had been a public defender of indigent clients for several years corroborated the views held by Rosedale's teenagers: "Old people are easy marks, and police protection in that area was very bad. They just let them do what they wanted to. The police get skittish about going over there as well. You can't blame them. But that kind of leaves the people at a disadvantage."

The judge who tried the infamous rape and murder cases occurring in Rosedale was more aggressive in defending the criminal justice system when I interviewed him in 1983. When asked what the courts and the legal profession could do to relieve the problems of Rosedale, he said to me:

> What the answers are I don't know. If society is looking for the legal profession to find answers, that won't ever happen. We ain't gonna find the answers. You guys find it. All we're doing is rubber stamping what society has already said: that these guys are bad. The legal profession is not geared to change the system. We'll change the rules of evidence and the method of appeal and the legal things. Cleaning up society's criminal problem, that's something that society will have to do, not the legal profession. But if you read the newspapers, they expect the legal profession to handle the whole matter. That's not even our job. That's the job of the home, church, and the schools.

In many respects, the judge's observations are not without merit. The problems of Rosedale are too complex to be remediated by the criminal justice system alone. At the same time, it was clear from our field studies that a positive working relationship between the police and the community had eroded during the course of racial transition. Perhaps more candidly than any other person interviewed, the officer in charge of the Rosedale beat explained how the relationship between the police and the community had changed over the years. A promoter of block-watch programs and community policing, the sergeant believed that "if everybody could get together and watch out for each other and get to know their neighbor, you could stop ninety-five percent of this stuff that's occurring simply by telling to police what you know."

He explained that prior to the brutal murders of Ethel Marlow and Clyde Robinson, it was nearly impossible for the police to establish any kind of working relationship with the residents of Rosedale. The elderly, held captive by their own fears and threats of retaliation from adolescents, simply stopped reporting crimes to the police. Black families and individuals, convinced that white police were not sensitive to their needs, also did little to cultivate a strong working relationship with the city's law enforcement officers. The sergeant maintained that the only way to stop the crime in Rosedale was "to get absolute trust in the police department; I know we had it in the past over there, and I think we'll get it in the future."

He thought that the changes taking place in Rosedale made it very difficult to give good police protection to the residents. His idea of proper law enforcement in an area like Rosedale entailed more than greater police presence in the community. Recommending that the police needed to get out and "meet the people," he urged establishment of a close working relationship with neighborhood institutions and leaders.

> But you have to have dedicated people to do that. Some of the younger cops, they think all you have to do is drive around in a police car, write a few tickets,

put someone in jail once in a while, and handle their calls—that's being a police-man. I think ninety percent of being a policeman is having confidence in the people that you're working around. If they trust you, they know you'll do your job. You'd really be surprised at the information you can get and how you're treated.

But the realities of life in Rosedale were far removed from the idealized vision of community policing promoted by the sergeant. His conception of what needed to be done was derived from knowledge of the way life once was in the neighborhood. Police work in Rosedale was dangerous. Professionalism, commitment to the ideals of law enforcement, and sustained involvement in neighborhood life were sentiments that died quickly on the streets of Rosedale. At the individual level, it was probably very difficult for working- and middle-class white policeman to identify with the poor black residents of Rosedale. Despite the sergeant's endorsement of stronger ties between the police and the community, the violent nature of street life in Rosedale surely made it difficult to put these ideals into practice.

Describing the family circumstances of many of Rosedale's youth, he said: "If you ever 'made' any of these kids' houses here, it would blow your mind. The houses, some of them, haven't seen a broom in a year. The roaches and stuff, you know, you walk in and you hear them crunch underneath your feet. In the summer weather it's so hot inside the house that you can't breathe, and the smell—you pray that they don't ask you to sit down." Many policemen were repulsed by life in Rosedale. The increasing fragmentation between the police and the community mirrored the class and racial lines separating those responsible for enforcing the law and those who needed protection. And even if the contempt that some policemen may have felt toward the African American residents of Rosedale could have been reduced, this would not have altered the magnitude of the crime problems taking place there. The chaos and disorder were so prevalent that traditional standards of police protection had to be altered and reassessed. In reference to the high rates of crime in Rosedale, one policeman conceded, "You just can't keep up with it." There was just too much drug traffic, too much theft, too much violence, and too few resources to stop any of it from happening. But the weakening ties between the police and the community were just one component of the larger puzzle revealing why established institutions no longer shaped the behavior of Rosedale's youth. Formal authority figures like the police could regulate behavior only when other agents of social control operated effectively. Within the neighborhood itself, the schools, churches, businesses, and families had also lost their ability to promote and maintain social order.

Our field research revealed fewer and fewer bonds linking individual adolescents to larger community and neighborhood institutions. Other agencies and institutions besides the police and the family maintain social order in urban neighborhoods. Light observed that merchants in established ethnic neighborhoods have a direct stake in curbing levels of delinquency.[25] All forms of legitimate business and commercial enterprise are negatively affected by street crime. Yet merchants in Rosedale realized they were no longer able to protect themselves from petty theft or wholesale burglary. Moreover, they were not able to provide safety to their customers. Without expensive investments in alarm technology, window bars, or private security forces, the merchants of Rosedale, like the police, were not able to reduce crime in the streets.

Several local merchants complained about the total disrespect for private property revealed by many black children. Both black and white entrepreneurs felt that youngsters in the neighborhood had little or no regard for private property. The executive director of the Black Business Association of Rosedale, a well-educated black man, explained that minority youngsters often walked into his office complex and demanded to use the bathroom or the telephone. If he honored their request, the toilet facilities were nearly always "trashed" and vandalized. If he explained to them that the facilities were private and not for public use, he often encountered verbal abuse, rude treatment, or retaliation. The plateglass window on the first floor of his office complex had been smashed five times during a twelve-month period. As a civil rights activist and successful businessman, he was convinced that a generation of welfare dependency and reliance on public-sector institutions had rendered the notions of private property and personal space meaningless among lower-class black children. As a result, he speculated, the notion of community and collective ownership of neighborhood institutions made little sense to the black youth of Rosedale.

Similar sentiments were echoed by numerous elderly residents of the area. Youngsters, they reported, defined private lawns and driveways as extensions of public streets. As public property, lawns and driveways could be expropriated as playgrounds, thoroughfares, shortcuts, dumping grounds, or places to congregate. Private businesses tended to be perceived as extensions of public restrooms. If facilities were not available, then parking lots and alleys could be viewed as places to urinate, especially if the restrooms were made inaccessible by those in a position to open them. Like the executive director of the merchants association, many of the elderly reported it was not uncommon for a youngster to request the use of their bathroom during the day or evening. Permission was seldom granted, and retaliation was not uncommon. Breaking streetlights was a frequent occurrence in Rosedale. As explained by one youngster, smashing streetlights was a game of skill played by several boys. They competed with each other to see who could hit the light with greatest accuracy with rocks gathered from parking lots or nearby gardens. One elderly respondent said: "I asked a little girl that seen them breaking lights. She said, 'Oh, it's only a bunch of boys; I don't know who they are; never see them only when they come here breaking lights out.'"

He went on to explain that pushing over stop signs and mailboxes was also a frequent sport in Rosedale. "Then down here on the corner, we have stop signs down there. A fellow heard a motor revving up and he went out to look, and they were just backing up over these stop signs with their car and pushing them over. He called the police. They come out and put them back up. But the next night, they come back and pushed them over again."

Another teenager explained to me that many youngsters liked to "get some weed and go down and tear up Rosedale Park." Describing a typical evening, he stated that several males would get high on marijuana and wine and rip up the public restroom in Rosedale Park. They would turn on all the water faucets, smash the plumbing and toilet fixtures, throw all the toilet tissue and paper towels in the water, and splat the soggy paper against the wall. Park benches would be broken, trash cans would be set ablaze, and anything wooden would be heaped upon the fire. When asked to explain why kids "trashed" the park, he replied, "They ain't got nothing else to do; they just try to be big shots and stuff."

Neither elderly whites nor black families were able to protect the collective possessions of community life: the parks, the streetlights, the public facilities. The merchants were unable to compel the youngsters of Rosedale to honor traditional notions of private property. And teachers and clergy were no more successful than the police, merchants, and residents in preventing crime and delinquency from occurring. Truancy and absentee rates were very high in the schools of Rosedale, especially among those youngsters known to engage in street theft, burglary, and vandalism. Among the youth we interviewed, nearly all knew at least one or two people who hung out on the streets: "They steal cars. They try to rob stores. They don't never come to school. They bring guns to school. They get put out of school. They just throw rocks at cars in the school lot and stuff like that." Among the youngsters who roam the streets of Rosedale, most were dropouts or those just serving time in the public schools. A girl of fourteen said: "They mostly be dropouts. And the dropouts are influencing the people in school to do the same thing they are doing; trying to walk the streets and trying to go to school. You can't walk the streets at night and go to school at the same time."

A boy of fifteen explained: "There's a lot of them just walking around, not doing anything. They will be just standing up at Rosedale Theater smoking weed and hanging out." Black churches also claim no special allegiance among the adolescents of Rosedale. A black social worker claimed:

> The church used to be a big influence on the black family. Most of these kids' parents were made to go to church. I don't know why that didn't stick, where

they thought they didn't need to send their children to church. I don't think there's anything so magical about church, and I'm not saying if they went they wouldn't get into trouble. But I do think that just being around people who have higher goals, higher ambition, and more of a sense of morality than what they are exposed to in the home would help a little.

In the face of declining community institutions and the increasing prevalence of serious social problems, the residents of Rosedale and the larger city of Fort Worth launched a major effort to revitalize the area. The revitalization effort spanned nearly a decade before it was abandoned.

9

THE STRUGGLE
TO CREATE
NEW INSTITUTIONS:
THE CRISIS DEEPENS

with Elise Bright and Richard Cole

I have great hopes of a resurgence in Rosedale. We need not have here in Fort Worth a South Bronx or an East Harlem or a Watts. . . . We don't have to face that future. We can do things for ourselves. I've retained an interest all these years. I've never let it waver. When Rosedale hurts I hurt. When it feels good I feel good.

—*Prominent Texas congressman who grew up in Rosedale, 1986*

Certainly nostalgia oriented me toward wanting to help the area where I grew up. Rosedale holds a lot of pleasant memories for me.

—*Texas state senator who grew up in Rosedale, 1986*

Fort Worth shouldn't sit back, watch, and allow one of its most important neighborhoods to die.

—*Rev. Jeremiah Jackson,*
community activist and chairman,
Rosedale Strategy Committee, 1986

IN THE AFTERMATH OF THE WILDING INCIDENTS OF 1982, political activists, public officials, business leaders, philanthropists, ministers, and agency heads finally mobilized to address aggressively the crisis in Rosedale. During the latter part of 1982 and throughout 1983, some of the

146

most prominent and powerful citizens in the metropolitan area pledged their support to rebuild the neighborhood.

Over and above the crime wave of 1982 and the deterioration of race relations that followed in its wake, the most immediate impetus to save the community was the announcement by the administration and trustees of Rosedale College of plans to relocate the institution across town in suburban southwest Fort Worth. Enrollment for the school was declining, and parents and students were complaining about the crime rate in the area. News of the college's plans to move was a major blow to area residents and commercial business owners. The college had been a cornerstone in the community since 1896. The Methodist church, which had donated the land in Rosedale for the college, opposed the move. Editorial writers urged the college to stay in Rosedale. The church elders, neighborhood residents, and neighborhood business owners did not want the school to abandon the neighborhood. They began to organize, conduct studies, and pursue other efforts to revitalize the Rosedale area, hoping to convince the college to remain in the community.

Toward this end, about sixty business, civic, political, and religious leaders met in one of Rosedale's churches in the latter part of 1982. Participants included a prominent Texas congressman who had grown up in Rosedale and a former mayor of Fort Worth who was then a member of the Texas state legislature. He also had grown up in Rosedale during its glory years.

Also present at the organizational meeting were longtime residents of Rosedale, local merchants, and high-profile corporate and civic leaders. The group agreed to create a strategic task force and draw up a specific set of recommendations to "turn Rosedale around," according to a local religious leader. The recommendations, he said, "will focus upon attracting business and jobs, upgrading housing, providing planned recreational activities for Rosedale's youth, and improving the community's image."

Enthusiasm, determination, and great public commitment characterized the early meetings to plan the revitalization of Rosedale. An activist African American minister expressed his belief that something positive could not fail to happen because a lot of high-powered people were involved in the effort to rebuild the neighborhood: "There is hope. There are a lot of strong-willed people showing an interest in what's going on here."

The minister who hosted the meeting proclaimed to the local press: "Change is certain. Whether that is a threat or a promise depends upon whether there is a vision and whether that vision is kept and implemented. I have a vision of a Rosedale that is a healthy, hospitable human habitat, with good schools and good churches, and a revived economy, and a rich, diverse mix of people of all hues, the poor becoming not-so-poor, along with a reentering middle class, young and old and in-betweens getting on together in a community they're proud of."

Reflecting the enthusiasm of those present at the meeting, a local HUD representative from Washington commented: "I haven't seen this much excitement since the Texas-OU game." Certain that change would come and the fortunes of Rosedale would be reversed, he predicted: "You can't stop it. Not with this group. It's too dynamic a group of people."

Over the next several years, extensive efforts were made to reverse the negative economic and political trends that had undermined the social and cultural institutions of Rosedale. Not surprisingly, the efforts ultimately failed. Plans for heroic interventions and enthusiastic proclamations about the power of positive thinking were slowly replaced by cynicism, pessimism, and the gradual realization that the problems of Rosedale were too severe to be fixed by boosterism and goodwill, federal grant dollars, and a strategic plan of action. The efforts to rebuild Rosedale followed two strategies: commercial redevelopment and housing renovation.

Commercial Redevelopment

The Rosedale Strategy Committee, a mayoral task force, was eventually formed in response to the work of the Allied Communities of the County, a countywide coalition of churches concerned with increasing public and private involvement in meeting the needs of the city's neighborhoods. The Strategy Committee was formed especially to address the problems of the Rosedale area, partly based on the findings of a city and United Way needs assessment conducted in 1983. The Strategy Committee consisted of four subcommittees: Long-Range Planning, Housing, Education and Employment, and Volunteerism.

In 1984, the Long-Range Planning Subcommittee began developing a series of redevelopment strategies for Rosedale. The subcommittee concluded that the most pressing problems facing the community were employment, housing, neighborhood networking (particularly with Rosedale College), poor community image, and lack of leadership.

During this time frame, Rosedale College officials continued to pursue plans to relocate the institution across town. The relocation plans were pursued until spring 1985, when it was revealed to the media that the college did not have funds to purchase the land and finalize the move. As a result, the board of trustees adopted a new resolution rescinding its previous agreement to move the campus, initiated a major capital and endowment campaign, and launched an effort to determine how the college could most effectively become a catalyst for renewal in the Rosedale community.

With the decision to remain in Rosedale, the college administration, led by its president, Ralph Meeks, became an active partner with the neighborhood and formally joined the Rosedale Strategy Committee. By July 1985, the college was heavily involved in the revitalization efforts in Rosedale.

President Meeks and the college's administrators prepared a proposal for matching grant funds and submitted it to various local agencies, including the city of Fort Worth, for support and commentary. In February 1986, after soliciting reactions from various agencies and constituencies, President Meeks submitted the proposal to two private foundations.

The proposed redevelopment plan requested $52,927 in funding for a two-year period and included a three-to-one match for revitalization efforts: The project would receive one dollar from a national foundation grant, one dollar from a local foundation, one dollar from the Community Development Block Grant (CDBG) program, and a one-dollar match from individual business owners. With these funds, the project would focus on the revitalization of Rosedale's business strip, located directly south of the college campus. This commercial strip contained historically significant buildings, a department store whose owners were willing to remain if there was a reasonable chance to revitalize the area, and two restaurants with potential citywide appeal. By the mid-1980s, the renovation of one building had already been completed and facade renovations on others were in progress. The Strategy Committee and Rosedale College concluded that redeveloping the commercial strip would be vital to spur the revitalization of the east and west corridors. In addition, the revitalization of the commercial strip would serve as a visible symbol to the rest of the Rosedale area, increase employment opportunities for local residents, and increase the tax base for the city.

The proposal received support from a prominent Texas congressman who had grown up in Rosedale during its glory years, the Mayor's Task Force on Rosedale, the Rosedale Business Association, the National Trust for Historic Preservation, the Texas Historical Commission's Main Street Project, the Historic Preservation Council of Tarrant County, and the Neighborhood Housing Services of Fort Worth.

The Structured Employment/Economic Development Corporation (SEEDCO), an intermediary organization of the Ford Foundation, initially responded positively to the proposal. However, before it would agree to make a positive funding decision on the proposal, SEEDCO wanted to have a written description of the specific relationship among all entities involved in the project, details of the commercial revitalization plan, and an itemized budget for the second year of the project.

The city of Fort Worth had informally set aside $175,000 in CDBG funds for the southeast quadrant of the city, an area that included Rosedale. The Strategy Committee requested that the city commit $160,000 of the CDBG funds for use in the Rosedale area. A portion of the funds would be used as a match to the anticipated Ford Foundation grant to hire a staff person who would encourage business owners to renovate their establishments on Rosedale's major commercial strip. The remainder of the funds would be used as a commercial revolving loan fund for the strip. These funds were to be administered by the Fort Worth Economic Development Corporation. The Strategy Committee further requested the city's planning department to prepare a revitalization plan for the commercial strip to guide interested parties in its renovation. The city of Fort Worth responded to the request by agreeing to hold the $160,000 for a reasonable amount of time. In addition, the city executed a contract with Rosedale College in the amount of $26,500 to operate the Rosedale Main Street Program for one year.

The funds were transferred from the CDBG Southeast Quadrant Economic Development Program account to a new account entitled the Rosedale Main Street Program account. However, the Rosedale Strategy Committee requested that the CDBG funds to be used for a revolving loan fund be deferred until the question of whether local banks would be willing to participate in the project (and leverage the CDBG funds) was resolved. On September 23, 1986, SEEDCO approved a one-year grant for $26,464 to Rosedale College for support of the commercial revitalization project. In addition, the grant was renewable in the second year for the same amount. The purpose of the Ford Foundation (SEEDCO) grant was to support the project-development phase of the commercial revitalization program. The funds were to be used for payment of the project manager's salary, training for the Main Street Program, and related administrative, consulting, equipment, and travel costs.

The Rosedale Main Street Program received funding from a number of other sources. Those sources included Rosedale College, the city of Fort Worth, Primerica Foundation of New York, the Meadows Foundation of Dallas, the Minnie Stevens Piper Foundation of San Antonio, the Garvey Texas Foundation of Fort Worth, and cash and in-kind donations from more than 100 local corporations.

Additionally, the Fort Worth Black Chamber of Commerce pledged its support of the project by initiating plans to establish a credit union in Rosedale. The credit union would take deposits from members and make personal loans to residents. The president of the Fort Worth Economic Development Corporation stated that Rosedale had not had a financial institution in the community since the mid-1970s. The credit union, if chartered, would help bring mainline financial institutions back to the neighborhood. Promoters of the credit union project boasted to the press that one major bank had already expressed some interest in opening a branch in Rosedale.

The Texas Main Street Project had specific criteria to define eligibility and the scope of assistance provided to self-initiated projects. Eligibility for assistance was based on the following criteria:

1. The community had to have a full-time, paid project manager.
2. The Main Street Program and its manager had to be recognized by a resolution of support by the city council.

3. The Main Street Project manager had to complete the Main Street training provided by the historical commission.
4. Monthly reports cosigned by the Main Street manager and a city administrator-manager had to be submitted to the Texas Main Street office.
5. The community had to be certified annually by the Texas Main Street office in Austin to confirm that the community met all of the criteria for designation as a self-initiated urban Main Street city.

In November 1986, the city of Fort Worth formally approved Rosedale's participation in the Texas Main Street Project and adopted a resolution supporting participation. In January 1987, the committee hired a project manager to oversee the revitalization efforts for Rosedale. In addition to a project manager, an assistant was hired, and an associate planner from the city of Fort Worth served as an adviser on a part-time basis. The staff reported to a twenty-three-member board of directors made up of a cross-section of merchants, residents, property owners, and college faculty as well as other professionals from throughout the city.

The new name of the project became Rosedale Main Street Project, and efforts to revitalize the community's commercial strip were officially started on January 2, 1987. The goals of the project were to (1) preserve the architectural and historical character of the Rosedale commercial area; (2) stimulate revitalization, redevelopment, and expansion of existing commercial properties; (3) increase employment opportunities for community residents; (4) market the commercial area in a coordinated way so as to attract more customers; and (5) attract new businesses to locate in the Rosedale commercial area.

To comply with the criteria set forth by the Texas Historical Commission's Texas Main Street Project, the first initiative made by the new project manager was to establish three committees: the Design Committee, the Promotion Committee, and the Economic Development Committee. The Design Committee worked to encourage appropriate, quality design in the maintenance, renovation, reuse, and new construction of buildings and public spaces. The Promotion Committee developed activities that would increase sales while marketing the area and improving its image through special events, sales and advertising, and media campaigns. The Economic Development Committee assisted in helping to retain and strengthen businesses, recruit new businesses, and increase the residents' buying power through job search and training.

The three committees of the Rosedale Main Street Project met from May to August 1987. The Design Committee focused on a sidewalk-improvement project to correct hazardous conditions of the sidewalks, curbs, and gutters in a three-block area along the major commercial strip and streets immediately adjacent to it. The Promotion Committee focused on preparing a marketing brochure containing information about Rosedale that would be used to attract new businesses and reinvestment activities to the area. The brochure contained information that prospective investors could review, such as demographics, economic conditions, other businesses and industries in the area, available properties, and available funding sources. The Economic Development Committee focused on establishing a low-interest revolving loan fund to assist existing businesses and attract new ones.

To fund these projects, the project manager secured $135,000 in CDBG funds from the city of Fort Worth. An amount of $80,000 of the $135,000 CDBG was needed for the sidewalk program, $3,500 was needed for the marketing brochure, and $50,000 was needed for the revolving loan fund program.

Meanwhile, the project director initiated contact with the Rosedale area businesses along the commercial strip. Twenty-three commercial businesses, three vacant buildings, two churches, one fire station, one student apartment building, two houses, and two churches were in the project target area. The project director and the Fort Worth Planning Department conducted a building inventory, a rehabilitation needs assessment, and a merchants survey to determine what needed to be done. Area merchants were encouraged to participate in property rehabilitation.

In December 1988, however, the project director was replaced because the board was not pleased with the progress being made. No new businesses had opened in the area during 1988, and few business owners seemed interested in making facade improvements or supporting marketing schemes. The termination of the project director was symptomatic of how far Rosedale had fallen before revitalization efforts were initiated and telegraphed the eventual collapse of the much-publicized commercial revitalization effort.

By 1990, the project had failed to demonstrate any positive effect on the area in terms of business expansion and actual increases in commercial activity. Funding for the Rosedale Main Street Project began to decline. In March, SEEDCO funded a $10,000 technical consulting assistance project for Rosedale merchants. However, in June 1990, SEEDCO ignored previous agreements to reimburse training expenditures, and it was behind on grant payments by over $17,000.

By 1991, SEEDCO was no longer a contributor to the project, the city of Fort Worth discontinued funding, and Rosedale College pulled out of the project and started its own economic development initiative. The credit union never materialized, and no branch banks relocated to the area. Rosedale Main Street requested an emergency grant from the Amon Carter Foundation, and a token amount was given to help the project through the end of the year. However, by January 1992, the Rosedale Main Street Project board had to accept the project director's resignation because of lack of operating funds.

Presently, the Rosedale Main Street Project has no director. In addition, all prior funding sources have severed their affiliation with Rosedale Main Street. The president of the Rosedale Business Association is currently trying to keep the Main Street Project alive. However, he is managing a business in the area and has little time to devote to the Rosedale revitalization program.

The Rosedale Main Street Project failed for several reasons. Numerous interviews were conducted with key people affiliated with the project from its inception.

Roger Marlin is executive director of a nonprofit organization in the Rosedale community that provides housing assistance, educational training, emergency assistance, and crisis counseling. He was a member of the Rosedale Main Street board during its first year. Marlin said that the primary goal of the Rosedale project was to provide revitalization to Rosedale's major commercial strip. However, there were severe economic downturns during that time that made realization of this goal difficult. When businesses were not retained or attracted to the community, the project refocused on housing issues. There were already several nonprofit housing services in the neighborhood, and they found themselves "bumping heads and competing for turf." In addition, Marlin said that many of Rosedale's residents were not made aware of the revitalization efforts. Community residents were not included in the organization of the project, and their involvement, in his opinion, was essential if the project was going to be successful.

Marlin thought that the first project director was very good; however, the president of the board overshadowed him. He contended that the president of the board was very domineering and actually held back the project. According to him, the project was poorly organized and lacked structure, and clear lines of authority between policymakers and management were not established. As a result, the first project director was fired and a new director was hired. Marlin felt the new director spent too much time attending meetings and accomplished little.

The Rosedale Main Street Project, according to Marlin, did produce some new sidewalks that were completed by the city in May 1992, and plans for facade improvements were drawn up. In addition, a free-lawn-equipment loan program was set up in the neighborhood. Marlin thought that these projects were not successful due to a lack of competent management and a lack of collaboration with other social agencies and efforts already under way in Rosedale. The projects seemed alien to residents of the community. Not one board member or project director lived in Rosedale, and the people in the community were not involved in the projects' implementation.

Marlin also noted that many of the problems came down to how the project used the funds it received. He said that a great deal of money was used to attend meetings and pay salaries; not much was spent on actually getting things done in the community. Marlin said that after a few years of paying for the project, funders were not pleased with its progress. The funders eventually lost interest and the project fizzled.

Alice Garson, owner and manager of the Vesco Printing Company, located in Rosedale, the current president of the Rosedale Main Street Project board, and acting project director, has mixed feelings about the project's success. Garson contends that all the advantages that have come to the community have been a result of the Rosedale Main Street Project. She argues that the businesses that have stayed are in better condition. However, she concedes there has been no profound change in the general appearance of the area or in the level of commercial activity.

According to Garson, SEEDCO had been the major contributor to the project. When the project was not realizing its objectives, SEEDCO wanted the goals to be revised. In order to continue providing funds for the initiative, SEEDCO wanted the project to expand into the housing area. However, the Liberation Community and Neighborhood Housing Services in Rosedale were already successfully providing housing services to the community. In order to qualify for SEEDCO funding, the project shifted its goals from business revitalization to housing revitalization. Garson thought this decision was a mistake.

Businesses were not locating in Rosedale because there was no economic base in the community. In response, the redevelopment strategy shifted to housing renovation, encouraging higher-income families to move in and improving the physical environment. These new goals angered the two housing agencies and the administration of Rosedale College. The existing housing agencies felt that the Rosedale Main Street Project was stepping on their toes by moving into housing revitalization. Garson said that SEEDCO wanted the project to be a clearinghouse for all the agencies located in the Rosedale community, thus combining all grants under one umbrella. Interagency conflict and competition over program scope and mission, however, were not only alien but largely irrelevant to the residents of Rosedale, according to her.

After Rosedale College pulled out of the project, the city of Fort Worth would contribute to the project based only on available matching funds. Garson said that in the initial phases of the project, the city required only letters of commitment to justify the matching funds. When the project could not show proof of the funds, however, the city simply pulled out. Garson concluded that the downfall of the project was the alteration of its mission. The project should have had a concrete mission statement and should not have deviated from it because of funding pressures.

Carla Thorn, the first president of the Rosedale Main Street Project, argued that the project was semisuccessful. She suggested an alternative measure of success for the Rosedale initiative: Success is achieved, according to her, if something happens that would not ordinarily happen. New businesses came in and fostered new jobs in the area. All that came, however, were not able to stay.

Thorn also pointed out that it was very difficult to gather enough participation in the Rosedale Business Association because most of the commercial businesses were run by one- or two-person teams that included the owner. These owners could not leave their businesses to attend meetings. These explanations notwithstanding, lack of interest on the part of business owners probably had more to do with poor leadership and ambiguous goals than with time pressures, according to Thorn.

Harry Marta, the second project director, observed that although the project had some successes—the lawn-mowing program, crime reduction, the closing down of some drug houses—the Rosedale project was not the brainchild of the merchants or the residents. It was initiated by the Strategy Committee. The merchants and movers and shakers of Rosedale did not have the opportunity to "buy into the program." Marta felt that the community viewed the project as something that was imposed on it and never identified with it.

The major downfall of the project, according to Marta, came as a result of conflicts between the goals of Rosedale Main Street and SEEDCO. SEEDCO had established milestones that the project had to accomplish quarterly. If the milestones were accomplished, SEEDCO would provide more funds. SEEDCO urged the board to become a housing-oriented community development corporation instead of a Main Street program. President Meeks and the administration at Rosedale College did not want to get into housing renovation but wanted to stay focused on commercial revitalization. But the board voted to go with the SEEDCO request, and this caused too much internal conflict.

Marta also reported that the board decided to have a retreat to reevaluate the goals of the program and to choose between the SEEDCO and the Rosedale College position. The merchants thought the project was being controlled too much by the college and decided to move the project office off the campus into a storefront location. At the retreat, participants decided to go with the SEEDCO request. Angered by the decision, President Meeks withdrew from the board, and the college withdrew from the project. This fragmented even further the tenuous coalition formed to rebuild Rosedale.

Brian Thomas, the director of Economic and Community Development for Rosedale College, agreed that the Rosedale Main Street Project was not successful because its primary goal was changed. The original goal of the project was architectural preservation of commercial buildings on the major business strip. The architectural preservation would return the buildings to the old Texas flavor that existed before Rosedale was annexed to Fort Worth.

According to Thomas, the Rosedale project was an economic development project to woo businesspeople into the buildings that had been renovated as part of the architectural preservation. This did not succeed because potential businesspeople did not want to locate to an area where most of the established residents were leaving. Thus, the project then turned to a neighborhood housing revitalization plan to both attract and hold residents in the neighborhood.

Thomas argued that the Rosedale Main Street group could not decide what it wanted to do or be. He described the project as being "dysfunctional and schizophrenic" because its direction and focus kept changing. The architects' interest was in the preservation of commercial buildings rather than in neighborhood housing revitalization. Community leaders were more concerned with the decline of socioeconomic conditions in the neighborhood. Thomas said that the project was successful with regard to its original objective—preserving the commercial and historical buildings on the strip. However, businesses could not support themselves in a blighted neighborhood, and as a result, the commercial strip was left with many empty and underutilized buildings.

Project leaders felt, according to Thomas, that it was prudent to change direction. They targeted housing and community development. But as a community development corporation, the project was not successful either. The Main Street Project was not equipped to deal with a housing and real estate slump. Thomas concluded that today the Rosedale Main Street Project is virtually nonexistent.

Billy Jenkins, executive director of the Amon Carter Foundation, believes that the Rosedale Main Street Project has been in "some state of existence" for the past eight years. However, some supporters, such as the Carter Foundation, feel they have made their contribution and cannot afford to gamble any more of their resources. There are simply not enough funds for the number of worthy projects competing for philanthropic dollars. The Carter Foundation has recently received a proposal from what remains of the Rosedale Main Street Project. However, Jenkins said that the foundation will not do anything until it can determine whether the project is still viable. It is unlikely it will fund the request.

Erik Chavez, assistant director of planning for the city of Fort Worth, worked with the project from its inception. He reported that until 1990 the city's planning department provided staff to function as consultants and researchers for the project. Staff members representing the Mayor's Task Force conducted merchant surveys, assisted with creating the revitalization plan, and assisted with infrastructure and streetscape design.

The planning department is no longer closely involved with the Rosedale Main Street Project because of limited staff and resources. In 1991, the Planning Department staff was reduced by 38 percent, and in 1992 the staff was reduced again by 15 percent. Since 1993, no efforts have been made to restore staff or funding to prior levels.

Chavez indicated that the city provided CDBG funds to assist existing and potential Rosedale businesses with an 8 percent loan. However, no businesses requested these funds. The forms and red tape required to realize a loan were formidable to many merchants.

The project was clearly successful in creating some organization in the community, according to Chavez. However, he feels there were too many people from outside telling the neighborhood what to do. Chavez added that current project problems are a result of a loss of focus resulting from SEEDCO demands and Rosedale College's withdrawal from the project.

Between May 1987 and October 1989, fifteen businesses located in the commercial strip. In 1987, the first year of the project, five businesses located to the neighborhood, including a theater, a restaurant, the Fort Worth Independent School District youth entrepreneurial print shop, a convenience store, and a beauty salon. These five businesses created 21 jobs. In 1988, three new businesses came to the commercial strip and created 6 new jobs, and in 1989, seven new business located on the commercial strip created 18 jobs. However, during the same period, thirteen businesses left the commercial strip, which resulted in 41 lost jobs. Thus there was a net gain of 3 jobs between 1987 and 1989.

Two of the businesses that left the commercial strip between 1987 and 1989 were anchor stores for the strip. Mott's five-and-dime store had been in the community forty-eight years. The store closed because it was showing no profit and had management problems. The Mitchell/Myers store tried to weather the economic downturn. The owners even remodeled the building. However, profits were not realized, and the store closed in June 1989.

A physical survey of the Rosedale commercial strip revealed that sixteen of the businesses that were present in 1987 were not there in 1993 and that the buildings vacant in both 1985 and 1987 were vacant in 1993. In addition, an on-site review of the area revealed that the buildings located at the addresses that were targeted for revitalization on the commercial strip remain in similar or worse condition than was described in 1985.

The Vesco Printing building, listed in good condition in 1985, was rehabilitated in 1988. The building received a new awning and a front door and was painted. However, the condition of the building has deteriorated. The Power House building located on Rosedale's Main Street received interior rehabilitation in 1987 at an estimated cost of $27,000. The building interior still needs major renovation work. The Zippy Carwash facility, valued in 1987 at $71,667, has been vacated and is deteriorating. Much of the plumbing has been vandalized, and the car-wash stalls are now used to conduct illegal enterprise. Thus it is difficult to characterize the Rosedale Main Street Project, a two-year planned economic development project, as a success.

Many contemporary policy analysts claim that strategic planning is required to achieve successful economic development.[1] A strategic economic development plan, according to them, can assist declining communities in becoming competitive in attracting prospective businesses. Failure in economic development occurs when planning lacks community participation and project ownership and when goals and objectives are too general. For an economically distressed community like Rosedale, however, it is not at all clear that a well-conceived plan, properly designed and implemented, would have produced any of the desired outcomes.

Clearly, it was difficult to determine what the Rosedale Main Street Project goals and objectives really were. Our analysis of its implementation revealed two different sets of revitalization plans and a set of objectives that were difficult to determine from the revitalization plans. Effective community redevelopment requires that neighborhood members participate in the creation of the plan. It is important that community members support the process and understand the time frame for intended results. Project administrators must appreciate that positive results must occur early to ensure continuing community support. In addition, realistic goals and objectives must be established and pursued throughout the life of the project, and these must be independent of the specific interests of funding sources.

In the case of Rosedale, the deterioration of community and neighborhood institutions occurred well before the emergence of efforts to stabilize the area. And efforts to stabilize the area were drawn out and increasingly entangled in bureaucratic red tape and conflict between competing agencies. The collapse of the private market had undermined normal investment activities in real estate, housing, and business development well before the redevelopment effort was ever implemented. The radical drop in disposable income among residents had made it difficult for them to support local businesses long before local politicians expressed their concerns about social problems in Rosedale. And the increasingly serious problems of adolescent crime and vandalism had transformed street life and neighborhood culture in the community well before city bureaucrats and planners began formulating a strategic plan of action.

From this perspective, it is not at all difficult to understand why the Main Street Project failed. Even if residents had developed a "sense of ownership" with the plan, most did not have the personal income, political resources, or personal wherewithal to implement it. Indeed, the abandonment of the project's original set of objectives reflects partial recognition of these facts on the part of external funding agencies. Even if agency infighting and protection of turf had been replaced by collaboration and cooperation, Rosedale's vital community and neighborhood institutions were either dead or seriously ill well before initiation of the Main Street Project. External political support, high-profile boosterism, and capital infusion from city hall, private foundations, and the federal government were heroic policy interventions, liberal life-support systems that were destined to fail in the end.

The Effort to Save Rosedale's Housing

Similar observations apply to recent efforts to salvage Rosedale's rapidly declining housing stock. Like the plan to revitalize its commercial strip, the proposed strategy to rebuild Rosedale's housing was launched with civic pride, political optimism, and public fanfare. Neighborhood Housing Services (NHS) had been active in Rosedale since 1979. Its activities had been only moderately successful during its first two years there. Ironically, the continued deterioration of the neighborhood and the political attention brought to the area by the Rosedale rapists and the wilding incidents of 1982 elevated the institution's political fortunes dramatically.

About the same time plans were announced to revitalize Rosedale's business sector, the local press carried major stories outlining an ambitious strategy to renovate the community's housing stock. During the latter part of 1982, an innovative program to finance the redevelopment of Rosedale's housing was drafted by many of the same individuals, groups, and agencies that had masterminded the commercial renovation plan.

Residents of Rosedale were declared eligible for mortgage and home improvement loans at an interest rate of approximately 9.5 percent, an extremely competitive rate at the time. The total amount of capital initially made available was $790,000. This amount was financed through grants from the Sid Richardson Foundation (a local private foundation), the Fort Worth Bank and Trust, and the Federal National Mortgage Association.

Neighborhood Housing Services was chosen to administer the loan program. Loans would be targeted to residents of Rosedale, especially those who would like to own rather than rent their homes. Politically, this program established NHS as the premier community agency responsible for housing renovation in Rosedale, a fact that later contributed to the interagency conflict and competition surrounding the shifting mission of the Rosedale Strategy Committee.

Barry Sears, a partner in Franks and Sears Real Estate, Inc., was at the time the president of Neighborhood Housing Services. He announced in late 1982 that local contributions to the loan program totaled approximately $293,000: "The city of Fort Worth contributed $200,000 and the Sid Richardson Foundation contributed $93,000." He went on to explain that NHS would receive $57,000 to administer the program. His firm would work in tandem with NHS to implement the program.

Sears explained that if a resident of Rosedale wished to make $10,000 worth of improvements to his home, he would probably receive a $3,000 interest-free loan under the program. The remaining $7,000 would be obtained as a loan at market rate. The combined package would bring the total cost of the borrowed money to approximately 9.5 percent, a figure about 5 percent below competitive interest rates in 1982–1983.

Because of the extremely favorable interest rate, the planning director for the city of Fort Worth predicted that demand for the loan program would be "intense": "The housing stock and its central location are the two things going for Rosedale. The houses [there] are of basically sound construction. You can get a lot of room for a reasonable price. And the neighborhood's history is something of a starting point. A lot of well-known people in Fort Worth grew up in Rosedale."

By the end of 1983 and well into 1984, enthusiasm for the housing-renovation plan was still in its honeymoon period. Those affiliated with NHS estimated that more than $2 million in private funds had been invested in the purchase and renovation of homes in Rosedale. Administrative officials within NHS became integrally involved in the wider effort to rebuild Rosedale, and enthusiasm about the neighborhood's future appeared contagious. By late 1983, the city had spent about $1.8 million in various projects ranging from street and sidewalk improvements to housing renovation and park rehabilitation.

Those involved in the housing effort were closely aligned with the commercial renovation planners. In 1984, merchants and housing advocates joined forces to criticize and change a city ordinance preventing front-end or head-in parking while a business was undergoing renovation. Reflecting their optimism about Rosedale's commercial future, the activists claimed that the ordinance would hurt business along the commercial strip. A spokesperson complained to the local media: "Many of the people who stop at the businesses along Rosedale do so on impulse. If the city prevents front-end parking, this will take away impulse buying."

By 1986, NHS had declared in an official publication that it had "stabilized" the neighborhood and the renovation of its housing stock was well under way: "Largely through the efforts of the NHS, the area was stabilized by 1986. Over the year, the NHS provided the technical assistance to help homeowners bring their homes up to minimum code standards; helped coordinate millions of dollars worth of public improvements; and in general served as an advocate for the area."

Among its many accomplishments, the following were most widely publicized in promotional literature and brochures released by NHS in 1990:

1. Two hundred and ten loans totaling $1,142,363 were made from the Revolving Loan Fund, enabling families to improve their homes.

2. A special home ownership program, created in 1985, helped twenty-nine families attain homeownership. NHS loaned $624,439 from its Revolving Loan Fund and banks loaned $371,503, a total of $995,942 in new-home ownership investment.

3. Technical assistance and homeownership counseling were provided to 2,000 families.

4. Rehabilitation cost estimates and construction monitoring services were provided for property owners.

5. Resident self-help programs such as crime watch, block cleanups, and paint projects were encouraged and supported by NHS.

6. City services were focused on points of need in the neighborhood as a result of the partnership effort.

A closer analysis of NHS's claims about stabilizing the neighborhood reveals the depth of the crisis in Rosedale's private housing market. In retrospect, it is clear that improvements in Rosedale's housing stock and continual efforts to reverse the decline in the community's physical appearance did not keep pace with the speed of demographic changes occurring there between 1980 and 1990. Residents who were unable to patronize the community's businesses surely could not be relied upon to maintain the quality of its housing stock or qualify for mortgage loans in the private marketplace. And despite fantasies about impulse buying, it was clear that few outsiders drove to Rosedale to shop or purchase community services.

Initially, white flight in Rosedale created a buyer's market for high-quality housing abandoned by prior residents. At first, Rosedale's newly purchased housing stock was owner-occupied. As white flight continued, and because the black middle class temporarily located in Rosedale before moving to new suburbs, the second wave of housing investors in Rosedale were absentee landlords. Between 1980 and 1990, the proportion of tenant-occupied housing in Rosedale dramatically increased. During this period, the average price of real estate in the community dropped from a high of $40,000 to $50,000 in the 1970s to a low of $15,000 to $20,000 by 1990.

As the quality of tenants deteriorated in the neighborhood, so did the incentives for landlords to maintain the integrity of the community's housing stock. Why bother to maintain the property if its value is rapidly decreasing? was a question frequently posed to us by local landlords and small-time real estate speculators. A primary objective of NHS, however, was to increase rates of owner occupancy in the neighborhood. This objective was not easily realized in a local housing market tipped largely in favor of outside investors, owners, and slumlords. But even these volatile market trends were undermined by a major downturn in the Texas real estate industry in the mid-1980s.

The initial downturn in the Texas economy resulted in foreclosures among the ranks of Rosedale's new homeowners. As distressing as these foreclosures were to local housing advocates, the real damage to the neighborhood was initiated by defaults among absentee landlords. Of the 783 vacancies reported in 1990, approximately 80 percent fell into the category of outside investors.

One of the negative features associated with the boom that preceded the downturn in the Texas real estate industry was an overbuilding of rental units in the suburbs. By 1987, the investors that had been drawn to Rosedale's bargain prices found it difficult to resist investing in other areas that offered lower rates and enabled them to offer appealing promotions such as free utilities and several months of free rent. As investors began to lose desirable tenants in Rosedale and were drawn to other areas, a cycle of disinvestment was initiated and the demand for rental units decreased. Many investors feared that they could not recoup their costs and cut back on maintenance as a result. When they reduced maintenance costs, their units became less marketable, commanded less rent, and sat vacant for longer periods of time. Some eventually were vandalized and fell out of the rental market altogether. Many investors cut their losses and walked away from their properties altogether.

As explained to us by a Rosedale College administrator, during the boom days of the 1970s, small investors came to Rosedale and acquired property from the original homeowners who were moving out to escape the in-migration of ethnic minorities. The new investors turned the property into rentals, but when the economy declined, the demand for rental housing also declined. Neighboring communities such as Rolling Plains and nearby cities such as Arlington offered better, safer rentals for less money. Investors found their properties continuously vacant; they stopped maintaining them and making payments. The vacant properties were eventually foreclosed, vandalized, covered with overgrown grass and weeds, and used as drug and gang houses. Rosedale became filled with vacant homes; according to the college official, one in every four homes was vacant and over 660 homes were turned over to HUD in the early 1990s.

Other individuals explained that many landlords scrambled to protect their investments by rapidly converting their units into Section 8 rental housing. Landlords attempted to hedge their bets against a volatile and highly competitive rental market in the metropolitan region; the federal rental subsidies would enable them to at least service their mortgage debts. Clearly, the interests of landlords and those objectives being pursued by housing advocates and redevelopment planners were not compatible.

The number of Section 8 rental units available in Rosedale increased rapidly during the latter part of the 1980s. As a result, many of those we interviewed expressed a widely held view that the quality of tenant drawn to

Rosedale had declined, as had the maintenance of those properties involved in the program. The president of the Black Business Association of Fort Worth, whose offices were located in Rosedale during the 1980s, bluntly described the impact of the Section 8 program on the neighborhood's housing stock: "I don't want to sound like a snob. But you've just got to deal with the fact that whenever you get low-income people, you are going to get high crime. Sometimes you have decent people in government housing, but not all the time."

He went on to explain that too many houses in Rosedale had been converted to Section 8 units during the late 1980s. Part of the problem, according to him, was the deterioration of the city's public-housing stock: "People are being dumped out of public housing and being shoved into areas like Rosedale. Homes are being destroyed in Southside, and those people are being pushed into Rosedale as well."

Expressing no great admiration for federal housing policy or the efforts of NHS, he observed:

And a lot of times they [government housing advocates] go into areas like Rosedale and give them [low-income tenants] X number of dollars to relocate, and they put it down on a house. They are low income and are not able to make repairs. They are not able to do the upkeep, so even though the house is occupied it continues to deteriorate. There is a house around the corner from me that would probably sell for about $40,000 to $50,000. They moved a woman who was on welfare in there. She is buying it and they moved her in. They [NHS] were supposedly subsidizing her housing note and she stayed there for about six months. And the house was just totally destroyed. And she just moved out, and she was in a pretty good neighborhood.

Others with whom we talked complained about the rapid increase in illegal aliens that moved to Rosedale in the wake of the housing slump that occurred in the 1980s. In 1988, a housing and community activist in Rosedale explained to me:

The other thing, I guess, would be there is a large concentration of undocumented workers in the last two years. The city has been so busy talking about the black drug problem in the area that they have totally ignored the illegal issue. The illegal problem has been growing in Rosedale for at least the last four years. I have been working with SEEK [a program for minority youth] for the last three years. They had an illegal problem then. What's happening is that they [the illegals] have been moving into Southside and they've been flushed out. They have been moving into Rosedale. Into low-income housing and into group housing.

He explained that houses occupied by "illegals" were always overcrowded and never maintained. Because the occupants were illegal aliens, it

was assumed they had virtually no incentive to maintain the property. Incentives did exist, however, to pack as many transient individuals as possible into the dwelling, an outcome that inevitably produced negative consequences for the maintenance of the community's housing stock.

By 1990, the community's private real estate market was again in sham-
bles. The private market for housing in the neighborhood had been nearly
eliminated by the real estate slump and by the rapidly changing demography in Rosedale. By 1991, city officials reported about 800 vacant houses
in Rosedale (3 to 4 on nearly every block). The level of home maintenance
in some of the owner-occupied properties was generally good; the absentee-
owner housing units were in a general state of disrepair and decline. This
element of Rosedale's housing problem was largely beyond the scope of
programs and policies envisioned by NHS or the other nonprofit organizations that targeted housing renovation as their major objective. And it was
also beyond the scope of the Rosedale Strategy Committee, despite its expressed desire to enter this controversial development arena.

In response to the latest crisis in housing, NHS, in association with
Rosedale College and other community agencies, announced a new plan to
address housing problems in the early 1990s. It proposed to initiate a new
cycle of reinvestment in the area by expanding previously successful loan
programs that provided homeownership opportunities for families in the
area and to make low-interest renovation loans available to current owners. These efforts and the related marketing activities, according to NHS officials, would build upon the considerable strengths of the area and place its
distressed real estate market on a positive trajectory.

The target area selected for the new plan shares a common boundary
with the thirty-block area identified by Rosedale College for its revitalization efforts. The target area was selected mainly because it is adjacent to
the Rosedale campus, just south of the major commercial strip in the community.

The strategy area contained a total of 240 lots with 239 residential properties as well as 6 vacant lots, 1 commercial property, and 1 church that occupied two lots. Overall, 51 percent of all houses were reported in good
condition, 32 percent were in fair condition, 13 percent were deteriorated,
3 percent were dilapidated, and less than 1 percent (one house) was in need
of demolition. At the time the housing survey was conducted (early 1990s),
15 percent of *all* the properties in the target area were vacant. Most significant, homeowners occupied just 36 percent of these properties, of which 68
percent were in good condition, 26 percent were in fair condition, and 4
percent needed to be demolished.

Absentee-owner properties constituted 64 percent of the target area, 2 percent were vacant lots, and less than 1 percent were zoned and used as commercial space. At the time of the new proposal, 36 investor-owned homes

within the target area were vacant. Of the 36 vacant properties, 9 were owned by banks or other financial institutions, 8 were owned by HUD, and among the remaining 19 vacant investor properties, only 2 had For Rent signs and 4 had private realtor For Sale signs. Of the 157 investor properties, banks owned 15 properties, 9 of which were vacant. The remaining 6 were rented or leased. Forty-one percent of the houses were in good condition, 45 percent were in fair condition, 18 percent were deteriorated, 3 percent were dilapidated, and less than 1 percent needed to be demolished.

According to NHS officials, their strategy was based on "starting revital-ization efforts in one of the strongest blocks, where homeownership was high and the housing stock was in good condition, and working outwards from there in a contiguous house-by-house, block-by-block process." NHS proclaimed that it was committed to creating a positive investment climate within the target area and would halt the pattern of disinvestment and pro-mote homeownership for the entire Rosedale community. NHS claimed to have developed a plan to market, rehabilitate, and finance existing proper-ties to moderate- and low-income buyers and to assist current homeowners in upgrading and stabilizing their properties.

By early 1993, it was clear that Rosedale's housing problem had slipped well beyond the influence of NHS or any other community agency or orga-nization interested in revitalizing the area. Although the latest NHS pro-posal to address the absentee-owner problem in the community received some favorable press, it was generally met with the same kind of polite skepticism that eventually undermined efforts to revitalize Rosedale's com-mercial sector. Unlike with earlier programs and plans, funds for the new effort were not forthcoming. The executive director of NHS eventually re-signed, and it remained without permanent administrative leadership for most of 1994.

Failures in housing and business development were not the only prob-lems that continued to ravage the community institutions of Rosedale. The arrest and conviction of the wilding gang in 1982 did not signal the end of adolescent crime in the neighborhood. Not surprisingly, criminal activity in the community continued to rise. Drug traffic increased as crack cocaine found its way onto the streets of Rosedale. The wilding episodes were re-placed by organized gang activities. Even worse, serious conflict between Asian, Chicano, and African American gangs over turf and drug markets made the streets of Rosedale as dangerous as they were in 1980.

Gangs and the New Wave of Adolescent Crime

The new crime problem in Rosedale was addressed with the same spirit of resolve and optimism that characterized initiation of the commercial and housing redevelopment plan. Of particular significance to those committed to reducing crime in the neighborhood was the "image" of Rosedale. Neighborhood leadership correctly assumed that perceptions of the community by residents citywide had been strongly and negatively influenced by the Rosedale rapist and the wilding incidents of 1982.

Intent on reversing negative views of the area, community activists launched a systematic effort to create a new image for Rosedale. They aggressively marketed the neighborhood's future to the wider community. On the heels of the announcement of plans to revitalize Rosedale's commercial strip and renovate its housing stock, a press conference was held by several neighborhood leaders. They complained to the press that the community was a victim of a distorted media campaign to vilify the area. According to those present at the conference, "a stereotype of Rosedale has been created by the media and [it] has taken on a life of its own."

An NHS activist present at the meeting declared to the press: "It's like Watts—millions of people who have never been to Watts have a perception of Watts based upon what they read in the newspaper. There are people all over Fort Worth and Dallas who have never been here but have some perception of Rosedale as being an armed camp. When people do come here they generally get a different picture." Suggesting that racial prejudice was at work, he warned that irresponsible press coverage of Rosedale could "hurt the recovery effort."

Like their associates and colleagues who were attempting to rebuild the community's business and commercial structure, those committed to reducing the crime rate introduced a series of special programs and policies. Many of the programs were designed to strengthen and expand family services in the area and deal with the problems of minority adolescents.

By the end of 1983, the metropolitan YMCA had been recruited to the area. It agreed to rent the abandoned fire station and provide day-care services within it. The facility planned to specialize in the provision of services to handicapped youngsters and the children of teenage parents so they could return to school.

Earlier in 1983, Neighborhood Health Services opened in one of the renovated buildings along Rosedale's main commercial strip. The community health clinic opened with the help of the Sid Richardson Foundation, the same private philanthropic organization that had generously invested in other community projects. The Amon Carter Foundation also made significant investments in the community health clinic. The clinic, organized as a nonprofit entity, began to provide health care to Rosedale's residents based on their ability to pay. By 1986, more than 1,100 patients had been treated.

A new multipurpose community center, boys' club, and day-care program were established through a combination of federal and private foundation grants and private donations. In 1985, a special program for unwed mothers was initiated at Rosedale High School. A director of one of the youth programs declared in late 1983, "We're really excited about it. We've been really impressed with the positive attitude of all the residents in the community."

By 1987, public optimism about reducing adolescent crime and turning the lives of Rosedale's youth in a positive direction was beginning to wane. Interviews with the director of Rosedale's Boys Club and with some of the youth who attended its programs clearly showed that the same social and economic forces that produced the wilding gang in 1981 had become even more potent five years later. In March 1986, it was obvious that the same forms of economic deprivation that lured Johnny Lee Brown and Harold Washington into crime remained integral to street life in Rosedale.

A sixteen-year-old female explained: "You've always got to know what you're doing, especially if you're out walking at night. It's like a jungle out there. It's people our age. They get to dropping out of school and get their minds corrupted. I guess they have to do it to have fun. Plus they get all drugged out and go crazy."

In mid-1986, the Fort Worth school district reported that only about 40 percent of Rosedale High School students enrolled as freshmen in 1981 were attending school there four years later. Most of the students who failed to attend school were dropouts, according to administrative officials. Teen pregnancy rates within Rosedale High were among the highest in the city. And about 35 percent of neighborhood residents between the ages of sixteen and twenty-five were unemployed, according to a survey conducted among more than 500 Rosedale households.

The director of the Boys Club presented an all too familiar profile of the youth he was attempting to influence. He explained that most of the youth coming to the center were black and poor. In the community, pimps and drug dealers flashed the fattest wallets and drove the biggest cars: "Our kids don't have real positive role models. That's why the club is so important. A lot come from single-parent homes with no dominant male figure. A lot of kids, when they talk to us, they call us Dad."

Other youth described the identical circumstances that I heard earlier while interviewing members of the wilding gang waiting to stand trial for capital murder in the county jail: "There ain't nothing on the streets. There ain't nothing but trouble. You don't go looking for trouble. Trouble will find you. Most of the kids will do it because other people will be influencing them. Kids will say, 'Hey, let's do this.' If they don't, they call you a punk or a chicken. They see adults, older people doing that stuff, and they think they can be bad like that. They see an older guy get away with robbing somebody and they're going to try it too."

The director of the Boys Club was realistic about his chances for success. He explained, "I'm not saying that we can counteract all the things that happen to them in every environment, but this club is part of their environment. If they weren't here, they'd be on the streets because they have no place to go."

When asked to explain what changes were most important to assist the youth of the community, he stood firm in his belief that the key problem for the adolescents of Rosedale was finding jobs for them: "Mainly their problems are financial in scope. Kids are seeking alternative ways to expand their economic base. Some drop out to get work. A lot of times it's done through violence. Most of the time it's through drugs. It's their use of the free enterprise system. They come here to learn just enough to make it out there, then drop out, just enough to get slick."

Summarizing his prognosis for the future, he said: "If we don't get to them now, it's going to be too late for a lot of kids." Crime statistics released for Rosedale in the mid-1980s showed that the hour was already too late. Between January and December 1984, there were 5 murders in Rosedale, 35 rapes, 149 robberies, 978 burglaries, 193 aggravated assaults, 874 thefts, and 135 auto thefts. One year later, murders were up by 100 percent, robberies increased by 21.5 percent, aggravated assaults increased by 6.5 percent, burglaries increased by 16.9 percent, and auto thefts rose by 68.1 percent. The only bright spots in an otherwise dismal crime report were minuscule drops in rape (5.7 percent) and thefts (3 percent). Residents took little consolation in these facts, however, since all statistics were based only upon reported crimes.

The crime report was most distressing to residents of the area. Between 1983 and 1986, more than fifty crime-watch groups had been established in Rosedale. Additionally, the tremendous publicity given to the revitalization efforts had resulted in a greater police presence in the neighborhood. Rosedale was reported to be one of the most heavily patrolled areas in the city. By mid-1986, nine police units had been assigned to the Rosedale beat or the adjacent areas.

When asked to comment about the crime rate in Rosedale, a member of the Fort Worth Police Department reported: "If the police department had the ability to do away with unemployment and all the social ills attributed to that in a certain area, then certainly we'd see a reduction in crime. But there are no utopias. There are no perfect worlds." I had heard this same message several years earlier.

Consistent with the breakdown of the housing and commercial redevelopment plans, efforts to reduce crime in the community and redirect the lives of Rosedale's youth followed a less than utopian script. As the market for crack cocaine expanded in the neighborhood, economic opportunities for youth also increased. Ironically, job opportunities in the illegal economy proved more interesting and lucrative than those available in the straight labor market. And as organized gangs took root in the fertile soil of Rosedale, a new set of crises emerged. In fact, by the early 1990s, organized gangs had emerged in every low-income minority community in Fort Worth.

Elisabeth Kübler-Ross describes a process through which individuals pass when they learn they have contracted a life-threatening disease.[2] *Denial* is the first phase of this process, followed by *anger, bargaining, depression,* and eventually *acceptance.* City officials appear to move through similar passages when dealing with the emergence of youth gangs. This was the case with city officials in Fort Worth before they finally mobilized to address the gang problem.

Evidence of serious gang activity was present in the city well before 1990, but most city officials denied the existence of the problem. The magnitude of crimes being committed in Rosedale between 1985 and 1990 suggested forces at work that were far more organized and widespread than the random mayhem perpetrated by the wilding gang of 1982. Acknowledgment of youth gangs, however, did not seriously enter public policy discourse in the city until 1991.

It took two more years for public officials to address formally the seriousness of the gang problem now fully before them. By that time, organized gangs were deeply rooted in the city's minority neighborhoods. During 1993, the city created a gang task force. In November 1993, the task force released a sobering, final report. A survey by law enforcement agencies and personnel established that approximately 210 gangs were operating in the county with as many as 2,800 members overall. The head of the task force, a Hispanic accountant, concluded what public officials had earlier denied: "There's no doubt it's gotten worse. Had the report not been developed, it would get worse. No one's addressing it from an entire-community approach. We want schools, neighborhoods, and everyone, to send a message to gangs—we will NOT tolerate you." To the residents of Rosedale, this message sounded all too familiar and rung a little hollow. They were well aware already that organized gangs had established control over the streets of Rosedale.

The task force report acknowledged that gangs in the city were organized by ethnic and racial groups. Moreover, each gang appeared to operate differently. Hispanic gangs were territorial in nature and engaged in drive-by shootings and violent rivalries more frequently than other groups. Asian gangs tended to prey upon other Asians, but the report warned that theft was their primary objective; easy and submissive targets of any ethnic group were becoming more frequent victims. White gangs tended to be racist in orientation and were disproportionately involved in racially motivated killings, beatings, and harassment.

The report also indicated that black gangs were primarily "profit-motivated" and extensively involved in the crack cocaine trade. The black gangs were organized as theft rings, some with ties and affiliations to national gangs such as the Los Angeles–based Crips and Bloods. In fact, some local black gangs operated like national franchises in the illegal economy. The assistant district attorney for the city said: "These gangs were so well organized that within five to ten seconds after the robbery started, they had people lying on the floor with their faces in the carpet."

Although predominantly African American, by 1995 Rosedale was a tri-ethnic neighborhood with growing Hispanic and Asian populations. Many of the elderly had died since my initial research in Rosedale in the late 1970s, but a small group of low-income whites remained there. They consisted of around 10 percent of the population in 1995. In terms of the growing gang crisis in the city, residents of Rosedale could only respond that all four gang types were present in the neighborhood. Conflict among the gangs became more and more prevalent between 1993 and 1995.

The increasing seriousness of the gang problem on the streets of Rosedale was evident in the crime statistics for 1991, 1992, and 1993. In 1991, Rosedale recorded an all-time high of 2,807 major crimes, including homicide, rape, robbery, and aggravated assault. Residents reported close to 1,000 burglaries and 900 thefts. Between 1992 and 1993, 18 murders were committed in Rosedale. During the same time period, 48 rapes occurred, along with 202 robberies, 430 aggravated assaults, 856 burglaries, 1,094 larceny thefts, and 320 auto thefts. Adolescents and young adults, typically males, were the primary perpetrators of crime in Rosedale. Media attention no longer focused on elderly white victims. Everyone left behind in Rosedale was a potential victim of crime.

To those who had worked so hard to save the community, by 1995 the message was becoming increasing clear. To those groups, agencies, and community activists who had tried so nobly to rebuild Rosedale's businesses, renovate its housing stock, and reconstruct its institutions, the community's vital signs were beginning to weaken and flicker. The diagnosis could no longer be denied. By the end of 1995, few of the prior advocates to rebuild Rosedale remained engaged in the struggle. Their prognosis for the community's future had moved well beyond denial, anger, depression, or bargaining. Like a physician viewing a seriously ill patient, they had come to accept the idea that Rosedale's problems were probably terminal. Gang graffiti was as prevalent as burglar bars and protective fences. Crack houses coexisted alongside residences occupied by children.

10

PUBLIC POLICY, SOCIAL CHANGE, AND THE FALL OF ROSEDALE

Shit happens.

—*Forrest Gump*

*In policy-making circles in Washington, the word "failed" has become perma-
nently grafted onto the War on Poverty and the Great Society. The general mental picture is one of a stupendous concatenation of wacky liberal ideas that were
launched for years, one after another, with unlimited funding, and that not only
didn't work, but actually made things worse by creating today's inner-city ghetto
underclass.*

—*Mark Abramowitz,* Washington Post, *May 1992*

THE CASE OF ROSEDALE OFFERS MANY LESSONS for those interested in
rebuilding urban neighborhoods. It also offers important lessons for those
desiring to manage racial transition and change in a more effective and humane manner. There are numerous ways to interpret the case of Rosedale. In
these final chapters, I will present my reactions to the story of Rosedale from
several vantage points. Each interpretation carries a distinct ideological and
philosophical perspective. Each perspective is accompanied by a set of assumptions identifying what went wrong in the community and who should
be responsible for making things right again. Some of the interpretations
portray Rosedale as a victim of institutional processes having origins outside
the community and beyond the reach of its residents. Other viewpoints im-

ply that the residents of Rosedale and local political leaders were authors of their own destiny and badly compromised the future of the neighborhood. I believe all interpretations hold some truth. I will leave to my critics and readers what portion of the truth each interpretation can rightfully claim.

Rosedale as a Victim of Social Change

The first interpretation is benign in its political assumptions and does not hold any group of individuals or political actors responsible for what took place in Rosedale. It does not require that major policy interventions be designed and implemented to manage or alter the fate of urban neighborhoods like Rosedale. The interpretation makes no moral judgments about race and racism. It is not premised upon any ethical or philosophical convictions promoting the rights of the elderly.

According to the interpretation, one may view the story of Rosedale as the inevitable result of economic and demographic changes. These changes have been altering the American urban landscape for at least four decades and are the product of larger population trends and corporate and individual decisions in the private marketplace. Many of these changes have been produced by global economic forces and the reorganization of the American industrial order.

Jane Jacobs in *The Death and Life of Great American Cities* observes that private market forces within urban regions initiate natural and systemic patterns of development, growth, and decline in cities.[1] Commenting on the processes through which slums emerge, she notes that many urban neighborhoods decline rapidly and remain depressed, whereas others experience redevelopment, rebirth, and regeneration. In fact, she claims, the creation of slums can serve positive developmental functions in cities because they provide a source of inexpensive housing for new immigrants: "If there were no slum dwellers or poor immigrants to inherit city failures, the problem of low-vitality neighborhoods abandoned by those with choice would still remain and perhaps would be even more troubling."[2]

This perspective is more fully developed in recent sociological analyses of regional growth and neighborhood deterioration. Drawing from invasion and succession theory, pioneered by what some social scientists call "the Chicago school" of urban development and change, contemporary analysts contend that "neighborhoods have a kind of life cycle. They begin new and full of promise, then tend to deteriorate and become less desirable."[3] Demographers Otis and Beverly Duncan identify various "phases" through which neighborhoods pass as control of urban space changes from one group to another.[4] According to them, racial transition consists of penetration, invasion, consolidation, and, finally, piling up. In the final phase, transition is complete and often accompanied by increasing rates of density, overcrowding, and the appearance of social pathologies.

Many urban planners and economists have also argued that natural patterns of neighborhood growth, development, and decline have functional and positive aspects for the city as a whole and should not necessarily be defined as dire social problems requiring expensive public-sector interventions and special development programs. The housing in neighborhoods abandoned by the middle class can "trickle down" to lower-income residents, usually at a reduced rental fee and a much lower purchase price. In fact, at about the same time that Rosedale began to decline as a viable urban neighborhood, some critics of liberal social programs for cities were introducing the concept of "urban triage" to the national debate over urban development policy.[5]

According to these policy analysts, certain areas of a city will inevitably decline. Rather than waste time and resources attempting to save these blighted geographic areas, it is more efficient, according to them, to simply let them decline and decay. Rather than squander limited developmental funds on blighted neighborhoods and continue to maintain a full array of public services and facilities there, city officials would be better advised to concentrate resources in communities with a higher potential to achieve revitalization. According to advocates of triage, public officials should simply abandon those areas with no chance of remaining prosperous.

Cities contemplating triage, according to advocates, could implement the idea in a manner that ranges from benign interventions (where limited or special funds are provided to selected communities) to draconian planning (where services and programs are deliberately terminated in order to encourage systematic evacuation). Summarizing triage policy, Peter Marcuse, Peter Medoff, and Andrea Pereira explain:

> If other neighborhoods are inevitably going to decline, given the macroeconomic and demographic circumstances beyond the control of public policy, then it could be argued that the continued expenditure of funds to preserve those neighborhoods at their old levels is only an attempt to hold back the tide. Better to accept and plan for the inevitable than to squander resources fighting it to no avail. There should be a net public savings from the strategy, it can be said: part of the savings could then be allocated to alleviating the hardships caused to those in the abandoned neighborhoods and assisting in relocating, retraining, or supporting in other ways their last remaining residents.[6]

Drawing from the triage argument, one might easily conclude that efforts to reverse or arrest Rosedale's fall from prior glory through heroic policy interventions were inefficient, a waste of public resources, and clearly destined to fail. Pursuing the logic of triage, one could also conclude that the signs of irreversible decay and decline were evident in Rosedale well before the initiation of major renovation efforts during the early 1980s. Save for the presence of Rosedale College and the fact that some prominent citizens and influential politicians grew up there, the neighborhood lacked the kinds of unique amenities and political resources that might qualify it for strategic renovation. Hindsight establishes that Rosedale was probably a poor candidate for neighborhood revitalization.

Unlike historic residential districts, the community lacked significant architecture. Most of the housing was of wooden bungalow design; small brick ranches and Cape Cod–type structures were also present. It was unlikely, therefore, that gentrification would emerge in the neighborhood. The original business district consisted primarily of 1920s storefronts close to the sidewalk with inadequate parking facilities. Although some grant funds were obtained on the basis of the historic and architectural significance of the storefronts, considerable lobbying efforts had to be expended in order to classify the commercial district in a manner that made it eligible for special funding. Many of those involved in the renovation effort privately conceded it was a stretch to classify Rosedale's storefronts as historically significant.

Critics of efforts to revitalize Rosedale, enlightened through hindsight, would undoubtedly argue that public officials responded more to political pressures than to rational planning arguments when they attempted to reverse the fortunes of the community. Rather than paying close attention to established demographic and migration trends and to obvious and severe downturns in the private housing market, officials appeared overly influenced by racial politics, the plight of the white elderly, and romanticized versions of Rosedale's grand history. Rather than reaching informed planning decisions about Rosedale's future, derived from hard-nosed cost-benefit analyses of current events and recent trends, officials chose instead to invest capital and energy in a losing enterprise. Influenced by high-profile politicians, corporate leaders, and liberal intellectuals, city officials compromised the future of other neighborhoods in the city by overinvesting in a futile effort to save Rosedale.

In the absence of moral and ethical counterpoints, the triage perspective is politically compelling. The logic of triage illuminates several components of the policy choices that were not made by those involved in efforts to revitalize Rosedale. Our case study makes it clear that cold economic reasoning and cost-benefit decisions did not characterize the early policy discussions about Rosedale's future. It was apparent that revitalization planning was influenced by the highly emotional press coverage and graphic depictions of the horrors experienced by the community's elderly white population. Policy choices were strongly influenced by efforts to retain Rosedale College in the community and to preserve the historical image of Rosedale held by its former residents and those influential citizens who had grown up there.

But in the face of consistent evidence that Rosedale could not be reclaimed, it eventually became clear to most parties that continued efforts to save the community were futile. Private foundations eventually withdrew financial support for various interventions. Federal, state, and local funds became increasingly difficult to obtain. By the early 1990s, technical support for planning and development was curtailed by the city. And although public funds were not expended to relocate the white elderly, most families ultimately insisted on relocating their aged relatives who remained there. Rosedale College played a major leadership role in efforts to renovate the neighborhood, but it should be remembered that earlier it too attempted to flee to the suburbs. But like many of the poor elderly who lacked the financial ability to move, in the end, the college was also left behind in Rosedale.

In retrospect, it matters little that the triage interpretation lacks a moral or ethical foundation as an interpretation of recent events in Rosedale. It matters little that a de facto triage policy was ultimately adopted by the city and other agencies and foundations involved in the renovation effort. And although triage planning clarifies the policy choices made or not made by public officials and community activists and enables critics to question the wisdom of the renovation effort, it is not necessary to apply the concept in order to view Rosedale as a victim of social change. During the 1960s and 1970s, urban neighborhoods in many American cities were rudely transformed by economic and demographic events beyond the influence of local officials and outside the reach of national urban policy. Americans are fond of believing that hard work and a positive attitude can alter the course of human events, but it is probably safe to conclude that the fate of Rosedale was inevitable, beyond the influence of any clever combination of national and local policy interventions no matter how sophisticated or well conceived these policies might have been.

The sources of these larger macroeconomic and demographic changes were numerous and were beginning to emerge long before Rosedale showed signs of neighborhood decline. The contemporary urban region emerged at the turn of the twentieth century as major cities became ringed with residential satellite communities outside their legal boundaries. From 1910 to 1970, nearly 95 percent of all population growth took place in metropolitan areas; more than half of this growth took place in the largest metropolitan regions.

The precursor of a metropolitan region with a declining central city and an expanding suburban fringe first began to emerge in the 1920s, a fact reflected in Rosedale's early debate over annexation. Before World War II, suburban growth involved only a limited number of households, was geographically restricted, and did not seriously threaten the dominance of the central city. This changed dramatically after 1945, when the suburban landscape exploded as veterans sought new housing in which to raise their families. The postwar suburbanization of America took place in nearly all the nation's metropolitan areas, thus starting the process that would culminate in the racial and socioeconomic polarization of the 1960s. Rosedale's fate, therefore, was shared by numerous urban neighborhoods throughout the nation and was determined well before the revitalization efforts of the 1980s or the demographic changes of the 1970s.

Suburbanization was driven not only by returning veterans but by a baby boom that would continue into the 1960s and that dramatically increased demand for housing, schools, and jobs. The exodus of white middle-income families to the suburbs was accompanied by the relocation of businesses, especially retailing, a fact that permanently altered the tax and revenue base of American cities.[7] At the same time, many central cities during the 1950s and 1960s were the destinations of a massive migration of blacks from the rural South. But unlike with prior immigration, African Americans were permanently segregated from the white population, first within selected neighborhoods and then within the central cities of metropolitan areas.[8]

Although the term "urban crisis" has been reserved for the 1960s, many central cities were in economic distress as early as 1955. By the end of the 1960s, the demographic and developmental patterns of metropolitan America were well established: growing metropolitan areas overall, within which suburbs coexisted uneasily with a declining and economically struggling central city. The central city was composed of a varying number of minorities, the poor, the elderly, and other socially disadvantaged groups. The culmination of this trend was accurately captured in 1968 by the National Advisory Commission on Civil Disorders, established to investigate the urban riots: The United States was "rapidly moving toward two increasingly separate Americas" composed of a "white society principally located in the suburbs . . . and a Negro society largely concentrated within large central cities."[9] The commission concluded that "within two decades, this division could be so deep that it would be almost impossible to reunite."[10]

Suburban population growth slowed in the 1970s but still accounted for most metropolitan growth. By 1977, African Americans had also begun to suburbanize in significant numbers. During the 1970s, the rate of the African American population in the suburbs increased faster than did that of whites and much faster than that of the black population in central cities.[11] Ironically, the beginnings of suburbanization among working- and middle-class blacks, a result of federal actions to end residential segregation, left some central-city neighborhoods with an intensified concentration of people with serious social and economic problems. During this process, many ghettos were transformed into slums. Rosedale was the prototype of this latter situation. Initially the destination of middle-class blacks, Rosedale deteriorated rapidly, and resegregation sealed the fate of the community as a casualty of social and economic change.

The restructuring of the American economy and the suburbanization of business and industry accelerated the demographic and employment changes occurring within the older, industrial cities.[12] Bluestone and Harrison report that between 32 million and 38 million jobs were lost during the

1970s.[13] The personal and social costs of deindustrialization were immense. In addition to lost wages and productivity, many workers and their families suffered physical and emotional disorders after losing their jobs. Cities lost revenues and became unable to sustain the provision of services to residents. Businesses closed in response to a drop in disposable income and ultimately in consumer spending. Higher levels of unemployment strained the demand on federal programs providing benefits to individuals and their families. The deindustrialization crises of the mid-1970s affected members of the white working class most severely, especially those living in older industrial cities.[14] By the end of the 1970s, it was clear that urban problems were no longer confined to minorities living in the core of America's metropolitan areas. Many of the negative traits associated with the central city had emerged over entire metropolitan regions, especially in the Northeast and Midwest. Rosedale was clearly in the path of these sweeping economic transformations, as deindustrialization affected Fort Worth more severely than Dallas.

Metropolitan growth revived in the 1980s: The nation's 284 metropolitan areas grew by 11.6 percent to reach 192.7 million residents by 1990, accounting for 77.5 percent of the U.S. population.[15] Although growth trends continued throughout the decade, they did not signal a revival of the central city but instead mirrored the rise of a dual or bifurcated economy.[16] By 1990, the urban landscape of the United States had evolved into a geography of metropolitan winners and losers. The largest metropolitan areas had become terminally fragmented, no longer tied together economically and socially by a dominant central city.[17] Los Angeles in 1992 best illustrates the growth of a bifurcated economy in which poverty and ethnic isolation persist in the midst of regional economic prosperity. The second largest metropolitan area with a 1990 population of 14.5 million, Los Angeles grew 26.4 percent in the 1980s. Far from being an effective economic strategy, downtown development simply provided corporations with the opportunity to move to newer quarters, leaving older buildings vacant in the process. There was no trickle down of jobs to south-central Los Angeles.

Much the same happened in other booming cities. Communities such as Lawndale in Chicago and Anacostia in Washington were still mired in poverty and blight. Even if the downtown redevelopment projects did not create new jobs, they did generate millions in new revenues for the cities. Much of these funds, however, simply replaced lost federal funding, cushioned inflation, covered the increasing costs of labor-intensive services such as firefighting and police protection, and financed programs dealing with new problems such as AIDS, the homeless, and the drug-related crime epidemic. In the 1980s, fragmented regional development and prosperity in Dallas–Fort Worth was similar to that found in L.A. And despite political rhetoric to the contrary, Rosedale became a lot like Watts.

Abramowitz points out that during the so-called urban boom of the 1980s, the number of Americans living in poverty increased from 27.4 million to 31.7 million, or 12.9 percent of the total U.S. population in 1990.[18] Of those 31.7 million people, nearly three-quarters, or 24.5 million, lived in metropolitan areas. Although much of the increase in the poverty population was in central cities, urban poverty was no longer a central-city phenomenon; by 1990, 42 percent of all metropolitan poor lived in the suburbs. In 1990, the suburbs of metropolitan areas contained a larger poverty population than did nonmetropolitan areas—10.2 million compared to 9.0 million. Two-thirds of the metropolitan poverty population was white (67.1 percent) and 32.9 percent was black. Hispanics (a nonracial census category) accounted for 23.6 percent of the metropolitan poor. The once attractive suburban community of Rosedale, by 1990, made its full contribution to the statistics describing national urban poverty.

Although there were more whites living in poverty in central cities than blacks—7.7 million compared to 5.8 million—the black poverty population was much more highly concentrated, 76.3 percent living in the central city.[19] Some 60 percent of Hispanic poor also lived in the central city. Conversely, slightly over half (51.2 percent) of all poor whites in the metropolitan areas lived in the suburbs. By the 1990s, then, although some of the most visible and worst concentrations of poverty were found in central cities, the geography of poverty in metropolitan areas was much more complex than it had been twenty years before, Rosedale again making its contribution to the trendy national data on poverty.

Another major change in the 1980s was that many central cities resumed their roles as hosts to new immigrants: Nearly 8.6 million people entered the country during the decade, "almost as many migrants as arrived from 1900 to 1910, the previous highwater mark of American immigration."[20] Historically New York, Philadelphia, and Boston have been the major magnets for immigration. In the 1980s, however, a greater number of immigrants came from Latin America and Asia; the large metropolitan areas on the West Coast and in the Southwest and Florida became immigrant magnets as well.[21] This immigration introduced new ethnic diversity into many metropolitan areas that was not without serious competition and conflict. By 1995, Rosedale mirrored the new ethnic diversity with a growing Hispanic and Asian population taking up residence alongside its poor African American neighbors.

Rosedale as a Victim of Liberal Public Policy

There are other ways to view and interpret the case of Rosedale. Larger demographic and economic changes surely altered the urban landscape, but they were not the only forces transforming American cities and their neighborhoods. Numerous public policies designed to bring about planned social change in cities were initiated after World War II. Planned social change is deliberate. Public policy intervention implies human volition and willful intent. Consequences typically follow deliberate policy interventions. Indeed, the purpose of deliberate intervention is to produce strategically planned consequences. Since the New Deal, public policy has been strongly influenced by a liberal political philosophy.

The purpose of liberal public policy is to use the government as an instrument of intervention in pursuit of the public good. Franklin Roosevelt eloquently described the political and moral premises of American liberalism in his second inaugural address, January 20, 1937:

> Our covenant with ourselves did not stop there. Instinctively, we recognized a deeper need—the need to find through government the instrument of our united purpose to solve for the individual the ever-rising problems of a complex civilization. Repeated attempts at their solution without the aid of government had left us baffled and bewildered. For, without that aid, we had been unable to create those moral controls over the services of science which are necessary to make science a useful servant instead of a ruthless master of mankind. To do this we knew that we must find practical controls over blind economic forces and blindly selfish men.[22]

In comparison to triage planning or trickle-down economics, liberal political philosophy is premised upon distinct moral and ethical imperatives. Unlike theories of social change that identify external forces that alter and shape human behavior and institutions, liberalism requires that interventions be designed to counter or mediate the negative effects of these forces. If these external forces, for example, produce negative economic consequences for individuals and families, it is the immediate responsibility of government to cushion the effects of these social events. It is the long-term responsibility of government to control or redirect these negative events and trends through strategic policy interventions or through social programs financed with public funds. Although acknowledging that changes in the private marketplace sometimes produce economic downturns and recessions, liberals believe that strategic government interventions can control the frequency with which these negative events occur. Not only can strategic policy interventions stabilize the marketplace and assist effective management of the business cycle, the government is morally and politically obligated to design interventions that ensure a minimum standard of living and provide equality of opportunity for all its citizens.

As Lowi explains, modern liberalism as a political philosophy has its origins in efforts to manage sharp downturns in the business cycle, especially those that emerged during the Great Depression.[23] Since the New Deal, however, a myriad of federal programs and governmental interventions have been enacted and implemented as part of the liberal policy agenda. These initiatives have extended far beyond initial efforts to implement

Keynesian economic theory in a manner that would enable government to manage the business cycle and remedy the worst effects of the Great Depression. They encompass government efforts to manage race relations, provide equality of educational opportunity, provide assistance to the poor and the elderly, service the educational needs of the population, provide special services for families and children, revitalize cities and their housing stock, and increase the employability of the urban underclass through special job-training programs, to mention only a few of the numerous liberal policy interventions enacted since World War II.

Despite its auspicious beginnings in the New Deal, liberal political philosophy and the public policies derived from it have been widely criticized over the past two decades. Whereas liberalism has strongly influenced the political debate over public policy since the New Deal, its current stature is tarnished. Partisan political debate over the appropriate role of government in private affairs has been especially heated over the past decade. And for more than one week in November 1995, the federal government was partially shut down, largely in response to partisan political debate over balancing the federal budget and sharp disagreement over various proposals to target for elimination the remaining vestiges of the liberal welfare state.

Much of current political debate over public policy and the course of American liberalism is directly relevant to the case of Rosedale. Critics of liberal public policy claim that governmental interventions reinforced rather than altered the negative social trends that undermined cities and their neighborhoods.[24] Rather than solving for individuals and families the increasingly serious problems of urban life, governmental interventions, according to critics, actually made them worse. Supporters of liberalism, however, strongly contend that without government intervention, cities and their inhabitants would be worse off than they are currently. In fact, most supporters of continued governmental interventions argue that the gutting of liberal social programs explains why urban problems have persisted and appear to have gotten worse in the 1990s. Many contend that budget cuts and further reductions in social welfare programs will increase the duration and amount of social pathologies presently found in cities.[25]

Irrespective of the perspective one brings to the current debate over welfare reform, the need to balance the federal budget, or the proper role of government in the private marketplace, it is clear that partisan political debate over liberalism has produced a serious policy quagmire for the nation. In order to elaborate on this policy quagmire, it is useful to review the liberal policy agenda and explain its relationship to the case of Rosedale. From 1948 through the early 1960s, federal urban policy focused on housing, a policy initiative actually begun under the New Deal but fully articulated in the Housing Act of 1948. Slum clearance and the building of public housing were translated into downtown revitalization through Urban Renewal with the 1954 amendments to the 1948 act. Modification of the interstate highway program in the late 1950s and early 1960s placed priority on building interstate highways in urban areas.

The Great Society programs that followed in the 1960s were less a response to urban development problems than to broader social issues: civil rights, poverty, equality of educational opportunity, and the health care needs of the elderly. The major programmatic interventions included the War on Poverty; the Economic Opportunity Act, passed in 1964; the Model Cities and Metropolitan Development Act of 1966; and the Housing Act of 1968.[26] The Comprehensive Employment Training Act (CETA) and Urban Mass Transit Grant Programs were initiated during the Nixon administration. The Carter administration essentially continued the "new federalism" initiated by President Nixon in 1972, shifted more block-grant funds to cities in the Northeast and Midwest, ordered the Department of Housing and Urban Development to use 75 percent of CDBG funds in low-income areas, and established the Urban Development Action Grant.[27]

All of these policy initiatives occurred at a critical time in Rosedale's recent history. The early phases of racial transition in Rosedale began during the 1960s. School desegregation became a major political issue in the Dallas–Fort Worth metropolitan area in the early 1970s. A court order to desegregate Fort Worth's public schools was issued in 1973. Throughout the 1970s, in response to the order, white flight from Rosedale intensified. By the late 1970s, the Rosedale rapist episode racially polarized the city, as did the wilding attacks that occurred in the early 1980s. By 1980, the deterioration of Rosedale's community institutions had become a serious social problem. A case can be made that liberal social programs contributed to the fall of Rosedale.

According to critics, liberal urban policy consistently lagged far behind the demographic and developmental trends that altered American cities and transformed them into metropolitan regions. Policy initiatives were sporadic and uncoordinated.[28] Urban problems were treated in isolation from their demographic, political, and economic causes. Urban renewal, according to critics, was implemented without regard to a growing historic preservation movement or the housing needs of the urban poor. Urban renewal was pursued in isolation from an overall downtown redevelopment plan and without adequate attention to the housing needs of those displaced by the "federal bulldozer."[29]

Federal housing programs, according to critics, were implemented without regard for school desegregation policy and other important initiatives in the civil rights arena. While the federal government sought to provide more shelter for low- and moderate-income families, housing officials and community activists paid little or no attention to the fact that most federal programs actually reinforced existing patterns of racial segregation or assisted in the resegregation of communities. Efforts to provide equality of educational opportunity and desegregate the nation's schools were actually undermined by HUD programs designed to expand the housing choices among the urban poor, such as Section 8 rental, public housing, and FHA and VA loan programs. It was not until the latter years of the Carter administration that efforts were finally made to bring a moderate degree of coordination among urban policies in housing, education, and civil rights.[30]

Community development programs, according to critics, were also implemented in an uncoordinated and unsystematic manner. In the face of long-term urban development trends, neither the Community Development Block Program nor Urban Action Grant funds could alter the growing polarization between city and suburb. Nor could they reverse the outward migration of people and capital to the suburbs. Federal revitalization programs were poorly conceived in Washington, badly coordinated among various governmental jurisdictions, and inadequately monitored at the local level.[31] Funds were often spent on questionable projects or maneuvered into programs not initially authorized by federal legislation.[32] The construction of highways assisted the growth of suburbs, thus undermining the vitality of the central cities. And the FHA and VA loan programs directly contributed to suburban rather than urban growth and development.

Social welfare policies, according to critics, were implemented without adequate attention to the erosion of jobs in the manufacturing sector and in isolation from job-training and economic development strategies. Many social welfare programs designed during the War on Poverty era made important contributions to the lives of the urban poor,[33] but they did little to bring the marginal classes of urban society closer to the economic mainstream. Programs to enfranchise the urban poor in city politics were not coordinated with established party processes. As a result, community action programs conflicted with local party machinery in many cities and produced what Daniel Moynihan called a "maximum feasible misunderstanding" over how to manage the War on Poverty.[34] Critics of the AFDC and food stamps programs argued that dependency on federal welfare undermined established family patterns, reduced the incentive to work, and perpetuated intergenerational poverty.[35] The relationship between the fall of Rosedale and the liberal policy agenda is illustrated most clearly through analysis of the way in which federal housing and school desegregation policies were implemented in the Dallas–Fort Worth metropolitan area.

Federal Housing Policy, School Desegregation, and the Fall of Rosedale

There is little doubt that federal housing and school desegregation policy contributed to suburban growth and development in the Dallas–Fort Worth metropolitan region and reinforced racial segregation in both cities. Various

components of the liberal housing agenda not only reinforced suburbanization but also contributed to the resegregation of urban neighborhoods and
their schools. Public-housing policy has typically been implemented without
adequate consideration of national and local goals in the educational arena.
In fact, housing policies during the 1930s and 1940s were explicitly racist in
intent and consequence.[36] Falk and Franklin maintain:

> Federal mortgage insurance through the Federal Housing Administration and
> the Veterans Administration assured the availability of long-term mortgages
> with low down payments and reasonable monthly payments to the average
> American homebuyer. FHA policies, however, promoted racially restrictive
> covenants in deeds of homes with insured mortgages until the *Shelley v.
> Kramer* decision (1948). . . . Federally assisted housing for lower income fami-
> lies was never built in the newer suburbs. The public housing agencies in the
> urban centers built substantial quantities of housing, but almost always in
> lower income or black neighborhoods.[37]

Because early federal housing activities were consistent with discriminatory practices taking place in the larger society, public policy directly contributed to the emergence of serious social problems in the educational
arena. Segregated schools are partly the product of segregated neighborhoods. When the Supreme Court ruled in 1954 that racial segregation in
the public schools was incompatible with the goal of equal educational opportunity, it was obvious that federal housing policies, along with the real
estate industry, private builders, and developers as well as mortgage finance
institutions, were among the main contributors to racial isolation in the
public schools. Although the schools themselves obviously contributed to
racial segregation, they were ordered by the courts to rectify inequities
largely originating in the housing and real estate industries and perpetuated
by the federal government.

Public housing has its origins in New Deal legislation, in particular the
National Industrial Recovery Act of 1933 (NIRA). The United States Housing Act of 1937 succeeded NIRA and provided the framework through
which low-rent public housing was provided to the nation. Falk and
Franklin maintain that most of the nation's public housing was constructed
between 1934 and 1960; this was also the most active and durable period
in federal housing policy.[38] During this period, decisions about site selection were made primarily by local housing authorities in association with
the federal government. Early federal programs provided the bulk of the
nation's public housing supply. "By 1973, 1,260,000 units of public housing, constituting approximately 1.5% of the nation's housing stock, were
under construction or under management."[39] Other major housing policies
were established during this time period as well: Urban Renewal, the Federal Housing Administration, and the Veterans Administration.

According to many historians and critical analysts, early housing policy was explicitly racist in nature.[40] "White" and "black" projects were the norm in public housing. The FHA and VA programs were riddled with racial biases: Falk and Franklin mince no words when they observe that "overtly segregationist policies were pursued by FHA and VA until 1948, and then continued in effect under the guise of 'sound underwriting practices' until the 1960s."[41] It is estimated that between 1950 and 1968 the urban renewal program destroyed about 2.38 million units.[42] The areas slated for "renewal" were usually located in low-income minority neighborhoods. The units that were destroyed were typically replaced with commercial structures or high-rent multifamily dwellings.

Dallas–Fort Worth, like most other urban regions, reveals a typical racist history when it comes to the programs initiated during this first phase (1934–1960) of federal housing policy. There is little doubt that FHA and VA policies strongly contributed to white flight and the associated suburbanization of the region. HUD officials maintain that the bulk of FHA and VA loans have gone to the suburban communities surrounding the Dallas–Fort Worth metropolitan area.[43] Fox and Jacobs, located in Dallas, is one of the largest suburban developers in the nation.[44] In response to charges that the firm helped engineer a white exodus from the central city, David Fox, president of the firm, responded in the late 1970s that FHA mortgage policies had largely underwritten a major proportion of the suburban housing market in the Dallas–Fort Worth metropolitan area.[45] Although it would obviously be incorrect to argue that FHA and VA policies were the primary causes of the blockbusting and white flight that occurred in Rosedale during the late 1960s and 1970s, it is reasonable to conclude they were contributing factors.

It is also clear that suburbanization in the Dallas–Fort Worth metropolitan area contributed to racial isolation in the city schools. The school districts surrounding the two cities are predominantly white in racial composition. The lack of housing mobility on a regional basis for minority families partially explains why the city schools became increasingly segregated during the 1960s and 1970s. Like many urban regions in the nation, the Dallas–Fort Worth metropolitan area is characterized by minority central cities surrounded by white suburbs. The conflict over Rosedale's neighborhood schools, therefore, was partially a product of federal and private housing policy.

The relationship between public-housing policies and racial segregation in Fort Worth and Dallas further illustrates this latter observation. Between 1937 and 1974, over 7,000 units of public housing were constructed in Dallas.[46] The bulk of these units (about 95 percent) were constructed as conventional multifamily structures. A much smaller proportion (about 5 percent) were single-family units. By 1980, 97 percent of all public-housing units in the city of Dallas were located in census tracts having a larger concentration of minorities and low-income families than the city as a whole. Comparable figures were reported for Fort Worth. By 1980, 87 percent of all public-housing units were located within the city limits of Fort Worth. Nearly all units have been one-race facilities for more than three decades, and no new facilities have been built since 1953.

The bulk of Dallas and Fort Worth's public-housing stock was constructed during the 1950s. In Dallas, six projects were completed between 1950 and 1954, representing a total of about 4,300 dwelling units. These units constituted about 4.7 percent of the new housing stock constructed in the city during the 1950s. According to 1950 and 1960 census data, about 65 percent of the units in Dallas were located in areas that were nearly 100 percent minority or in areas with minority concentration ratios in excess of the city average. By 1980, African American families composed over 90 percent of the tenant population in these projects; comparable figures are found for public-housing units located in Fort Worth. Public housing, either by design or outcome, concentrated minority families within specific geographic areas of both cities.

Although no public-housing projects were located in Rosedale, the concentration of minorities in these types of dwellings had direct ramifications for educational policy in the metropolitan area. The degree of racial isolation in public housing has obvious implications for segregation in the public schools.[47] Since public housing typically has a fairly high proportion of tenants with school-age children, the educational facilities serving these areas were, by the mid-1970s, largely one-race institutions. Whereas public-housing policy should not be singled out as the primary cause of racial isolation in the public schools, it is safe to say that early site selection procedures strongly contributed to problems that later emerged in the educational arena. Because Rosedale still contained a supply of white children, it was initially targeted as a critical part of the school desegregation plan adopted by the Fort Worth Independent School District in the early 1970s. By the late 1970s, however, so many white families with children had left the neighborhood that Rosedale became an irrelevant component of the school district's busing plan.

The second major period in federal housing policy began in 1960 and ended during the mid-1970s. During this period, site selection was primarily in the hands of private developers. This period witnessed the passage of the Section 202 program, initially designed to provide housing for the elderly. Through federally guaranteed loans and other incentives, the private sector began to play a stronger role in the delivery and provision of housing. Also during this period, Section 221(d)(3) was passed, making below-market-interest-rate (BMIR) loans to profit and nonprofit entities interested in constructing multifamily housing units. The Section 235 and 236 programs also became part of the federal housing agenda. These programs made it possible for private developers to build single-family and multifamily units with financial support from the Department of Housing and Urban Development. Additionally, rental-supplement programs were formulated in 1966. These programs generated a tremendous amount of activity in the housing construction industry. Falk and Franklin estimate that in 1970, the peak of activity during this period, "total subsidized housing starts constituted 29.3% of the year's total new housing production."[48]

The implementation of these programs in the Dallas–Fort Worth region did not reinforce racial segregation as directly as did public housing. Analysis shows, however, that although units were not initially placed in minority census tracts, most were adjacent to segregated areas. Most of these areas eventually became one-race communities. Between 1960 and 1973, for example, about 4,364 units were constructed in Dallas under the 221(d)(3) BMIR program. These units represent around 2 percent of the new housing stock added to the city of Dallas between 1960 and 1970. Some units within these structures were also designated to be included as part of the Section 8 set-aside program. Most of the BMIR units, about 86 percent, were initially located in predominantly white neighborhoods. Officials in the Dallas area HUD office indicate, however, that by 1980, 21 percent of the BMIR units were located within "concentrated" census tracts.[49]

Examination of placements associated with the 221(d)(3) rental-supplement program reveals similar patterns. Between 1969 and 1975, 1,282 units were made available through this program in Dallas. This amounted to about 0.6 percent of the new housing units added to Dallas's supply between 1960 and 1970. About 62 percent of the units were initially placed in tracts with very high concentrations of African American residents. As of June 1980, however, these units were 99 percent African American in tenant racial composition. At that time, HUD officials reported that 91 percent of all 221(d)(3) rental-supplement units were located in "concentrated" areas. Figures for Fort Worth showed comparable patterns for both BMIR and 221(d)(3) programs.[50]

The various federal "leasing" programs were established during the mid-1960s. Although several of the programs were modified significantly in 1974 with the passage of the Housing and Community Development Act, the various Section 8 plans have their origins in 1960s legislation. Like the previous programs established during what has been called the "second phase" of federal housing policy, the several Section 8 schemes were implemented in a way that reinforced racial segregation in the Dallas–Fort Worth metropolitan area.

The Section 8 set-aside program provided an additional 2,790 units to Dallas's housing supply between 1963 and 1972. A lesser amount was added to Fort Worth's housing supply during this period. Of those units made available in Dallas, about 50 percent were initially placed in predominantly black census tracts. As of June 1980, African American residents composed nearly 100 percent of the tenant population in these units. Like many of the 221a(d)(3) projects, however, further analysis showed that the remaining 50 percent were often located in areas revealing a high potential to change from white to black. Very similar patterns were found in the geographic distribution of Section 8 rental units in Fort Worth.

By 1980, officials at the Dallas Housing Authority and HUD personnel reported that participation in the Section 8 existing program had substantially increased in both Dallas and Fort Worth. By the end of 1970, African Americans composed about 51 percent of the Section 8 tenant population; whites accounted for about 45 percent of tenants, Hispanics about 3 percent, and 1 percent fell in the residual "other" category. Housing officials indicated, however, that about 75 percent of the white tenants were elderly. And although the spatial distribution of tenants was not available for analysis, housing officials estimated that fairly high levels of concentration characterized the entire Section 8 program. That is, black tenants probably resided in predominantly African American neighborhoods, and white tenants found apartment accommodations in white areas of the city.

Under the 236 subsidy production program implemented between 1970 and 1973, the owner of rental units could pass on the benefit of lower interest rates to economically depressed tenants. These units constituted a small proportion of the increase in residential dwellings added to Dallas's and Fort Worth's housing stocks during the 1970s. Only about 10 percent of these units were located in complexes found within predominantly African American neighborhoods. Reflecting the racial composition of the neighborhood, nearly 100 percent of the tenants in those units were African Americans as of June 1980. The vast majority of units supplemented through the 236 program—over 7,590—were found in predominantly white areas of the metropolitan area. Closer examination shows, however, that many of these areas were placed very close to communities in the midst of rapid racial transition.

All the programs initiated during the second phase of federal housing policy, then, showed a high degree of association with racial segregation in the metropolitan region. In one way or another, federal programs concentrated housing opportunities for minority families. Because spatial deconcentration of minority housing opportunities was not a goal associated with the implementation of these programs, racial isolation in the public schools was an inevitable consequence.

The implementation of federal housing policy reinforced racial isolation in the public schools and contributed directly to the educational problems experienced in the community of Rosedale. Throughout the 1970s and 1980s, the suburbs between Dallas and Fort Worth were extremely reluctant to participate in federal housing programs; some jurisdictions rejected federal housing assistance altogether because the social costs of integration were considered too high. Statistics show very few federally assisted housing units being constructed in the suburbs between the two cities and only a modest number of Section 8 rental units being available in these communities.[51] In the late 1970s and early 1980s, both Dallas and Fort Worth experienced highly visible political turmoil and widespread public opposition over federal plans to locate new public-housing projects in suburban communities.[52] Angry white residents in four different Fort Worth suburban neighborhoods forced the city to table plans to locate public-housing projects in their communities.

The school desegregation plan was implemented in Fort Worth in the mid-1970s, but patterns of white flight, reinforced by federal housing policy, were established well before that time and nearly complete by 1980. As long as white residents could flee to the suburbs, the problems of racial isolation in the public schools were not going to be solved through busing, magnet schools, or other widely promoted educational reform programs.[53] As long as suburbs refused to participate in federal housing programs, they could escape the social costs of school desegregation. Legally, the federal government could do little to order suburbs to participate in the regional implementation of housing and educational desegregation plans. Whereas the Millikan case provided some legal precedent upon which to base school desegregation policy within a single district, it did not address policy across school districts; nor did it address racial isolation in neighborhoods or in public-housing policy.[54]

By the early 1980s, as part of its housing-assistance plan, the federal government was requiring cities to make concerted efforts to scatter new housing construction in either integrated or predominantly nonminority areas. This policy, however, was an extremely difficult one to implement in the Dallas–Fort Worth metropolitan area. Although new federally assisted housing could be scattered throughout the two cities, it could not be scattered throughout the metropolitan region without the cooperation of suburbs.

By 1982, development of the Area-wide Housing Opportunities Plan (AHOP) had been pending in the Dallas–Fort Worth area for nearly five years. The North Central Texas Council of Governments (COG) had been attempting for several years to broker a plan that might be acceptable to the various localities that composed the region. The suburbs in the Dallas–Fort Worth region were not particularly interested, however, in becoming involved in efforts that might increase their minority populations. Neither were suburban political leaders particularly interested in attracting public-housing projects to their communities. And the regional COG was not particularly interested in alienating its wealthy suburban members.

At a conference on site selection and school desegregation held at the Institute of Urban Studies, University of Texas at Arlington, in 1981, the mayors of Arlington and Fort Worth exchanged barbs on the topic of public housing. The mayor of Fort Worth observed that Arlington was a rather peculiar place to hold a conference on the topic of site selection, school desegregation, and public housing. The conference should have been held, he contended, in either Dallas or Fort Worth, where the housing and school desegregation problems actually occurred. The suburbs, he observed, were hiding from the real problems of urban life and were not carrying their fair share of responsibility on the question of minorities, school desegregation, and public housing. The mayor of Arlington, in response, talked about the beautiful weather, the budding trees in the community, and what a fine day it would be to go fishing.

By the mid-1980s, school desegregation and busing had taken their toll on the white residents of Rosedale. Although the school desegregation plans in both Dallas and Fort Worth made extensive use of one-way busing and magnet schools, neither city could retain enough whites in the district to achieve racial balance in its public educational institutions. By 1985, Rosedale High School was again a one-race school. In October 1984, the school district reported that 82.2 percent of students at Rosedale High School were of African American descent, 10.5 percent were white, 6.0 percent were Hispanic, and 1.3 percent were Asian. The school district also reported that between 1979 and 1985, the number of students attending Rosedale High School dropped from 1,293 to 1,032. Between 1976 and 1985, the number of students graduating from Rosedale High School dropped from 324 to 185. And by 1985, it ranked ninety-fifth out of 116 public schools in the city in the rate of transiency among its student body.

The 1980s brought further shifts in national urban policy. After assuming the presidency in 1980, Reagan began to move rapidly to privatize public-sector institutions and programs and to disassemble the liberal policy agenda. As part of a widespread movement to privatize the production and distribution of public goods and services, many of the social programs of the preceding thirty years were systematically dismantled during the 1980s. Between 1981 and 1983, expenditures allocated to nondefense programs steadily dropped as both a percentage of the gross national product and in absolute dollar figures.[55] The major targets for budget reductions included social security, Medicare and Medicaid, higher education and student loans, aid to disadvantaged school districts, unemployment insurance, housing assistance and grants for urban development, grants for job training and creation, financial aid to the poor and the elderly, grants for urban social services, and legal assistance to the poor.

The federal budgets for 1984 and 1985 also revealed significant cuts in social program expenditures. Budget reductions in 1986 targeted the Department of Housing and Urban Development; the Small Business Administration; the community development block-grant program; the Urban Development Action Grant program; Aid to Families with Dependent Children and other social welfare services and benefits; Medicare and Medicaid; education, training, and employment assistance programs; and urban transportation for additional cuts in federal assistance.[56] The federal reorganization of social programs was coupled with the transfer to state and local governments of the responsibility for administering those programs, but according to federally mandated funding levels.

At the same time that federal funding of urban and social programs was being cut, the federal deficit burgeoned. In 1983, an Urban Institute report examining the American economy predicted that the annual federal deficit was on a course that would ultimately exceed $200 billion by 1984 and $300 billion by the end of the decade.[57] These projections proved accurate through 1986. In 1985, the deficit was approximately $212 billion; it rose to $221 billion in 1986. With the passage of the Gramm-Rudman bill, efforts were made to bring the federal deficit under control, thus creating even more political pressure to cut urban programs. In 1987, the deficit dropped to $149 billion, and it remained relatively stable through 1989. In 1990, however, the federal deficit exceeded $220 billion, and in 1991 it increased to a record $268 billion. By 1992 the Bush administration presided over the largest deficit in history.

The 1980s were also a critical period in Rosedale's most recent developmental history. During that time, most of the programs to rebuild the community were designed and implemented. The commercial redevelopment strategy was launched during the latter part of 1980, as was the effort to renovate the community's housing stock. Numerous program interventions were conceived at the local level and implemented with the financial assistance of state, federal, and private foundation grants. It is important to note that Rosedale's redevelopment strategy was executed during a period of major shifts in public policy and throughout an era in which massive cuts in federal spending occurred. The impact of these cuts on Rosedale's redevelopment strategy was significant, especially by 1990. Additionally, public support for liberal public policy had significantly eroded by the early 1990s.

Irrespective of declining federal funds and growing skepticism over the effectiveness of the liberal policy agenda, there were critical flaws in the various redevelopment strategies themselves. Like the implementation of housing policies at the national level, local development strategies were problematic and did little to alter the magnitude of the community's growing problems. Although the Community Development Act and the "new federalism" gave regional jurisdictions greater autonomy to design local solutions to urban problems, they did not ensure that homegrown interventions were going to be more effective than national solutions. In the face of larger economic and demographic changes, local officials were equally powerless to implement their development plans no matter how ingenious or resourceful those plans might have been. Moreover, by the mid-1980s, available funds to accomplish redevelopment were simply not available. The fiscal crisis made it virtually impossible for the city to prevent the fall of Rosedale.

The commercial revitalization plan was destined to fail without dramatic increases in the disposable income of Rosedale's residents. Without jobs and steady employment, the residents of Rosedale were simply not in a position to support local merchants. Likewise, there was precious little likelihood that residents living outside the community would travel there to shop. Government grants assisted in the revitalization of storefronts, but the image of Rosedale as a high-crime community did little to enhance its appeal as a place to travel in order to patronize local businesses. Limited public finds enabled the community to repair sidewalks and improve the community's infrastructure, but the image of Rosedale as a crime-infested neighborhood did little to facilitate window-shopping or browsing in the newly renovated shops along the major commercial district.

Whereas the new federalism created greater autonomy at the local level, the block-grant program did little to increase the participation of local residents in development planning or to reduce turf conflicts among competing community agencies and social service programs. In many respects, the block-grant program simply transferred political and financial dependency of community residents from the federal to local and state governments. The homegrown commercial redevelopment plan did not empower the residents of Rosedale any more than did federal housing policy, Urban Renewal, or Model Cities.

The primary problem with Rosedale's economic revitalization plan was that it did not create any permanent economic institutions within the community or create any new jobs. No wealth was created in the community; nor was any permanent cash flow created in the form of wages, rents, or profits. Once external grant funds were expended or grant funds were no longer available, the activities with which they were associated also ceased to exist. The private market in Rosedale was hopelessly shattered, and temporary cash infusions from external grant funds did little to repair the local economy or reinvigorate spending in the neighborhood.

The capital invested in Rosedale's housing market was largely derived from grants and private foundations. Home mortgage funds and home improvement loans were typically made available at below-market rates and independent of private market forces or normal evaluations of credit and ability to pay. Because few residents of Rosedale had incomes sufficient to make mortgage payments or maintain a home, many residences were eventually sold to absentee landlords. Rents obtained by absentee landlords did not remain in the community and were, therefore, seldom invested in the support of local merchants or services. The artificial market created by below-market housing programs made available through Neighborhood Housing Services and related nonprofit development agencies did little to create permanent economic institutions in the community or restore the private-housing market.

In the face of strong competition from the suburban housing market, absentee landlords were forced to turn to Section 8 housing programs in order to meet their own mortgage obligations. Section 8 too created an artificial housing market and sustained the diversion of rental income outside the community. Faced with few incentives to maintain their properties, absentee landlords were able to defer maintenance, an option made possible because federal funds subsidized their mortgage debts. And if routine maintenance was not required to attract tenants, job opportunities for local plumbers, electricians, and carpenters were reduced.

In the face of increasing federal deficits and declining support for liberal public policy, Rosedale's revitalization plans had little chance for success. In the absence of federal financial support for local policy interventions and with increasing skepticism over the government's ability to solve urban problems, it is not at all surprising that efforts to revitalize Rosedale failed. It is easy to recognize deficiencies in the liberal policy agenda; it is far more difficult to identify a productive course of action to resolve the underlying racial conflicts that undermined the community of Rosedale. Racism was a major factor contributing to the fall of Rosedale. Very few American cities have managed racial transition and change in an effective manner.

The case of Rosedale raises as many issues about community development policy and strategies of neighborhood revitalization as it does about race relations in American society. Ultimately, however, neighborhood decline might be a much less serious social problem if we were able to control the process of racial transition more effectively. It is perhaps fitting, therefore, that I have saved the most difficult policy questions raised by the case of Rosedale for the final chapter.

11

RACE RELATIONS, SOCIAL JUSTICE, AND THE FUTURE OF URBAN NEIGHBORHOODS

We have to get together and remove the evils, the vices, alcoholism, drug addiction, and other evils that are destroying the moral fiber of our community. We ourselves have to lift the level of our community, the standard of our community to a higher level, make our own society beautiful so that we will be satisfied in our own social circles and won't be running around here trying to knock our way into a social circle where we're not wanted.

—*Malcolm X, 1964*

When we let freedom ring, when we let it ring from every village and every hamlet, from every state and every city, we will be able to speed up that day when all of God's children, black men and white men, Jews and Gentiles, Protestants and Catholics, will be able to join hands and sing in the words of an old Negro spiritual, "Free at last! free at last! thank God almighty, we are free at last!"

—*Martin Luther King, Jr., 1963*

Can we all get along?

—*Rodney King, 1992*

RACIAL OPPRESSION IN AMERICAN SOCIETY has claimed the lives of many people. Slavery was conceived and sustained by violence. The war bringing slavery to an end was the most violent in our nation's history. Lynchings and beatings were common in the South, especially during the late 1890s and early 1900s. Race riots have been a prominent part of American urban history. Between 1906 and 1943, serious race riots occurred regularly in cities, with major disturbances erupting in Springfield, Ohio; Atlanta, Georgia; Springfield, Illinois; Tulsa, Oklahoma; East St. Louis, Missouri; Washington, D.C.; and Chicago.[1] During the 1940s and 1950s, Detroit, Los Angeles, Chicago, and Harlem were the sites of extreme racial conflict.[2] And in the 1960s and 1970s, Detroit, New York, Newark, Watts, Bedford-Stuyvesant, Philadelphia, and Boston were only a few locations where urban racial violence claimed lives and property.[3]

Racism has severely affected the civil rights of minorities, undermining their opportunities to earn a decent living, pursue educational goals, and exercise other routine liberties taken for granted by members of the majority. Racism has hunted and claimed other quarry as well. The community of Rosedale was a casualty of America's racial legacy. Rosedale did not pass through the period of racial transition in a smooth or harmonious manner. Residential integration was not desired or pursued by the white residents of Rosedale. Racial harmony was never identified by them as a valued objective. Most of the white residents made it clear through their deeds and actions that they were not willing to coexist in the same community with African Americans.

When it became clear to the white families of Rosedale that federal policies to ensure equality of educational opportunity and open housing could no longer be resisted, they simply moved to the suburbs. In the suburbs, they could continue living in white neighborhoods and send their children to neighborhood schools that were largely exempt from federal desegregation orders.

Like all accounts of racial victimization, the story of Rosedale is a tragic one. As stated in the opening chapter, the story of Rosedale is rooted in racial oppression and inequality. It is about insensitivity and neglect. The case of Rosedale chronicles the failure of public officials, business leaders, and community residents to manage the process of racial change in an effective and humane manner. The story documents the failure of both white and African American citizens, of both white elderly and minority underclass families, to forge any sense of solidarity, respect, and mutual support during the process of institutional and cultural change. The fate of Rosedale is not unique. Numerous other urban neighborhoods in American cities have been equally ineffective in managing racial change, have suffered comparable heartbreak, and have shared similar destinies.

We know from recent history that very few cities have managed racial change in a competent and constructive fashion. Urban planners and sociologists tell us that the case of Rosedale is the norm rather than the exception. The major fair-housing law in the United States is Title VIII of the Civil Rights Act of 1968. The act was recently expanded in 1988 under the

Fair Housing Amendments Act. Urban planner Richard Smith maintains that after twenty-five years of experience with Title VIII, efforts to achieve racial integration have accomplished very little: "While levels of discrimination in US cities have, arguably, declined, levels of segregation have been reduced only minimally and much of this reduction appears to derive more from the deconcentration of ghetto areas than from the creation of integrated living patterns."[4]

Although Donald DeMarco and George Galster are generally optimistic about the future of integrated neighborhoods, they reach similar conclusions. They report that most multiracial neighborhoods are only temporary aberrations and will eventually resegregate and become one-race communities.[5] According to them, stable and integrated communities require a unique set of policy interventions and innovative political leadership. After examining recent evidence describing the process of racial and ethnic change in the Los Angeles metropolitan area, urban geographer William Clark pessimistically concludes: "The process of neighborhood transition is not creating mixed integrated tracts in very large numbers and, although there are differences between the old automatic patterns of white to minority neighborhood transition, there is still a strong tendency for continuing change to minority predominance once it has been initiated."[6]

Sociologist Harvey Molotch argues that public policies designed to manage the process of racial transition will probably fail. Taking a position similar to Jane Jacobs's and consistent with the logic of triage theory, Molotch suggests that urban neighborhoods inevitably age and decline and eventually lose their attractiveness to white, middle-class consumers.[7] Middle-class consumers have many more housing options available to them in comparison to minorities entering the housing market. Normal housing turnover, made possible by residential mobility among white consumers, creates housing opportunities in neighborhoods vacated by them. As a result of strong but normal market processes, racial change in many urban neighborhoods is very difficult to reverse or control through strategic policy interventions.

Economist George Galster views efforts to achieve stable, integrated communities in a similar manner. Racial steering in the real estate industry to increase the volume of housing choices available to middle-class whites makes residential integration a desirable but elusive policy objective.[8] He observes: "Whites' preferences for predominantly white neighborhoods must be understood as a contingent product of twentieth-century urban racial history. This history is characterized by decades of racial residential separation, explicitly enforced by a host of private and public actions, institutional practices, and statutes, coupled with large secular growth in urban black populations."[9]

In order to manage racial transition more effectively, urban neighborhoods need the support and wisdom of external agencies and political bodies.[10] Public officials have regional or metropolitan responsibilities and are not usually able to invest the time and resources necessary to address problems occurring in one area or neighborhood. The problem of gathering sufficient external support to reverse neighborhood decline, an event that often accompanies racial transition, was clearly evident in the Rosedale case. Public recognition of Rosedale's problems was eventually mobilized, but long after racial change was in its advanced stages.

In East Cleveland the rate of racial change and community transformation and decline was comparable to that occurring in Rosedale. Urban planner Dennis Keating reports that between 1960 and 1965, 159 out of 172 real estate parcels in one part of this community changed hands at least once.[11] Although white residents were wary of the racial changes confronting the community, they took no direct action to deal with the issues before them. In the face of increasing evidence that racial transition was occurring in the schools and in the neighborhoods, panic selling was initiated in the early 1960s. According to Keating, city leadership failed to act decisively and made only inept attempts to manage the rapid escalation of real estate transactions in the community. Committed to a free market economic philosophy and convinced that any form of public intervention in the community might block minority access to newly emerging housing opportunities, the city manager made only token efforts to curb white flight.

The city did initiate contacts with the local real estate community and asked that it not contribute to the process of white flight by encouraging panic selling or assist in blockbusting activities. These efforts were not effective. Keating reports that the city manager's office failed (1) to make public pronouncements designed to show leadership in the face of rapid racial transition, (2) to alleviate white fears over the process of racial change, and (3) to deal forcefully with the real estate industry, whose practices were accelerating the process of white flight and resegregation.[12] The local clergy also took no stand on the changes taking place; nor did the local media address the issues in a constructive manner.

As a result of a conspiracy of silence and a complete absence of local leadership, according to Keating, the resegregation of East Cleveland took place in three stages. In the early 1960s, those whites who did not desire to live with blacks and who were able to leave the community did move. During the mid-1960s, those white residents who feared significant loss of equity in their housing investment and increasingly worried about the economic effects of blockbusting practiced by the local real estate industry also left the area. The last stage of resegregation occurred in the late 1960s and early 1970s, when East Cleveland lost its remaining white residents. Initially supportive of integration, they stayed as long as they could but eventually left the community discouraged and disillusioned.

Like Rosedale, the community of East Cleveland attempted to mitigate the worst effects of white flight but waited too long to be effective. And like

Rosedale, its efforts to restore and rebuild the community were not successful, despite passage of the 1968 fair-housing law. Keating reports that in 1990 the population of East Cleveland was 92 percent African American. It had the highest rate of poverty of any suburb in Cuyahoga County, and the median sales price of a house in the community was the lowest of all suburbs in the county. In the late 1980s, the state of Ohio was compelled to take over the finances of East Cleveland in the face of political corruption and deteriorating public services. A 1993 survey of residents measuring satisfaction with local government showed that among the thirty-five largest suburbs in Cuyahoga County, East Cleveland registered the lowest ratings.

A Conflict of Rights

Freedom of choice is a fundamental American value. The right to live where one chooses, to pursue educational and employment opportunities consistent with one's abilities, and to associate with whomever one desires are basic rights protected by our legal system. Freedom from religious persecution is also a protected legal right, as is protection from discrimination based on one's racial or ethnic origin. On the matter of achieving racial integration in our communities and neighborhoods, however, it is clear that a fundamental conflict of rights exists within the American population.

Advocacy planners, veterans of the civil rights movement, and public officials committed to achieving racially stable communities acknowledge the potential conflict of rights between freedom of choice and public policies designed to promote residential integration. The nub of this important policy dilemma is succinctly posed by economist George Galster and public official Donald DeMarco: "Should we strive to do more than eliminate housing market discrimination and, if so, what sorts of affirmative, prointegrative efforts are appropriate?"[13] They maintain that explicit antidiscrimination efforts will probably be insufficient to achieve socially desirable amounts of residential integration. More is required if the nation is to overcome high rates of residential segregation within its metropolitan regions.

Galster and DeMarco coined a new term that they think more effectively summarizes the goal of prointegrative public policy: stable integrative process (SIP). SIP is defined by them as "a dynamic in which homeseekers representing two or more races actively seek to occupy the same vacant dwellings in a substantial proportion of a metropolitan area's neighborhoods over a period of time."[14] After reviewing a large body of research findings, they concede that promoting stable integrative processes depends on the substantial reduction of prejudice and discrimination among the majority population: "History has provided ample evidence to reinforce the common belief that desegregation is synonymous with inevitable resegregation and decay."[15] Consistent with this belief, the story of Rosedale shows that most residents were willing to abandon their community rather than pursue or accommodate residential integration.

In 1963, Martin Luther King, Jr., stood in the shadows of the Lincoln Memorial and shared with us his dream of racial harmony for America. Significant progress has been made in the civil rights arena since his famous speech. African Americans exercise voting rights in significant numbers and have become an influential interest group in local, state, and national politics. Racial gaps in educational attainment levels are slowly closing. Blacks and whites casually mingle in public places, shopping malls, downtown stores, and restaurants and at sports and entertainment events. Although much remains to be accomplished, the nature of intergroup relations has dramatically changed over the past four decades.

Public opinion polls also show a reduction in racial tension. In 1958, just 35 percent of whites indicated they would vote for a well-qualified African American candidate. In a recent Gallup poll (June 1997), 93 percent of white respondents said they would support a well-qualified African American candidate for political office.[16] In 1958, only 4 percent of whites expressed approval of interracial marriages. By 1997, 63 percent of whites were expressing approval of marriages between races. And 80 percent of white Americans indicated in 1958 that they would leave their current neighborhood if blacks entered it in significant numbers. In 1997, only 18 percent of whites stated they would flee their communities if African Americans moved there.

Despite these attitudinal trappings of progress, approximately 80 percent of Americans still reside in segregated communities. Churches remain highly segregated. Forty-five percent of African Americans in 1997 still report experiencing discrimination, and nearly 70 percent of black men between eighteen and thirty-four report that they encounter discriminatory treatment regularly. The majority of both groups (54 percent of whites and 58 percent of blacks) continue to believe that race relations will remain a serious problem in the United States well into the future.[17]

The case of Rosedale shows how difficult it is to achieve common ground between African Americans and whites and the serious social and institutional consequences that follow from this failure. Achievement of common ground was in the interest of all those left behind in Rosedale, but efforts in that direction were consistently undermined by racial antagonism, hostility, and distrust. The story of Rosedale makes it clear that we still have a long way to travel as a nation before achieving the vision articulated by Martin Luther King over three decades ago.

On a more positive note, my research experiences in Rosedale showed that the female children of the community occasionally provided brief hope that Dr. King's dream might actually be possible to achieve. An elderly white woman in Rosedale explained to me that her racial views had changed because of her association with a young African American girl:

We've always been glad to have children in the neighborhood. And now these colored back of me, they have children. And I've never seen them out of their fence only one time. I was going down the alley to the mailbox here on the corner to put my utility bills in and I saw one of the cleanest and nicest dressed little colored girls and she said, "Good morning" or something. And I spoke to her and we walked a few steps together, you know, and I said, "I've got to go this way," and she said, "I've got to go this way, and it's very nice to have met you." She was just so cute. Now they live back here on the corner. So I believe that colored are just like white.

Other elderly citizens of Rosedale reported similar experiences with female children: "The Mexicans that were such bad housekeepers, they had three little girls that were very fond of me. And they came and sat on my porch with me if I was out on the porch. And I'd read Bible stories to them. They'd come and ask me to read a Bible story to them, and they were real nice little children. And I believe the Mexican man was a pretty nice man." One white woman spoke lovingly about her experiences with two African American girls:

They've got two real sweet little girls, twelve or thirteen years old. They come over here and visit with me. The one little girl, she's always making me things. She made me a picture and brought it to me. It was a valentine. It was the cutest thing. It's right yonder in that Kleenex box. I want you to see it. I asked her, I said: "Who made that?" She said, "I did." She made me another picture. She had cut out the trees and she colored the back part for the sky and sun. And there's a row of trees that she cut out, and there were little tiny flowers that she colored to put along the trees. And there were children playing in the picture. I hung it in the living room.

In light of the terror spread by teenage males in Rosedale, these small but very positive joys experienced with female children created an oasis of compassion and kindness within the otherwise harsh and barren human landscape of the area. An elderly white woman said:

I try to help the little black children next door. I don't do enough. For Thanksgiving they didn't have anything. They were going to a party, so I bought a hat and a little cape for the younger girl and let the older girl have a dress which she hasn't brought back. But I didn't want her to especially. It was a pretty good dress and I try to see, like when they're going on a picnic, I try to give them a little job. The mother has a lot of pride, and I'll let the little girl come over and sweep my floor and give her a dollar so she'll have something to take to the picnic. I think they love me and I know I do them and they are real sweet.

A few of Rosedale's elderly spoke positively about their African American neighbors: "I had two very dear black families that helped me. When they didn't see me out and about, they would come up to my back door and check and see if I was alright. One of them even went to the store and bought us groceries." Another reported: "You know, when that rapist was going around, they came over here and told us that anytime we needed help to just give them a buzz or knock on the door or do something."

All too often, however, even the most elementary forms of human contact were tainted by racial biases. Proudly proclaiming his commitment to racial equality, one elderly white man was unable to comprehend the racist implications of the story he was telling:

> I know all of these people personal here at the center. There was a colored woman that came in. She's a good woman, I know. And one of our white women met her and embraced her. Well, that's common among the whites, but that's a little unusual between the two races. And I made the remark to one of the boys here: "Now, that's an example of good Christian fellowship. How many of these other white women would hug that nigger and welcome her here. Not many. She practices what she preaches." And most of these people here are good Christian people. That's the reason I like to associate with them.

Possibilities of racial harmony glistened like gems within the rough terrain of life in Rosedale, but they were extraordinarily rare. And without a basis upon which to establish common human ground between whites and blacks, efforts to engineer residential integration through enlightened public policy and appeals to a higher morality or shared humanistic values were futile exercises. In the minds of most whites, residential integration equals community deterioration. The logic of this social equation was too compelling to be reversed by aggressive federal interventions, too persuasive to be transformed by Christian goodwill, and too predictable to be altered by making simple adjustments in one's racial attitudes.

Social Justice and Residential Integration

The nation remains sorely divided on the desirability of achieving residential integration. As a culture, we are legally and morally committed to freedom of choice. Our legal system strives to ensure that all of our citizens can choose to live wherever they can afford to purchase housing. But when African Americans move into a neighborhood, our legal system cannot compel whites to remain there. And as the case of Rosedale clearly establishes, serious, undesirable institutional and social costs accompany white abandonment.

In pursuit of racial justice and harmony, we have failed as a nation to establish an accepted set of principles that enable us to resolve competing and conflicting claims between minority and majority. The moral and ethical quagmire is complicated by the fact that individual acts of racism can be camouflaged behind the cloak of freedom of choice. Racially biased whites can extricate themselves from addressing the issue of racial justice by simply moving to another segregated geographic location. Suburban development has provided a wide range of market choices for white consumers. Only the most impoverished are left behind in changing neighborhoods. Without the assistance of the civil rights movement and the aggressive federal interventions that accompanied it, it is highly unlikely that the very worst aspects of racial discrimination and segregation would have been addressed voluntarily by state and local government or through the goodwill of our citizens and public officials. What, then, can be done to promote socially desirable amounts of integration within our communities while simultaneously protecting freedom of choice? What can be done to protect the rights of minorities while simultaneously preventing the creation of incentives that produce majority flight and abandonment?

Despite widespread evidence to the contrary and the immense difficulties involved, some communities have successfully managed racial transition and change. Others have prevented or reduced white flight, but in a manner that has increased racial hostility and intergroup conflict. Even among the limited number of success stories within our cities, no community has completely transcended or eliminated conflict between minority and majority during the process of residential transition and change.

Sociologist Jonathan Rieder profiles the intense intergroup conflicts that erupted in the Brooklyn community of Canarsie during the process of racial transition and change.[18] The Jewish and Italian residents of Canarsie mobilized in opposition to the liberal policy changes confronting them during the 1970s. In response to school desegregation orders and expanding interest among the black middle class to live in Canarsie, many residents initially mobilized to block residential integration. In an effort to prevent white flight and panic selling, many citizens of Canarsie attempted to control the sale of housing to African Americans through violence, intimidation, and the establishment of a clandestine market in housing. Informal ethnic and social networks frequently prevented the sale of homes to potential African American buyers. Organized boycotts of Canarsie's public schools by residents opposed to busing also characterized the response of this community to racial transition and change.

Whereas the case of Canarsie provides no blueprint detailing how successful integration can be managed, it does explain very clearly the depth and strength of the belief among whites that community decline will inevitably follow in the wake of racial transition and change. As explained by Rieder, "Busing edicts and racial tipping undermined the faith of whites in the stability of their neighborhoods."[19] The case of Canarsie makes it painfully clear that busing and open housing are two of the most unpopular liberal policy initiatives of the past three decades. Given the experiences of Canarsie and numerous other urban communities, it is highly unlikely that contemporary elected officials and civil rights leaders will be able to mobilize much public support for renewed interest in civil rights as a major public policy issue facing American society.

Other communities, however, have managed to achieve more positive results in their efforts to manage residential change. Cleveland Heights, Ohio;
Shaker Heights, Ohio; and Oak Park, Illinois have earned strongly positive
reputations as national leaders in managing residential integration.[20] Several consistent themes characterize these three success stories: (1) early intervention and planning, (2) progressive leadership and guidance by public
administrators and community officials, (3) stabilization and strong community support of public schools, (4) the provision of housing and loan services to stabilize the private housing market, and (5) systematic promotion
and marketing of the community by residents and public officials.

African American movement into Cleveland Heights began in the late
1960s. Unlike in Rosedale and East Cleveland, residents responded early
and directly to real estate initiatives promoting blockbusting. An ordinance
banning For Sale signs was passed by the city as well as other aggressive
measures directed toward curbing the negative sales practices of local brokers. According to Dennis Keating, progressive Jewish and Catholic elements within Cleveland Heights effectively mobilized community support
to manage integration in a constructive and positive manner.[21]

Among the more positive interventions undertaken by the residents to
manage more effectively the process of racial transition and change, Keating identifies the following as critically important: (1) initiation of a preferred realtor program based on a firm's past record of compliance with
fair-housing provisions, (2) implementation of a vigorous code enforcement
program designed to counter the perception that property values decline in
response to racial transition, (3) the monitoring and review of local lending
practices to ensure equal access to credit, and (4) establishment of various
community review bodies to monitor and evaluate the city's compliance
with fair-housing practices.[22] Of special significance was a lawsuit filed and
won against a local real estate firm for having engaged in racial steering
and blockbusting.

In addition to directly addressing local real estate practices, residents of
Cleveland Heights took strong measures to maintain high standards in the
local school system and in the delivery of government services. Keating
concludes that Cleveland Heights, in partnership with community organizations committed to racial justice, "has forged a long, enduring community consensus in which racially integrated housing, neighborhoods, and
public schools are accepted and supported by the city's residents."[23] Although the city's management of racial change has not been devoid of conflict and expensive litigation, Cleveland Heights remains a national leader
in open housing and community stability.

The case of Shaker Heights is similar to that of Cleveland Heights. In the
wake of racial change, the city banned use of For Sale signs as a strategy to
reduce potential blockbusting efforts by local realtors. Initially, many

African American realtors strongly objected to this policy on the grounds that it severely limited black access to the area and undermined their business and sales opportunities. The city took early and positive actions to address racial change in its educational and housing policies. In 1966 and 1968, the board of education voluntarily addressed racial isolation in the schools by initiating a busing and magnet school plan. Citizen groups created progressive organizations designed to recruit and disperse potential African American homebuyers throughout the region. Efforts were also made to attract African Americans with housing alternatives throughout the region in order to undermine racial concentration.

According to DeMarco and Galster, efforts to manage racial integration were successful in Shaker Heights because of (1) a deliberate and strategic advertising campaign to promote the community as stable and racially diverse, (2) the delivery of housing and counseling services designed to promote racial diversity within all the community's neighborhoods, (3) the provision of mortgage services and loans in areas where one race is underrepresented, and (4) strong monitoring and enforcement of open housing laws.[24] They summarize the success of Shaker Heights: "Experience and marketing surveys have convinced Shaker that a high percentage of mid- and upscale homeseekers will buy into a racially diverse community if safety and order prevail, schools produce award-winning scholars, home values are appreciating at a favorable rate compared to the competition, and community values and lifestyles are comfortable."[25]

Oak Park, Illinois, also experienced the initial waves of racial change during the early 1960s. A nearby white community, Austin, did not successfully address racial transition, and by 1980 nearly three-fourths of its population was African American. Like the Cleveland suburbs of Shaker Heights and Cleveland Heights, Oak Park adopted a positive strategy of affirmatively marketing the area as a racially diverse, stable community: "White homebuyers and renters were encouraged to consider living in Oak Park's southeast area, while blacks were encouraged to look elsewhere in Oak Park where they were underrepresented."[26] The leaders of Oak Park also responded with early intervention and planning.

Oak Park initially experimented with the establishment of a controversial racial quota system in response to widespread fear that once a hypothetical tipping point was reached, an irreversible process of white flight would soon follow. Although the quota policy was narrowly defeated and never implemented, it did elevate community discourse over the best way to manage racial transition and change, and it promoted other more positive solutions to the emerging social crisis. Rather than establish a quota system, Oak Park adopted a combination of several policy interventions designed to more effectively manage racial change in the community: (1) implementation of a strict housing code enforcement program, (2) establishment of progressive housing rehabilitation procedures, (3) creation of an innovative home equity assurance program in which participants were guaranteed 80 percent of the difference between the assessed valuation of their home and the actual sales price, and (4) provision of financial incentives to apartment owners who increased racial diversity in their buildings.[27]

All three of these communities directly addressed racial transition during its early phases, well before white flight could become a major social problem. Most of the policies and strategic interventions, in one way or another, were directed toward maintaining established social institutions: public schools, local businesses, community and housing standards, property values, city services, and law and order. More recently, policy researchers Philip Nyden, Michael Maly, and John Lockhart reported that nine other cities have registered similarly positive experiences.[28] In addition to maintaining community institutions and standards, residents and public officials of Oak Park, Shaker Heights, and Cleveland Heights recognized the importance of maintaining class homogeneity during the process of racial transition. Deliberate efforts were made to recruit and cultivate African American homeseekers from middle-class backgrounds. The maintenance of class homogeneity helped stabilize the community and prevented radical shifts in culture and lifestyles, events that characterized the decline of Rosedale and East Cleveland. Although racial diversity was pursued in these three communities, social class diversity was not.

As in Shaker Heights, Cleveland Heights, and Oak Park, the first wave of African American homeseekers who entered Rosedale had middle-class backgrounds. Like their white counterparts, they too abandoned Rosedale in response to housing opportunities in the suburbs. Rosedale's failure to retain members of the black or white middle class was pivotal to its rapid and precipitous decline. It is clear that middle-class African Americans are no more enthusiastic than middle-class whites about living in high-crime neighborhoods dominated by street thugs and adolescent gangs. It is also clear that the institutional instability and leadership vacuum created when the African American middle class abandons urban neighborhoods is as devastating to a community's future as is the loss of the white middle class. And as the case of Rosedale clearly establishes, white racism and traditional forms of prejudice and discrimination are not the only reasons behind our failure as a nation to achieve residential integration in the 1990s.

African American Youth and the Future of Race Relations

A social problem of crisis proportions has been emerging within our cities for the past two decades. In 1994, African Americans accounted for 31.3 percent of the nation's total arrests.[29] This group accounted for 33.1 percent of all arrests for crimes against property and 44.7 percent of arrests for violent crimes. More significant, among youths under eighteen years of age, African Americans accounted for 50.2 percent of all arrests for violent crimes in 1994.

Other statistics convey the gravity of this increasingly serious social problem among African American youth. The homicide rate among black youth is rising at an alarming pace. The homicide rate among African American teens was 46.4 deaths per 100,000 youths in 1985; by 1992 it had risen to 128.5 deaths per 100,000 youths. In 1992, black males between twelve and twenty-four experienced violent crime at rates higher than any other age or racial group in American society.[30] Their rate of violent victimization was almost double that reported among white youth. Between 1973 and 1992, the rate of violent victimization among African American youth increased by 25 percent, and it is still rising.

The likelihood of becoming a victim of violent crime has risen sharply among young black males. One out of every 10.3 African American males between twenty and twenty-four was a violent-crime victim in 1973; by 1992, the rate had risen to 1 of every 8 persons. Among black males between sixteen and nineteen, 1 of every 11 was a victim of violent crime in 1973; by 1992, the rate had risen to 1 of every 6 persons. Black youth are more likely than any other racial or age group to be a victim of crime involving weapons. Among young black male victims of crime, the probability of facing a weapon exceeds 50 percent. Too many young African American males are armed and dangerous.

The FBI's Uniform Crime Report shows that even though black males between twelve and twenty-four compose only 1.3 percent of the population, they accounted for 17.2 percent of single-victim homicides in 1992.[31] The Uniform Crime Report also establishes that an African American male in this age range is nearly fourteen times more likely to become a homicide victim than is a member of the general population. The murder rate for older black males was 67.5 per 100,000 individuals in 1992, a figure approximately eight times that found for the general population.

The problem of substance and alcohol abuse is extremely serious among young African American males. Street gangs involved in drug trafficking have emerged in most major American cities. In many cities, young African American males are extensively involved in drug sales and distribution through organized gang activities. Facing an uncertain future in the declining labor markets of cities experiencing deindustrialization and decline, many African American youngsters find opportunities for illegal enterprise to be extremely appealing. Some researchers contend that in cities such as Detroit, gangs and their illegal activities provide more job opportunities than major employers in the region, for example, General Motors.[32]

There are more youth gangs in operation today than in the 1950s, a watershed period in public recognition of the problem. More important, today's gangs are more violent and more inclined toward criminal activities than at any prior point in recent history.[33] Despite the increasing presence of gangs in African American communities, we have available fewer and fewer resources to understand their growth and development and less will to treat the causes that produce and sustain them. More important, the increasing rates of violence among African American youth, the increasing presence of gangs in inner-city communities, and the escalation of drug trafficking and other forms of illegal enterprise pursued by gangs have taken their toll on racial tolerance within the larger society.

A terrible irony within the contemporary civil rights movement has been posed by the escalating rates of violence among African American youth. The increasing absence of civility flaunted by a growing proportion of African American youth is slowly but systematically eroding the monumental achievements of the civil rights movement and the social programs that accompanied it. The case of Rosedale clearly reveals how traditional forms of prejudice and discrimination contributed to the community's decline. But the case of Rosedale also establishes that an elementary social contract was hopelessly shattered by the uncivil behavior of its youth.

Irrespective of the social and psychological circumstances influencing the behavior of the wilding gang members responsible for the violent murders of Rosedale's elderly residents, little sympathy can be marshaled for them. And whereas some form of compassion can be mobilized to understand that racial victimization influenced the personalities of the Rosedale and *Roots* rapists, it is small compensation to the victims and their families. In light of the outrageous behavior displayed by the young predators of Rosedale, it was extremely difficult for public officials and community leaders to sustain rational discourse and dialogue about the virtues of racial harmony and residential integration. The violent and careless behavior vaunted by some of Rosedale's youth contributed to the community's demise as surely and forcefully as the racial biases that sabotaged and frustrated efforts to retain its middle class.

As a microcosm of a much wider set of social problems and issues, the case of Rosedale is painfully instructive. It is clear that the violence and criminal behavior being pursued by an increasing number of African American youth and the accelerating presence of gangs in inner-city communities have undermined the nation's interest in participating in the "great and unprecedented conversation about race" recently proposed by President Clinton.

In June 1997, the president addressed the graduating class at the University of California at San Diego and introduced his plan to address the racial divide in American society. In that speech, he condemned the "tendency to wrongly attribute to entire groups, including the white majority, the objectionable conduct of a few members." He recommended to the graduates: "If a black American commits a crime, condemn the act—but remember that most African Americans are hard-working, law-abiding citizens."[34] Later in his speech, he also stressed the importance of individual responsibility and the maintenance of law and order:

> Beyond opportunity, we must demand responsibility from every American. Our strength as a society depends upon ... people taking responsibility for themselves and their families, teaching their children good values, working hard and obeying the law, and giving back to those around us. ... No responsibility is more fundamental than obeying the law. It is not racist to insist that every American do so. The fight against crime and drugs is a fight for the freedom of all our people, including those—perhaps especially those—minorities living in our poorest neighborhoods. But respect for the law must run both ways.[35]

The case of Rosedale shows how difficult it will be to achieve the goals articulated by the president in his San Diego address. In order to extend a compassionate hand to all of our citizens left behind in our nation's cities, the "year of honest dialogue" proposed by the president must entail frank and candid discussion of the ways in which youth violence, gangs, and drugs have influenced the direction of race relations in contemporary American society.

On June 15, 1997, more than 1,000 African American men marched in downtown Louisville, Kentucky, the city in which I currently reside. They marched in celebration of Father's Day and pledged to stand up against neighborhood crime. The rally came in the wake of a series of murders involving young black men. Since Father's Day, six more murders have occurred, all involving young African American males. Drug and gang violence have arrived in Louisville, a community deeply committed to the idea that these problems are big-city issues. As I write these final sentences for this book (June 27, 1997), the headlines in the local paper read: "Two Killed, Four Wounded Within 3 Hours."

At the Father's Day rally in Louisville, veteran civil rights leader Reverend Walter Malone thundered from the podium: "We didn't come here just to have a good time. Gang violence and drugs have no place in our community, and we have the power to take them out. We aren't waiting on government or any private group to give us a future. We're coming out on our own! There are some things that black people must do for themselves!"

It is fitting that the male organizers of the Louisville march selected Father's Day to take their righteous stand against gangs, drugs, and violent crime. Their challenge was clear: Black fathers need to take care of some important business at home and get their sons off the streets. Our collective future as a multicultural nation depends upon doing whatever is necessary to help them achieve this objective.

NOTES

Chapter One

1. Donald L. DeMarco and George Galster, "Prointegrative Policy: Theory and Practice," *Journal of Urban Affairs* 15, no. 2, 1993, pp. 141–160; George Galster and Edward W. Hill, *The Metropolis in Black and White* (New Brunswick, NJ: Center for Urban Policy Research, 1992); Dennis Keating, *The Suburban Racial Dilemma: Housing and Neighborhoods* (Philadelphia: Temple University Press, 1994); Juliet Saltman, *A Fragile Movement: The Struggle for Neighborhood Stabilization* (Westport, CT: Greenwood Press, 1990).

2. Carole Goodwin, *The Oak Park Strategy: Community Control of Racial Change* (Chicago: University of Chicago Press, 1979); Keating, op. cit.; Saltman, op. cit.

3. Oscar Handlin, *The Uprooted* (New York: Gosset and Dunlap, 1951); John Higham, *Strangers in the Land* (New York: Atheneum, 1963); Charlotte Erickson, *American Industry and the European Worker* (New York: Russell and Russell, 1957).

4. Stanley Lieberson, *Ethnic Patterns in American Cities* (New York: Free Press, 1963); Gerald Suttles, *The Social Order of the Slum* (Chicago: University of Chicago Press, 1968).

5. Mark Fried, *The World of the Urban Working Class* (Cambridge: Harvard University Press, 1973); Herbert Gans, *The Urban Villagers* (New York: Free Press, 1962).

6. Nathan Glazer and Daniel Patrick Moynihan, *Beyond the Melting Pot* (Cambridge: MIT Press, 1963); Colin Greer (ed.), *Divided Society* (New York: Basic Books, 1974); Mark R. Levy and Michael Kramer, *The Ethnic Factor* (New York: Simon and Schuster, 1972); Lieberson, op. cit.

7. David Ames et al., "Rethinking American Urban Policy," *Journal of Urban Affairs* 14, no. 3/4, 1992, pp. 197–216; Sar Levitan and Robert Taggart, *The Promise of Greatness* (Cambridge: Harvard University Press, 1977).

Chapter Two

1. David Harvey, *Social Justice and the City* (Baltimore: Johns Hopkins University Press, 1973), p. 135.

2. Douglas S. Massey and Nancy Denton, "Hypersegregation in U.S. Metropolitan Areas: Black and Hispanic Segregation Along Five Dimensions," *Demography*

26, no. 3, August 1989, pp. 373–391; George Galster and Edward Hill, *The Metropolis in Black and White* (New Brunswick, NJ: Center for Urban Policy Research, 1992). "By the Numbers: Tracking Segregation in 219 Metropolitan Areas," *USA Today*, November 11–13, 1991, p. 4.

Chapter Three

1. Robert Nisbet, *The Sociological Tradition* (New York: Basic Books, 1966), pp. 47–48.

2. Émile Durkheim, *The Division of Labor in Society* (New York: Free Press of Glencoe, 1933); Ferdinand Toennies, *Community and Society,* translated and edited by Charles Loomis (East Lansing: Michigan State University Press, 1957); Max Weber, *The Theory of Social and Economic Organization,* translated by A. M. Henderson and Talcott Parson (New York: Oxford University Press, 1947).

3. Suzanne Keller, *The Urban Neighborhood* (New York: Random House, 1968); Maurice Stein, *The Eclipse of Community* (New York: Harper & Row, 1960); Joseph Vidich and Joseph Bensman, *Small Town in Mass Society* (Princeton: Princeton University Press, 1988); Robert Nisbet, *The Quest for Community* (New York: Oxford University Press, 1953).

4. Herbert Gans, *The Urban Villagers* (New York: Free Press, 1962).

5. Gerald Suttles, *The Social Order of the Slum* (Chicago: University of Chicago Press, 1968), p. 6.

6. Ibid., p. 8.

7. Marc Fried, *The World of the Urban Working Class* (Cambridge: Harvard University Press, 1963); Gans, op. cit.

8. Martin Anderson, *The Federal Bulldozer* (New York: McGraw-Hill, 1964); James Q. Wilson (ed.), *Urban Renewal: The Record and the Controversy* (Cambridge: MIT Press, 1966).

9. Kai Erikson, *Everything in Its Path: Destruction of Community in the Buffalo Creek Flood* (New York: Simon and Schuster, 1976).

10. Ibid, p. 191.

Chapter Four

1. William James, *The Principles of Psychology* (New York: Dover, 1918).

2. Yona Ginsberg, *Jews in a Changing Neighborhood* (New York: Free Press, 1975).

3. Gerald Berreman, "Caste in India and the United States," *American Journal of Sociology,* September 1960, p. 122.

4. Ibid., p. 125.

5. Allison Davis, B. B. Gardner, and M. R. Gardner, *Deep South* (Chicago: University of Chicago Press, 1941); John Dollard, *Caste and Class in a Southern Town* (New Haven: Yale University Press, 1937); Gunner Myrdal, *An American Dilemma* (New York: Harper & Row, 1944).

6. Dollard, op. cit., p. 375.

7. Davis, Gardner, and Gardner, op. cit., p. 25.

8. Myrdal, op. cit., p. 65.

9. Myrdal, op. cit., p. 1356.

10. William Grier and Price Cobbs, *Black Rage* (New York: Basic Books, 1968); Calvin Hernton, *Sex and Racism in America* (New York: Grove Press, 1965); LeRoi Jones, *The System of Dante's Hell* (New York: Grove Press, 1976).

11. William J. Cash, *The Mind of the South* (New York: Knopf, 1941), p. 118.

Chapter Six

1. Eldridge Cleaver, *Soul on Ice* (New York: Dell, 1968).

2. Nicholas Groth et al., "Rape: Power, Anger, and Sexuality," *American Journal of Psychiatry* 134, no. 11, 1977, p. 1241.

Chapter Seven

1. Émile Durkheim, *The Division of Labor in Society* (New York: Free Press of Glencoe, 1933); Robert Merton, *Social Theory and Social Structure* (New York: Free Press, 1968).

2. Travis Hirsch, *Causes of Delinquency* (Berkeley: University of California Press, 1969); Sue Titus Reid, *Crime and Criminology* (New York: Holt, Rinehart & Winston, 1976); Lewis Yablonsky, *The Violent Gang* (Baltimore: Penguin Books, 1967).

3. Elliot Liebow, *Tally's Corner* (Boston: Little, Brown, 1967).

Chapter Eight

1. Robert Pear, "Number of Poor Americans Grows by 1.2 Million," *Courier Journal*, October 5, 1993, p. A8, New York Times News Service.

2. William Wilson, *The Truly Disadvantaged* (Chicago: University of Chicago Press, 1987), p. 63.

3. Charles Murray, *Losing Ground: American Social Policy, 1950–1980* (New York: Basic Books, 1986).

4. Wilson, op. cit., p. 71.

5. Ibid., p. 90.

6. Daniel Patrick Moynihan, *The Negro Family: The Case for National Action* (Washington, DC: Office of Policy Planning and Research, U.S. Department of Labor, 1965).

7. Lee Rainwater and William Yancey, *The Moynihan Report and the Politics of Controversy* (Cambridge: MIT Press, 1967).

8. Andrew Billingsley, *Black Families in White America* (Englewood Cliffs, NJ: Prentice-Hall, 1968); E. Franklin Frazier, *The Negro Family in the United States* (Chicago: University of Chicago Press, 1939); John Scanzoni, *The Black Family in Modern Society* (Boston: Allyn and Bacon, 1971); Robert Staples, *The Black Family* (Belmont, CA: Wadsworth, 1971).

9. Rainwater and Yancey, op. cit.

10. Christopher Lasch, *Haven in a Heartless World: The Family Besieged* (New York: Basic Books, 1977), p. 161.

11. Carol Stack, *All Our Kin* (New York: Harper & Row, 1970).

12. Scott Cummings and Michael Price, "Race Relations and Public Policy in Louisville: Historical Development of an Urban Underclass," *Journal of Black Studies* 27, no. 25, 1997, pp. 615–649.

13. Allison Davis, B. B. Gardner, and M. R. Gardner, *Deep South* (Chicago: University of Chicago Press, 1941); John Dollard, *Caste and Class in a Southern Town* (New Haven: Yale University Press, 1937); Gunner Myrdal, *An American Dilemma* (New York: Harper & Row, 1944).

14. Ibid.

15. Elijah Anderson, *Streetwise* (Chicago: University of Chicago Press, 1990).

16. Ibid., p. 2.

17. Ibid., p. 3.

18. Ibid.

19. Ibid., p. 73.

20. Marian Wright Edelman, "Threat to Black Youth Greatest Since Slavery," *Courier Journal*, February 6, 1994, p. 5; Carl Nightingale, *On the Edge* (New York: Basic Books, 1993).

21. Robert Merton, *Social Theory and Social Structure* (New York: Free Press, 1968); Richard Cloward and Lloyd E. Ohlin, *Delinquency and Opportunity: A Theory of Delinquent Gangs* (New York: Free Press, 1960).

22. Émile Durkheim, *The Division of Labor in Society* (New York: Free Press, 1933).

23. Travis Hirsh, *Causes of Delinquency* (Berkeley: University of California Press, 1969).

24. Lewis Yablonsky, *The Violent Gang* (Baltimore: Penguin Books, 1967), p. 169.

25. Ivan Light, *Ethnic Enterprises in America* (Berkeley: University of California Press, 1972); Ivan Light, "The Ethnic Vice District," *American Sociological Review* 42, June 1977, pp. 464–470.

Chapter Nine

1. Edward J. Blakely, *Planning Local Economic Development* (Thousand Oaks, CA: Sage, 1994); Thomas S. Lyons and Roger E. Hamlin, *Creating an Economic Development Action Plan* (New York: Praeger, 1991).

2. Elisabeth Kübler-Ross, *On Death and Dying* (New York: Macmillan, 1969).

Chapter Ten

1. Jane Jacobs, *The Death and Life of Great American Cities* (New York: Vintage Books, 1961).

2. Ibid., p. 274.

3. Richard Taub, D. Garth Taylor, and Jan D. Dunham, *Paths of Neighborhood Change* (Chicago: University of Chicago Press, 1984), p. 4.

4. Otis Dudley Duncan and Beverly Duncan, *The Negro Population in Chicago* (Chicago: University of Chicago Press, 1957).

5. See Nancy Kleniewski, "Triage and Urban Planning: A Case Study of Philadelphia," *International Journal of Urban and Regional Research* 10, no. 4, 1986, pp. 563–579; and Peter Marcuse, Peter Medoff, and Andrea Pereira, "Triage and Urban Policy," *Social Policy*, Winter 1982, pp. 33–37, for excellent overviews of triage planning.

6. Marcuse, Medoff, and Pereira, op cit., p. 34.

7. J. Mikesell, *Fiscal Administration: Analysis and Application for the Public Sector* (Homewood, IL: Dorsey Press, 1982).

8. George Galster and Edward W. Hill, *The Metropolis in Black and White* (New Brunswick, NJ: Center for Urban Policy Research, 1992); N. Glazer and D. P. Moynihan, *Beyond the Melting Pot: Negroes, Puerto Ricans, Jews, Italians, and Irish in New York City* (Cambridge: MIT Press, 1963).

9. Kerner Commission, *National Advisory Commission on Civil Disorders* (New York: Bantam Books, 1968) p. 407.

10. Ibid.

11. B. Chinitz, "A Framework for Speculating About Future Urban Growth Patterns in the US," *Urban Studies* 28, 1991, pp. 939–959.

12. R. A. Beauregard, "Space, Time and Economic Restructuring," in R. A. Beauregard (ed.), *Economic Restructuring and Political Response* (Newbury Park, CA: Sage, 1989), pp. 209–240.

13. B. Bluestone and B. Harrison, *The Deindustrialization of America* (New York: Basic Books, 1982).

14. Scott B. Cummings, "Vulnerability to the Effects of Recession: Minority and Female Workers," *Social Forces,* March 1987, pp. 834–357; Scott B. Cummings, "Private Enterprise and Public Policy," in S. B. Cummings (ed.), *Business Elites and Economic Development* (Albany: State University of New York Press, 1988), pp. 3–21.

15. U.S. Bureau of the Census, "Metropolitan Areas and Cities," *1990 Census Profile*, no. 3, September 1991.

16. Gregory Weiher, "Rumors of the Demise of the Urban Crisis are Greatly Exaggerated," *Journal of Urban Affairs* 11, 1989, p. 229.

17. R. Kling, S. Olin, and M. Poster (eds.), *Post Suburban California: The Transformation of Orange County Since World War II* (Berkeley: University of California Press, 1991); J. Garreau, *Edge City: Life on the Frontier* (New York: Doubleday, 1991).

18. M. Abramowitz, "The Urban Boom: Who Benefits?" *Washington Post,* May 10, 1992, p. H1.

19. Ibid.

20. F. Barringer, "New Census Data Reveal Redistribution of Poverty," *New York Times*, May 29, 1992, p. A14.

21. W. H. Frey, "Metropolitan America: Beyond the Transition," *Population Bulletin* 45, no. 1, 1990.

22. Franklin D. Roosevelt, "Franklin D. Roosevelt on the Democratic Welfare State," in Albert R. Chandler (ed.), *The Clash of Political Ideals* (New York: Appleton-Century Crofts, 1949), pp. 275–276.

23. Theodore, J. Lowi, *The End of Liberalism* (New York: W. W. Norton, 1979).

24. D. Falk and H. M. Franklin, *Equal Housing Opportunity: The Unfinished Agenda* (Washington, DC: Potomac Institute, 1976); C. Murray, *Losing Ground: American Social Policy, 1950–1980* (New York: Basic Books, 1984).

25. Cummings, *Business Elites and Urban Development;* W. J. Wilson, *The Truly Disadvantaged: The Inner City, the Underclass, and Public Policy* (Chicago: University of Chicago Press, 1987).

26. S. A. Levitan and R. Taggart, *The Promise of Greatness* (Cambridge: Harvard University Press, 1987).

27. D. R. Goldfield and B. A. Brownell, *Urban America: A History* (2d ed.) (Boston: Houghton-Mifflin, 1990).

28. W. Gorham and N. Glazer (eds.), *The Urban Predicament* (Washington, DC: Urban Institute, 1976); M. Kaplan and F. J. James (eds.), *The Future of National Urban Policy* (Durham, NC: Duke University Press, 1990); L. K. Loewenstein (ed.), *Urban Studies: An Introductory Reader* (New York: Free Press, 1971).

29. M. Anderson, *The Federal Bulldozer: A Critical Analysis of Urban Renewal, 1949–1962* (Cambridge: MIT Press, 1964); M. Fried, *The World of the Urban Working Class* (Cambridge: Harvard University Press, 1968); H. J. Gans, *The Urban Villagers: Group and Class in the Life of Italian-Americans* (New York: Free Press, 1972).

30. Falk and Franklin, op. cit.

31. J. L. Pressman and A. Wildavsky, *Implementation* (Berkeley: University of California Press, 1980).

32. W. Tabb and L. Sawers, *Marxism and the Metropolis* (New York: Oxford University Press, 1978).

33. Levitan and Taggart, op. cit.

34. D. P. Moynihan, *Maximum Feasible Misunderstanding: Community Action in the War on Poverty* (New York: Free Press, 1975).

35. Murray, op. cit.

36. Falk and Franklin, op. cit.; Robert Forman, *Black Ghettos, White Ghettos, and Slums* (Englewood Cliffs, NJ: Prentice-Hall, 1971); Lillian Rubin, *Busing and Backlash* (Berkeley: University of California Press, 1972).

37. Falk and Franklin, op. cit., p. 52.

38. Falk and Franklin, op. cit.

39. Ibid., pp. 9–10.

40. Falk and Franklin, op. cit.; Forman, op. cit.; Rubin, op. cit.

41. Falk and Franklin, op. cit., p. 10.

42. Martin Mayer, *The Builders* (New York: W. W. Norton, 1978); see also *The Politics of Housing*, special issue of *Society*, July-August, 1972.

43. Scott B. Cummings (ed.), *Racial Isolation in the Public Schools: The Impact of Public and Private Housing Policies* (Arlington, TX: Institute of Urban Studies, 1980); Mayer, op. cit.

44. Mayer, op. cit.

45. Ibid.

46. Eloise Hajek, "An Analysis of the North Central Texas Entitlement Jurisdictions Community Development Block Grant Proposals Under the First Four Years of the Housing and Community Development Act of 1974," master's thesis, Institute of Urban Studies, University of Texas at Arlington, 1980; North Central Texas

Council of Governments, *Federally-Assisted Housing Opportunities for Low Income Persons in North Central Texas* (Arlington, TX: COG, 1979); William Rotert, *Expanding Housing Opportunities and Related Issues* (Dallas: U.S. Department of Housing and Urban Development, Regional Office, June 1980).

47. Gary Orfield, *Must We Bus?* (Washington, DC: Brookings Institution, 1978).

48. Falk and Franklin, op. cit., p. 13.

49. North Central Texas Council of Governments, op. cit.; Rotert, op. cit.

50. North Central Texas Council of Governments, op. cit.

51. Falk and Franklin, op. cit.

52. North Central Texas Council of Governments, op. cit.; Rotert, op. cit.

53. Cummings, *Racial Isolation in the Public Schools.*

54. Falk and Franklin, op. cit.; Orfield, op. cit.

55. Aaron & Associates, "Non-defense Programs," in J. A. Pechman (ed.), *Setting National Priorities* (Washington, DC: Brookings Institution, 1983).

56. "Summary of Fiscal 1986 Budget Resolution," *Congressional Quarterly*, August 31, 1985, pp. 1702–1705.

57. G. Mills and G. Palmer, *The Deficit Dilemma* (Washington, DC: Urban Institute Press, 1983).

Chapter Eleven

1. Joseph Boskin, *Urban Racial Violence in the Twentieth Century* (Beverly Hills, CA: Glencoe Press, 1976).

2. Ibid.

3. Ibid.

4. Richard Smith, "Creating Stable Racially Integrated Communities: A Review," *Journal of Urban Affairs* 15, no. 2, 1993, p. 116.

5. Donald DeMarco and George Galster, "Prointegrative Policy: Theory and Practice," *Journal of Urban Affairs* 15, no. 2, 1993, pp. 141–160.

6. William Clark, "Neighborhood Transitions in Multiethnic/Racial Contexts," *Journal of Urban Affairs* 15, no. 2, pp. 170–171.

7. Harvey Molotch, *Managed Integration: The Dilemmas of Doing Good in the City* (Berkeley: University of California Press, 1972).

8. George Galster, Fred Frieberg, and Diane Houk, "Racial Differential in Real Estate Practices: An Exploratory Case Study," *Journal of Urban Affairs* 9, no. 3, 1987, pp. 199–215; Michael Collins and George Galster, "Discriminatory Marketing of Racially Mixed Neighborhoods in Memphis," *Journal of Urban Affairs* 17, no. 4, 1995, pp. 339–355.

9. George Galster, "Assessing the Causes of Racial Segregation: A Methodological Critique," *Journal of Urban Affairs* 10, no. 4, p. 402.

10. Philip Nyden, Michael Maly, and John Lockhart, "The Emergence of Stable Racially and Ethnically Diverse Urban Communities: A Case Study of Nine U.S. Cities," *Housing Policy Debate* 8, no. 2, 1997, pp. 491–534.

11. Dennis Keating, *The Suburban Racial Dilemma: Housing and Neighborhoods* (Philadelphia: Temple University Press, 1994).

12. Ibid., pp. 77–95.

13. DeMarco and Galster, op. cit., p. 141.

14. Ibid., p. 142.

15. Ibid., p. 148.

16. Paul Shepard, "Blacks and Whites Are a Nation Apart on Race Relations," *Associated Press Courier Journal*, June 11, 1997, p. A6

17. Ibid.

18. Jonathan Rieder, *Canarsie: The Jews and Italians of Brooklyn Against Liberalism* (Cambridge: Harvard University Press, 1985).

19. Ibid., p. 57.

20. There are several excellent accounts of these three communities, including Keating, op. cit.; Carole Goodwin, *The Oak Park Strategy: Community Control of Racial Change* (Chicago: University of Chicago Press, 1979); and Juliet Saltman, *A Fragile Movement: The Struggle for Neighborhood Stabilization* (Westport, CT: Greenwood Press, 1990).

21. Keating, op. cit., pp. 114–139.

22. Ibid.

23. Ibid., pp. 137–138.

24. DeMarco and Galster, op. cit.

25. Ibid., p. 151.

26. Keating, op. cit., p. 212.

27. Ibid., pp. 211–214; see also Goodwin, op. cit.

28. Nyden, Maly, and Lockhart, op. cit.

29. Kathleen Maguire and Ann Pastori (eds.), *The Sourcebook of Criminal Justice Statistics for 1995, 1996* (Washington, DC: U.S. Department of Justice, Bureau of Justice Statistics, 1997).

30. Lisa Bastien and Bruce Taylor, *Young Black Male Victims: National Crime Victimization Survey, 1994* (Washington, DC: U.S. Department of Justice, Office of Justice Programs, 1996).

31. Ibid.

32. C. S Taylor, *Dangerous Society* (East Lansing: Michigan State University Press, 1990).

33. Ronald Huff (ed.), *Gangs in America* (Thousand Oaks, CA: Sage, 1996); Lewis Yablonsky, *Gangsters* (New York: New York University Press, 1997).

34. William Clinton, "Remarks by the President at University of California at San Diego Commencement," Washington, D.C., Office of the Press Secretary, June 14, 1997.

35. Ibid.

INDEX

Absentee landlords, 161, 162,
    164–165, 191
Abramowitz, Mark, 171
African Americans, 186, 187
    as candidates, 198
    elderly, 129, 133–137
    fathers, 207
    female children, 198–199
    gangs of, 169–170
    males, 50, 61, 62, 75–77, 127, 133,
        205, 207
    in suburbs, 176
    white beliefs about, 52, 53–54, 55
    youth, 4, 13, 50, 70, 76, 133, 135,
        139, 165, 167–168, 204–207.
        See also Elderly whites, and
        black youth; Gangs; Wilding
        incidents
    See also Families, black female-
        headed
Agriculture, 20
AHOP. See Area-wide Housing
    Opportunities Plan
Airports, 25–26
Allied Communities of the County,
    148
American Dilemma, An (Myrdal),
    53–54
Amon Carter Foundation, 152, 156,
    166
Anderson, Elijah, 133
Anger, 41, 70, 95–96, 97, 122
Anomie, 138
Architectural preservation, 156
Area-wide Housing Opportunities Plan
    (AHOP), 188
Arlington, 25, 26, 162, 189

Asians, 22, 165, 178
    gangs of, 169
Automobiles. See Crime,
    automobile/property theft;
    Parking

Banks, 152, 165
Berreman, Gerald, 51
Black Business Association, 163
Black Chamber of Commerce, 88, 89,
    150
Black Community Crusade for
    Children, 137
Black menace, 55
Blockbusting, 35, 41, 184, 196, 202
Bluestone, B., 176–177
BMIR. See Loans, below-market-
    interest-rate
Boosterism, 19
Boston, 7
Bush administration, 190
Businesses, 2, 18, 19, 20, 22, 41,
    43–44, 47, 139, 143, 158, 174,
    176, 177
    during commercial redevelopment,
        157, 191
    See also Commercial redevelopment
Busing, 22, 25, 44–45, 46, 185, 189,
    201, 203

Canarsie (Brooklyn), 201
Carter administration, 181, 182
Cash, William, 54
Caste systems, 51–52
CDBG. See Community Development
    Block Grant
Census tracts, 22, 27(table), 186

Chamber of Commerce. *See* Black
Chamber of Commerce
Chicago, 177
Chicanos. *See* Hispanics
Children, 4, 26, 29, 43, 45, 46, 59, 76,
143, 170
female, 198–199
in poverty, 126, 127, 137
responsibility for, 131, 136
See also African Americans, youth
Churches, 2, 48, 56, 66, 116, 139,
144–145, 147, 148, 198
Cities. *See* Metropolitan areas
City services, 44, 177
Civility, 206
Civil rights, 181, 182, 198, 201, 206
Civil Rights Act of 1968, Title VIII,
194–195
Clark, William, 195
Class issues, 52, 120, 142
and racial transition, 204
Cleaver, Eldridge, 84, 95
Cleveland Heights, Ohio, 202, 204
Clinton, Bill, 206–207
COG. *See* North Central Texas Council
of Governments
Collective trauma, 37
Commercial redevelopment, 148–159,
160, 190, 191
Community, sense of, 1, 17, 28–47, 59,
133, 134, 135, 139, 143
Community Center, 4
Senior Citizen's Center, 4, 5—7, 31,
56, 63, 134
Youth Center, 4
Community Development Act, 190
Community Development Block Grant
(CDBG), 149, 152, 157, 181, 182,
191
Community development programs,
182, 190
Community standards, 41–43, 128,
136, 193, 203
Cotton industry, 18
Crack cocaine, 165, 168, 169,
170
Credit union, 150, 152

Crime, 9, 14, 50, 53–54, 63–67, 68–83,
102, 105, 120, 138, 158, 162, 207
automobile/property theft, 72, 73,
74–75, 116, 168, 170
economic deprivation as cause of,
129, 131–132, 168
efforts to reduce, 165–168
household crime, 70, 71, 72, 75–80,
117, 168, 170
psychological effects of, 69–70, 74,
75, 78, 85
reporting, 141
statistics concerning, 71, 72, 73–74,
74(table), 168, 170, 204–205
street crime, 70, 71, 72, 80–83,
122–123
unreported, 72
violent, 205. *See also* Murders;
Rape; Violence; Wilding
incidents
Criminal justice system, 113, 114,
140–141. *See also* Police

Dallas-Fort Worth metropolitan area, 4,
23–26, 177, 181, 182, 184, 186
crime in, 73, 74(table)
Dallas, 24, 184–185, 187, 188
Fort Worth, 18, 19, 24, 145, 149,
150, 151, 152, 154, 156, 159,
177, 181, 185, 186, 187, 188, 189
perception of safety in, 60, 61(table)
populations in, 24
real estate development in, 23
*Death and Life of Great American
Cities, The* (Jacobs), 172
Deep South (Davis, Gardner and
Gardner), 53
Deficits. *See under* Federal government
Delinquent subcultures, 114
DeMarco, Donald, 195, 197, 203
Depression (psychological), 14, 70,
114
Discrimination, 195, 198. *See also*
Racism; Segregation
Dollard, John, 53
Domestics, 20
Drive-by shootings, 169

Drugs, 14, 116, 117–118, 123, 132, 205, 206, 207. *See also* Crack cocaine
Duncan, Otis and Beverly, 172

East Cleveland, Ohio, 196–197
East Side Lions Club, 88–89
Economic development plans, 158
Education, 2, 33(table 3.5), 46, 182. *See also* Schools
Elderly whites, 4–7, 13, 29, 39, 45, 128, 174, 175, 198, 199
and black neighbors, 198–200
and black youth, 6–7, 10, 57, 120, 130
homes of, 22–23. *See also* Residences, security measures in
as irrelevant, 11
males, 60, 83, 86, 87, 200
numbers of, 8
victimization of, 7, 11, 50, 51, 93, 111, 139–140
See also Rosedale, elderly in; Women, white/elderly white
Employment, 33(tables 3.4, 3.5), 127, 132, 148, 149, 168
discrimination in, 128
jobs created/lost, 157, 176–177
See also Unemployment
Erikson, Kai, 37, 39
Ethical neutrality, 9
Ethnic communities, 29
Exercise, 62–63

Fair Housing Amendments Act, 195
Falk, D., 183, 184, 186
Families, 29, 120, 125
black female-headed, 127, 129, 130
intergenerational breakdown in black, 133
See also Parents; Poverty, and family structure
FBI Uniform Crime Report, 205
Fear, 7, 8, 13, 48–50, 52, 53, 54–55, 59–63, 65–67, 72, 79, 82
and daylight/evening hours, 61(table)
See also Residences, security measures in

Federal government, 36, 37, 41, 44, 45, 46, 163, 179, 181, 183, 194
deficits, 190, 192
social program expenditures of, 189–190
Federal Housing Administration (FHA), 182, 183, 184
FHA. *See* Federal Housing Administration
Ford Foundation, 149
Foreclosures, 162
For Sale signs, 202–203
Fort Worth. *See under* Dallas-Fort Worth metropolitan area
Fort Worth Star Telegram, 103
Fox, David, 184
Fox and Jacobs firm, 184
Franklin, H. M., 183, 184, 186
Freedom of choice, 197, 200, 201
Freetown, 20, 21, 30, 72, 140
Friendships, 40–41

Galster, George, 195, 197, 203
Gangs, 14, 102, 104, 105, 133, 165, 168–170, 205–206, 207
task force for, 169
Gans, Herbert, 29
Ghettoization, 38, 50, 59, 139, 176
symptoms of, 12
Ginsberg, Yona, 50
Grandparents, 130
Great Depression, 3, 20, 179, 180
Great Society, 171, 181
Grieving, 36–38
Guardian Angels, 103
Guns, 65, 87, 89–90, 91, 98, 123, 205

Hammond, 21, 30, 140
Harrison, B., 176–177
Harvey, David, 23
Health issues, 62–63, 166
Highways, 181, 182
Hirschi, Travis, 138
Hispanics, 22, 24, 26, 72, 165, 178, 187, 199
gangs of, 169

Historical issues, 52–53, 55, 174, 178, 194, 197. *See also* Rosedale, history of
Homicide. *See* Murders
Housing, 2, 22, 46, 176, 181, 191, 202
    public housing, 163, 180, 182–185, 188, 189
    renovation of, 148, 153, 154, 155, 156, 158, 159–165, 190
    Section 8 rental housing, 162–163, 182, 186–187, 188, 192
    Section 221(d)(3), 185, 186
    trickle down of, 173
    See also Real estate; Residences
Housing Act of 1948, 180
Housing and Urban Development, Department of, 186

Illegal aliens, 163–164
Illegitimacy, 130
Immigrants, 1, 172, 178
Incomes, 26, 27(table), 33(table 3.5), 34(table), 158, 177, 191
India, 51
Industrialization, 28, 29
    deindustrialization, 177
Infant mortality, 138
Inflation, 177
Institutions, 142–143, 158, 204
    absence of permanent, 191, 192
Insurance, 69
Integration, 21, 39, 54, 55
    residential, 55–56, 197, 200–204.
        See also Segregation, resegregation
    See also under Schools
Interviews, 11, 134, 139, 153

Jackson, Jesse, 126
Jacobs, Jane, 172, 195
James, William, 49
Jews, 50, 139, 201
Job training, 2

Keating, Dennis, 196, 197, 202
King, Martin Luther, 193, 198
Ku Klux Klan, 10, 21

Lasch, Christopher, 128–129
Liberalism. *See* Public policy, liberal
Liberation Community, 154
Lifestyles, 203, 204
Loans, 159, 160, 164, 182, 184, 191, 202, 203
    below-market-interest-rate (BMIR), 185, 186
Lockhart, John, 204
Los Angeles, 177
Louisville, Kentucky, 207
Lowi, Theodore J., 179
Lynchings, 53, 193

Main Street Program. *See* Rosedale Main Street Project
Malcolm X, 193
Males, elderly, 32. *See also* Elderly whites, males
Malone, Walter, 207
Maly, Michael, 204
Marcuse, Peter, 173
Marriages, interracial, 198
Mattapan, New Jersey, 50
Media, 63, 73, 84, 88, 103, 111, 166, 170, 174, 196
Medoff, Peter, 173
Methodist Church, 147
Methodology, 11, 15, 31
Metropolitan areas, 126, 175, 177
    central cities, 178, 206
    See also Dallas-Fort Worth metropolitan area
Mexicans, 57, 199
Middle class, 43, 47, 139, 161, 173, 176, 195, 204
Millikan case, 188
Mind of the South, The (Cash), 54
Molotch, Harvey, 195
Mortgages, 32, 34, 35, 159, 191, 192, 203
Moynihan, Daniel Patrick, 128, 182
Murders, 7, 68, 70, 71, 72, 85, 86, 87, 88, 102, 104, 105, 106, 107–108, 131, 168, 170, 205, 207
Murray, Charles, 127
Myrdal, Gunnar, 53–54

National Advisory Commission on
   Civil Disorders, 176
Natural disasters, 37, 47
Neighborhood Health Services. 166
Neighborhood Housing Services
   (NHS), 154, 159, 160–161, 163,
   164, 165, 192
Neighborhood life, 40–41, 65–66,
   134–135
New Deal, 179, 180, 183
New federalism, 190, 191
NHS. *See* Neighborhood Housing
   Services
Nisbet, Robert, 28
Nixon administration, 181
North Central Texas Council of
   Governments (COG), 188
Northside, 72
Nyden, Philip, 204

Oak Park, Illinois, 202, 203–204
Ohio, 197, 202
Ordered segmentation, 30

Parents, 13–14, 115, 116, 118, 120,
   121, 125, 129, 131, 132, 134,
   135–136, 137. *See also* Families,
   black female-headed
Parking, 160, 174
Parks, 144
Pawnshops, 116
Pereira, Andrea, 173
Plano, 25
Plea bargains, 112, 113
Police, 7, 8–9, 57, 61, 63, 71, 72, 73,
   77–78, 88, 93, 102, 103–104,
   105, 110, 111–112, 121, 124,
   140, 168
   relationship with community,
      141–142
Population growth, 21, 24, 25, 175,
   176
   metropolitan, 177
Poverty, 26, 27(table), 114, 128,
   129
   in cities, 126, 177, 178, 182
   and family structure, 127, 128

   in suburbs, 178, 197
   See also under Children
Power House building, 157
Prison sentences, 100–101, 112–113
Private property, 143, 144
Public opinion polls, 198
Public policy, 2, 3, 12, 13, 22, 39, 46,
   173, 194, 195
   and freedom of choice, 197
   liberal, 178–182, 189, 201
   shifts in, 190
Purse-snatchings, 80–81, 82

Quota system, 203

Race riots, 194
Racial etiquette, 55–57
Racial transition, 4, 35, 36, 42, 46–47,
   52, 138, 141, 171, 172, 181, 187,
   192, 195, 201
   and class homogeneity, 204
   successful efforts concerning,
      202–204
Racism, 50–51, 114, 128, 129, 183,
   184, 192, 194, 200
Rape, 53, 59, 71, 72, 83, 84–101, 103,
   168, 170
   anger rapes, 95–96
   rape complex, 54
   See also Roots rapist; Rosedale rapist
Reagan, Ronald, 189
Real estate, 158
   brokers, 21, 35, 41, 46–47, 195
   investors in, 162. *See also* Absentee
      landlords
   and Texas economy, 161–162
   values, 23, 25, 35, 38–39, 161, 197,
      203
Recreation, 66–67
Religion. *See* Churches
Residences, 18, 19,, 170
   condition of, 164–165
   homeownership, 32, 33(table 3.3),
      134, 161, 164, 165
   length of residencies, 31–32
   possessions in, 68–69
   security measures in, 22–23, 63–65

selling of, 35. *See also* Real estate, values
tenant-occupied, 21, 46, 47, 135, 161, 162–163, 164, 204
vacancies, 162, 164, 165
See also Housing; Integration, residential; Real estate
Responsibility, 137, 207. *See also under* Children
Revitalization program, 145, 146–165, 174
Rewards, 88, 104
Rieder, Jonathan, 201
Rights, 197–200. *See also* Civil rights
Role models, 133, 167
Rolling Plains, 21, 162
Roosevelt, Franklin, 179
Roots rapist, 84–85, 93–97, 206
Rosedale
  elderly in, 31–34(tables), 31–36, 49, 52–53, 61(table), 63–67, 72, 73, 138. *See also* African Americans, elderly; Elderly whites
  history of, 17, 18–20, 22, 26
  image of, 147, 166, 191
  incorporation and annexation, 19
  inevitable fate of, 172, 191
  racial composition of, 26
  socioeconomic characteristics of residents, 27(table), 33(table 3.5), 34(table)
Rosedale Boys Club, 167–168
Rosedale Business Association, 155
Rosedale College, 18, 147, 148–149, 150, 152, 155, 158, 164, 174, 175
Rosedale High School, 166
  Marching 100 band, 45
  racial composition and number of students attending, 189
Rosedale Main Street Project, 150–159
  committees of, 151–152
  failure of, 153–159
Rosedale rapist, 8, 84, 85, 93, 97–101, 159, 166, 181, 206
  arrests concerning, 90, 91–92
  and copycat rapists, 88
  statements of, 97–99

Rosedale Strategy Committee, 148, 149, 150, 155
Ross, Elizabeth Kubler, 169
Rural to urban migration, 129–130, 130–131, 176

Schools, 2, 18, 121–122, 132, 176, 185, 187, 194, 202
  boycotts of, 201
  dropouts from, 144, 167
  integration of, 22, 44, 45, 46, 181–182, 182–183, 188, 189, 201. *See also* Busing
  magnet schools, 189, 203
  See also Rosedale College; Rosedale High School
Sears, Barry, 159–160
SEEDCO. *See* Structured Employment/Economic Development Corporation
Segregation, 1, 22, 24, 51, 52, 53, 186, 195, 198
  and public housing policies, 184–185
  resegregation, 176, 181, 183, 195, 196, 197
Senior Citizen's Center. *See under* Community Center
Sexuality, 54, 57, 59–60, 95
Shaker Heights, Ohio, 202–203, 204
Shopping, 66
Sid Richardson Foundation, 159, 166
Smith, Richard, 195
Social change, 172–178
  planned, 179
Social control, 128, 129, 134, 138
Social science, 28, 52, 127
  Chicago school of, 172
Social security checks, 77
Social welfare, 2, 180, 182
Soul on Ice (Cleaver), 84, 95
Southside, 20, 21, 30, 72, 140, 163
Stadiums, 26
Stereotypes, 50, 58, 166
Street lights, 143–144
Structured Employment/Economic Development Corporation

(SEEDCO), 149, 150, 152, 154, 155, 157
Suburbs, 23–26, 162, 182, 187–188, 194, 204
  poverty in, 178
  suburbanization, 175–176, 184, 200–201
Supreme Court, 183
Suttles, Gerald, 29–30

Taxation, 19, 149, 176
Technology, 28, 29
Teen pregnancies, 166, 167
Texas Main Street Project, 150–151
Transportation, 18, 22, 23, 25–26
Triage theory. *See* Urban triage

Underclass, 129, 171
Unemployment, 24, 128, 167, 168, 177
United States Housing Act of 1937, 183
Urban crisis, 176
Urban renewal, 36, 37, 180, 181, 183, 184
Urban triage, 173–175, 195

VA. *See* Veterans Administration
Values, 47, 114, 133, 134
Vesco Printing building, 157
Veterans Administration (VA), 182, 183, 184
Vigilante action, 103
Violence, 13, 14, 70, 79, 82–83, 86, 97, 98, 99, 105, 122, 131, 137, 194, 201, 205, 206, 207

victims of, 205. *See also* Elderly whites, victimization of
See also Murders; Rape; Wilding incidents

War on Poverty, 2, 171, 181, 182
Washington, D. C., 177
Weapons, 205. *See also* Guns
Welfare dependency, 127, 143, 182, 191
Welfare reform, 180
White flight, 22, 26, 35, 41, 43, 45, 46, 55, 128, 138, 161, 181, 184, 188, 196, 200, 201
White supremacy, 51
Wilding incidents, 83, 102–125, 146, 159, 166, 181, 206
  arrests concerning, 105, 109, 110
  case histories of youths involved, 114–125
  defined, 102
Wilson, William, 127, 129
Women, 14, 34, 126, 127
  arming of elderly, 89–90, 91
  black elderly, 133–134
  white/elderly white, 6, 31, 53, 54, 55, 59–63, 71, 84, 96, 104
  See also Families, black female-headed

Yablonsky, Lewis, 138
YMCA, 166

Zippy Carwash facility, 157–158